Skills for Simple Living

edited by Betty Tillotson

Hartley
&Marks
PUBLISHERS

Published in the U.S.A. by
Hartley & Marks, Inc.
79 Tyee Drive, Point Roberts
Washington
98281

Published in Canada by
Hartley & Marks, Ltd.,
3663 West Broadway
Vancouver, BC
V6R 2B8

Printed in the U.S.A.

Text illustrations by Cindy Davis
Cover illustration by Cindy Davis

All the material in this book was drawn from the pages of *The Smallholder*, a unique quarterly
magazine. Subscriptions may be obtained by writing to *The Smallholder*, Argenta, BC, Canada,
V0G 1B0. Subscriptions are $14 for 6 issues, $26 for 12.

ISBN 0-88179-035-4

LIBRARY OF CONGRESS CATALOGUING-IN-PUBLICATION DATA
Skills for Simple Living: how-to letters from the home front for tomorrow's world /
edited by Betty Tillotson.
p. cm.
Includes index.
isbn 0-088179-035-4 (pbk.: alk. paper) : $12.95 ($15.95 can.)
1. Home economics. 2. Conservation of natural resources.
I. Tillotson, Betty, 1925- .
TX147.S5S 1991
640--dc20 91-39934
CIP

Contents

Foreword

We've reached the deadline for depleting our natural resources, and for using methods which pollute the earth and make us ill. We know we must now begin to live our daily lives differently, and to follow in the steps of experienced guides.

The letters in this book come from people who have lived with environmental awareness for a long time. They were published over a period of twenty years in an extraordinary monthly magazine called the *Smallholder*, and they share a wealth of useful inventions and solutions for every sphere of domestic life. While many ideas come from country households, the majority are valuable for suburban and urban dwellers as well.

The emphasis is always on safe, natural materials, and on practical ways to transform and re-use, rather than to discard. And their warm and open style draws us into a friendly network of people trying to live the simple, good life.

Helen Nearing, Harbourside, Maine
(Co-author of *Living the Good Life:
How To Live Sanely & Simply
in a Troubled World*)

CRAFTS

 SPINNING WITH A SPINDLE

I wanted to learn how to spin on a spindle, so I made one using an 18″ long dowel made of birch for the shaft and a piece of ½″ thick plywood for the whorl (Figure 1). I've also made a whorl from a scrap piece of fir. The head of the shaft should be long enough to hold easily and twirl, and the end should be tapered to fit into the hole in the whorl. I used a knife to carve the hook into the end of the shaft after an angular saw cut was made. For the plywood whorl, I used a compass to get a 3″ radius on a square piece, then sawed off the corners and rasped it round. For plain lumber, it was just as easy to round it to shape with a sharp hatchet.

I found the large whorl preferable to a smaller one because it enabled me to spin 4′ of yarn at a time without stopping. With a smaller spindle, shorter in length with a smaller whorl, I had less momentum. I prefer to have the spindle made in two pieces that are detachable to facilitate the removal of the yarn after spinning. In making the first whorl, I filed just a little too much with the rat-tail file in the hole and had to make another whorl.

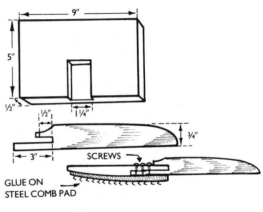

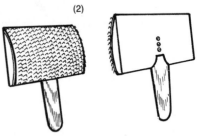

(2)

Before you begin spinning, you must card the wool. If you don't have carders, you can tease the wool by picking it apart with your fingers and arranging it as evenly as possible to prepare for spinning. I made my carders by buying steel combs on leather and copying the wooden back boards from a pair of cotton carders we already had (Figure 2).

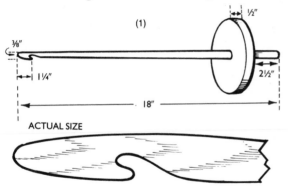

ACTUAL SIZE

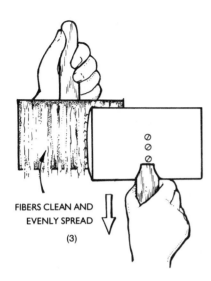

FIBERS CLEAN AND
EVENLY SPREAD

(3)

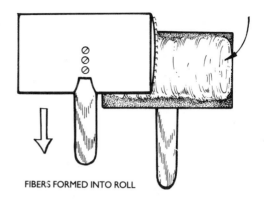

FIBERS FORMED INTO ROLL

To card, put one carder on your lap (left) with the handle away from you, combs up. Hold the other one in your right hand (if you are right-handed) with the handle towards you, combs down (Figure 3). Put some wool between the carders and spread it over the left carder. Don't spread too much wool— you'll soon see what quantity is best. Hold the left carder steady and pull with the right, going over the wool several times. When the fibers seem clean and evenly spread, turn the left carder so that the handle is towards you, then comb the wool onto the other carder by pulling the right carder towards you (Figure 4). Then push the right carder away from you onto the left carder, and there will be a roll of wool ready to be spun. It's easier to start spinning with a roll the size of the yarn you wish to make, so in this case, have the rolls about one inch thick. I prefer to make a large roll and pull the wool to the size I want as I spin. The size of the yarn depends on how thin I pull the wool.

Hold the top of the shaft in one hand and twirl it. It doesn't matter which direction you twirl it; just be consistent in whichever direction you turn it.

Hold the roll with your left hand, and after starting the twirl with the other hand, lightly slide the roll up with the thumb and index and middle fingers of the right hand. Twirling will make the yarn as it slips through the fingers (Figure 5).

Go as far as the arm will reach (and the momentum continues), then stop the spindle. Undo the yarn over the hook and slide it down to the base of the shaft above the

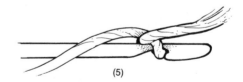

(5)

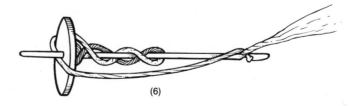

(6)

whorl. Wind the yarn up the shaft, then down to hook onto the shaft below the whorl, then back up to the notch. Put a half-hitch on the hook, and you're ready to start again (Figure 6).

Take the unspun part of the first roll and spread the next roll over it so that they overlap. Always leave a bit of the roll unspun so that the next roll can be easily attached. Spin so that the fiber of the two rolls intertwines. Spin until the spindle is full.

Remove the whorl and slide the wound yarn down.

I use thick yarn for toques and kids' bulky knit sweaters (needles made from ⅜" dowels). I spin thinner yarn on a wheel and two-ply it for socks.

H. K.

 DYEING WITH LICHENS

In case you are new at nature dyeing, let's start at the beginning and take it step by step. If you have never heard of a lichen, by the way, it's pronounced LI-KEN. You have probably seen millions of them. They are the grayish green mosslike little plants that grow all over the trees in our woods. Real mosses are quite different, and they won't yield a dye no matter how you treat them. But a lichen is an ancient plant form composed of two different minute plant organisms, a fungus and an algae. Each one feeds the other, so they live and thrive under varied climatic conditions. Their job in the cycle of life is to reduce stones and woody plants to humus. They are helpful in many other ways as well, and for

the nature-dye lover they produce soft rich colors, from yellow to orange to brown. By using a trick or two, you can make them green and red and purple.

Of course lichens have proper Latin names—hundreds of them—but since I use them for pure pleasure, their Latin names are incidental. Instead I use descriptive names so that you can identify them on sight. Later you can get beautiful scientific books for a serious study.

The easy way to begin, assuming you have some washed and spun sheep's wool, or commercial wool in white skeins, is to find a lichen-covered tree. Fruit trees are best, but alder, birch and maple are good too. Take along a dull knife and a plastic bag and scrape all kinds of lichens that are growing together into the plastic bag. Now you have a number of different forms. There will be a small gray-black scaly type that covers the bark of the tree. That is the kind I call crusty lichen. It dyes orange-brown. Among the crusty you will see a taller kind, almost white, which has a staghorn shape, branching in all directions. I call this one staghorn, and it dyes beige-brown. There will likely be little clumps of greenish white hairy lichens. Sometimes they are bushy and short; sometimes they hang down and are six or eight inches long. Both kinds are white hairy lichen. These give a great variation in color from beige to burnt orange, depending on the tree and the elevation and climate.

If you live away from a seacoast, there is a black hairy lichen, which dyes a good light beige. Best of all, there is a greenish yellow lichen found on old pine trees and even on fence rails; it dyes a beautiful clear yellow. It is my favorite lichen, and I wish it grew here in the coastal forests. One can call it yellow lichen, but it deserves its Latin name of Letharia vulpina (meaning death to wolves, although I can't imagine why a wolf would want to eat it). Again assuming you have gathered a cupful of mixed lichens, put them in a small granite or Pyrex dish, cover with water (rainwater is best), add the wool, and simmer for 20 or 30 minutes. Remove the small skein, rinse well in warm water, shake off the bits of lichen, and dry. If you are lucky, you will have a little sample of wool in a warm orangey brown color that will delight you.

Try lots of samples, and then get a book and learn to use mordants, which will give you lovely soft green shades with lichens. If you want to get reds and purples, you can learn how to ferment lichens with ammonia and time and patience, and you then have orchil dyes.

Of course lichens are only one of the many dye plants that grow in fields and forests — or even in your own flower garden. The leaves or flowers or fruit or roots all have possibilities, but they require a mordant of alum, tin, copper, or chrome.

A walk in the country can produce a basketful of possibilities. I think you will find it a delightful hobby.

K. W.

 DYEING WITH GARDEN PLANTS

I am a gardener because I am interested in plants — their growth habit, their foliage, and the beauty of their flowers. In 1947, I tucked away three garden magazines carrying articles on obtaining dyes from plants and 20 years later dug them out when I was given some wool fleeces.

So began my nature dyeing. I use only plants from my garden and the countryside — except for cochineal (an insect), which is necessary for good reds. Almost all dye-yielding plants of the temperate zone give yellows and beige. Some give olive green with iron mordant, moss green with copper mordant, or orange with tin mordant. (A mordant is a substance that fixes the color.)

The plants may be used fresh, or dried and stored away from the light. Barks and roots are better cut up and then dried. Some dyers have good results with plants or concoctions put in their freezers.

Garden plants I have used and liked — all yellow:
- *Flowers: Anthemis,* coreopsis (annual and perennial), *Helenium,* African marigold, gloriosa daisy.
- *Roots:* iris, rhubarb (lovely yellow), beets.
- *Skins and leaves:* onion skins, alum, spinach.
- *Stems and twigs:* barberries.

Some I plan to try are asters, dahlias, zinnias, calendula, tomato vines, lily of the valley leaves.

Turmeric, a spice, is not a fast color, but a pinch can brighten a yellow. It is very strong, and it can be bought at a grocery.

Native plants growing in British Columbia's Kootenays and Okanagan:
- Soopolallie (*Shepherdia canadensis*) — berries.
- Pearly everlasting (*Anaphalis margaritacea*) — whole plant — green with copper.
- Ragwort (*Senecio*) — yellow, alum.
- Yarrow — in bud and whole plant — moss

green.

- Mullein—leaves—fast yellow, alum, gray-green, copper.
- Juniper berries—ripe blue—beige, alum.
- Goldenrod—flowers as they come into bloom—gold, chrome, yellow, alum.
- Horsetail *(Equisetum)*—yellow, alum. Good for top dyeing.
- Birch—bark—tan and reddish brown; leaves—yellow, alum.
- Tansy—as flower buds open or whole plant—acid yellow.
- Dock *(Rumex crispus)*—root from a mother plant that has seeded—dark yellow, alum.
- Alder bark or cattail—black with iron.
- Elderberry—purple and red. I have seen a beautiful reddish lilac from berries of red elderberry. Leaves—green; berries—blue.

The list seems endless—yellows and golds can be had from the above by using alum or chrome for mordant. Some will give olive, moss, yellow, and gray-greens with iron or copper mordant. Madder gives red-salmon, browns with iron, orange with tin mordant.

Some dyes are substantive, requiring no mordant.

Sumac—bark and twigs or berries—tan; walnut hulls—brown; Oregon grape roots—yellow. Some lichens (there is a yellow one growing on old fences and pine trees). Lungwort *(Pulmonaria officinalis)*, found on trees in damp, shady ravines—brown. Lichens should be gathered with discretion. Most are very slow growing.

Imported dye stuff: Cochineal—pinks, wines, scarlet; indigo, blues.

The process of dyeing can become very involved. Colors vary, depending on the season plants were gathered, soil they were growing in, and temperatures they're dyed at.

Mordants

Dyeing involves two processes: dyeing, and mordanting to fix the color. Most frequently used mordants:

Metallic salts

- Alum—potassium aluminum sulfate. 6 Tbsp. = ½ oz.
- Chrome—potassium (or sodium) dichromate. 1½ tsp. = ½ oz.
- Iron—(ferrous sulfate). 1 tsp. = ¼ oz.
- Tin—stannous chloride. ½ tsp. = ⅛ oz.
- copper sulfate

Acids

- Acetic acid—vinegar
- Tannic acid
- Tartaric acid—cream of tartar. 2 Tbsp. = 1 oz.

Mordanting Wool (1 lb.)

1. With alum: Prepare a water bath of four gallons. Heat it. Dissolve completely three ounces alum and one ounce cream of tartar in a small vessel and add to the water bath. Immerse wetted wool. Raise the temperature gradually, but don't boil. Then simmer for an hour. Rinse.
2. With chrome: Chrome is sensitive to light. Dissolve a half ounce of chrome in a cup of boiling water. Add to a four-gallon bath. Immerse wetted wool and cover the vessel. Bring slowly to boil, then simmer for an hour. Rinse.

For fine wool, simmer for three-quarters of an hour, not over 200°F.

Wool must be washed and wet, since lanolin will prevent dye from penetrating. Use enamel or galvanized tin utensils, and use only for dyeing. Do not use your current cooking utensils. Pots used for indigo should be kept for that purpose only. The same goes for spoons and cups. Use rainwater where possible except for madder.

Have fun. You may not get the color you expect, but most colors are pleasing and many are beautiful.

J. W.

COMBING A FLEECE

Having just been introduced to combing a fleece instead of carding it before spinning, I'd like to pass this method on. Combing a fleece is quiet and peaceful, and it does away with a rather expensive machine. You need a plastic or metal dog's comb, and a cardboard box cut in half in which to put the combed fleece.

Fibers can be pulled from the fleece in sections. Pick a small section from the outside (as opposite to the shorn) end. If you are right-handed, transfer it to your left hand. Grasp the section in the middle, and with your comb in your right hand, comb outwards until all the fibers are separated. Turn the fleece around and comb the other end. Now lay this fluffy piece inside the box, shorn end against the wall.

When the box is full, spin away, always feeding the fleece through shorn end first. My sister from New Zealand taught me this method, and it works well as long as the wool is in fairly good condition.

Another tip from her that I haven't tried yet is about dyeing the fleece. She had little plastic net bags, like onion bags, only smaller. By putting unspun wool pieces inside, they remain undisturbed during the dyeing process and are easy to spin afterwards. I suppose one could make little bags out of the big onion bags.

Is it true that lichen takes seven years to grow? If so, when collecting lichen for dyeing wool, it would be advisable to collect only part of it, leaving the rest for future harvesting.

B. K.

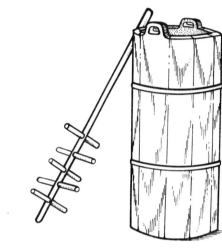

HOW TO RECLAIM WOOL

In the olden days, nothing could be wasted. After you got through the whole process of spinning and weaving your clothes, you'd likely wear them for many years and then sew them over for your children, and whatever was left when they were finished with them would be reclaimed, mixed with new wool at times, and spun again, and the process would start all over again. Old knitted items—socks, mittens, sweaters, etc.—would be cut in long strips and then plucked apart by hand; usually this was an occupation for children. The woven cloth would be cut up in little squares and the threads drawn out, then everything would be put in a big kettle, boiling water was poured over, and the cloth was stirred and mashed till it became wool again.

Another process was to put it in an old butter churn, pour hot water over it, and then "churn" the cloth with a stick into which holes had been made and sticks put in crosswise (see figure). After the wool was dry, it could be mixed with new wool again and spun. This yarn often got nubby and still had particles of color. It was usually used as weft in dress materials and wool capes.

W.

PURPLE MARTIN HOUSE

Purple martins, which are about eight inches long, are a large member of the swallow family. They can be recognized by their forked tail, which is not as pronounced as the familiar barn swallow's tail but has a glossy purple color. They live in colonies of four or more pairs and can be attracted to your area if you build specially constructed martin-type "apartment houses." Keep an eye out that no other species gets started in the house, or the martins won't go near.

Here is how to construct a martin house:

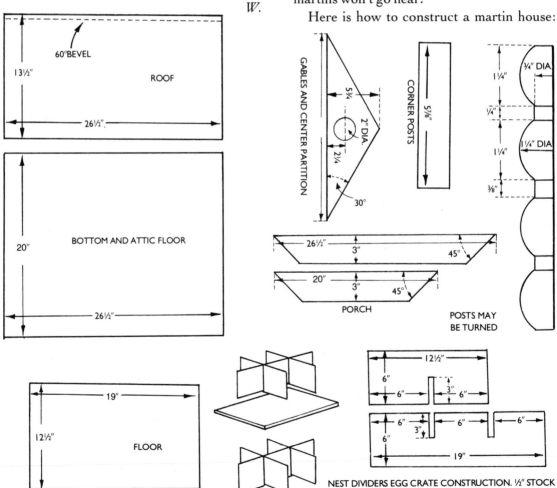

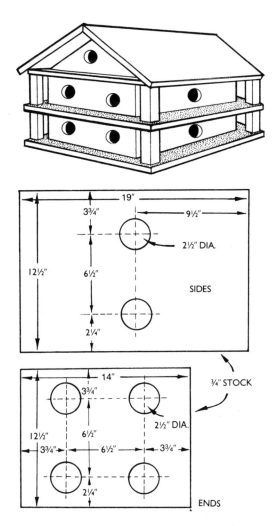

of March, so the house should be ready by then. Martins consume vast amounts of mosquitoes.

B. G.

SOCK-TOP GAITERS

Here's something I learned myself: Gaiters made from old sock tops. Probably not a new invention, but very useful in keeping snow out of boots and keeping pants legs dry. (Pants are tucked in the top of the sock and the bottom is pulled over the boot top.)

S.

CATFACE CRADLE

Quite a while ago, someone asked how to make the Catface Mountain community cradle. Here is how I made a cradle for friends four years ago. It is only one of numerous variations on this theme—a box in which to safely keep an infant. (You could, of course, find a nice box or basket.)

We arrived at this design after an evening of discussion around the dining table, with some hypothetical measuring and sketching and a certain amount of hope that the size would be adequate for six months or so of use. It was. The choice of materials was based on what I had on hand: some nicely marked imbuya planks (also marketed as Brazilian walnut) and some ⅜″ × 3″ tongue-and-groove red cedar. Use what you have or

Here is how to construct a martin house: The size of each compartment ought to be 6″ × 6″ × 6″. The entrance holes should be about 2½″ diameter and about 2″ from the floor to keep the young ones from falling out. There should be a 4–6″ porch for sunning, and the house should be painted white or aluminum to reflect heat. It should be well vented throughout. It is suggested that the house be about 40′ from anything and 15–25′ high. Perhaps the vent on the barn roof could convert nicely into a martin house. The martins arrive in the north towards the end

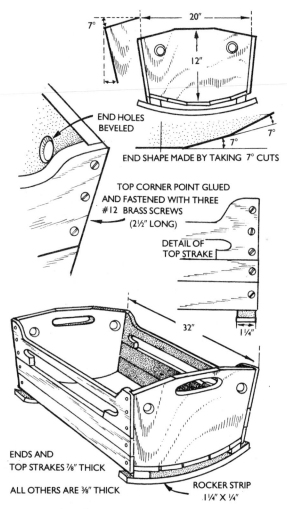

END HOLES
BEVELED

END SHAPE MADE BY TAKING 7° CUTS

TOP CORNER POINT GLUED
AND FASTENED WITH THREE
#12 BRASS SCREWS
(2½" LONG)

DETAIL OF
TOP STRAKE

32"

ENDS AND
TOP STRAKES ⅞" THICK

ALL OTHERS ARE ⅜" THICK

ROCKER STRIP
1¼" X ¼"

There are handholds on each end, and the top strakes of each side are shaped to be easy on the hand. The 1″ holes in the ends have had lines spliced in so that the cradle can hang from a beam overhead. This has proven quite successful—one may sit reading and occasionally tug on a cord to sway the cradle. In addition, an array of objects may be hung from the overhead lines to provide optical stimulation. (This one has had shells, bells, driftwood, feathers, and colored yarn—use your imagination.)

Don't skimp on the length of fastenings. These, along with the glue, assure a strong and lasting object fit for use. There are, of course, other choices for fastenings, such as dowels glued into holes and then cut off flush with ends carefully split and wedges glued in. Or a series of small holes could be made and the strakes lashed on with strong cord.

The cradle I made has served five children in four years. It needs a bit of polishing but is otherwise sound. It remains in service, and I hope it will go on for a long time. The design is all right, but use your imagination. There are infinite possibilities (well, quite a few anyway). And start early; give yourself time to do a nice job.

D. D'A.

can easily obtain. For the small amount of material required, even expensive hardwoods don't amount to much real cost in an item that is a durable and useful bit of furniture. Fastenings are brass screws, and all joints are glued as well (belt and braces). Finish is several coats of beeswax, well rubbed. The intent was to avoid any potential hazard to a child from toxic finishes. I suspect that I could have sealed the wood first with a thinned coat of shellac without risk.

Dimensions: 32″ long, 20″ wide, 12″ deep.

MUSICAL INSTRUMENTS TO MAKE

Winter's evenings are a great time for making all the odd and lovely things we've seen and shared with others over the summer. This winter I want to make some instruments for our family. Aside from the usual musical instruments that you can buy, it's nice to have smaller and more durable ones for little folks to play.

Here are a few I've made or seen around.

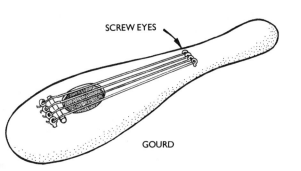

Gourd Mandolin

Materials:

- 1 dry gourd, long and oval
- knife for cutting sound hole
- 8 screw eyes
- nylon fishing line (4 lb.), cut into 4 pieces for strings
- dowel for a bridge ($\frac{1}{4}$" × 3")
- triangular file

To make:

Select a gourd that is long and narrow. On the flattest side of the gourd, cut a sound hole a third of the way from the oval end. With a spoon or your hand, clean out the gourd, removing all the seeds and membranes. Dry thoroughly. Attach four screw eyes, evenly spaced, at each end of the gourd. Leave enough space at the stem end for holding, and make sure the strings will cross the sound hole. Tie strings to screw eyes, pulling tightly. Using triangular file, make four evenly spaced grooves on the dowel. Place grooved dowel under the strings for a bridge.

To play:

Play like a mandolin by fingering with the left hand and strumming with the right hand over the sound hole. The strings can be tuned by screwing the screw eyes a bit one way or the other.

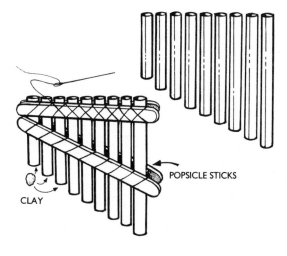

Panpipes

Materials:

- 41" plastic tubing (firm) or bamboo (thin tubes make a thin sound; large tubes are more mellow)
- knife
- clear plastic tape
- strips of bamboo or ice cream sticks
- string
- needle
- Plasticine clay

To make:

With the knife, cut the tube or bamboo to the lengths you want. Here are the measurements for a C scale:

- C—6$\frac{3}{4}$"
- D—6"
- E—5$\frac{1}{4}$"
- F—4$\frac{3}{4}$"
- G—4$\frac{1}{4}$"
- A—3$\frac{3}{4}$"

- B—3½"
- C—3¼"
- D—3"

Lay down a length of tape, sticky side up, and arrange the tubes in order on the tape. Tape them front and back so the tubes will stay in place while you sew the sticks onto both sides of the tubes, as illustrated.

Insert the clay in the end of the tubes, filling the end of each pipe until it makes the note you want. The clay can be pushed in further to make the pitch higher or lower.

To play:
Holding panpipes in hand, blow across the open ends of the tubes.

COCONUT

Coconut Thumb Piano (Zanza, Mbira, Kalimba, or Kaffir Harp)

In the African Congo where these originated, coconuts were the usual base for these lovely little instruments. I've seen lots of sophisticated ones made from all sorts of exotic woods and metals, but I thought this one was quite nice.

Materials:

- coconut
- 3 coping saw blades or 8" flat spring steel wire
- tin snips
- ¼" piece of wood to fit top of coconut half (plywood, cedar, whatever)
- glue
- metal
- tape

- hammer
- saw

To make:
Cut the coconut in half lengthwise. Let coconut dry until meat shrinks. Remove meat. Cut piece of wood to fit the hole. Sand the edges of the coconut and the wood. Drill a hole ¼" in diameter, centered in the wood for sound. Cut the coping saw blades with tin snips into 3", 2½", and 2" lengths. (A friend here used copper telephone wire, hammered flat, for the "keys." Because it had steel inside the copper, it had the necessary spring. And it was really nice looking.) Cut a metal strip ½" × 3". Place a 2" long finishing nail on the wood and line up your metal keys across it. Place the metal strip over the end of the keys and nail in place. Glue wood in the coconut.

To play:
Hold instrument by cupping in hands and gently depress and release the tone bars with your thumbs.

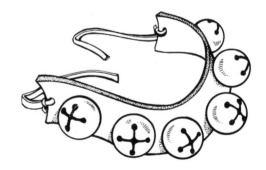

Indian Dancing Bells

Attach bells to strip of rawhide or sheepskin with thonging. Kids love these. Wear them anywhere—neck, waist, knee, ankle.

Navajo Drum Rattle

Materials:

- fresh thin willow, about 18" long, strong
- rawhide and lacing

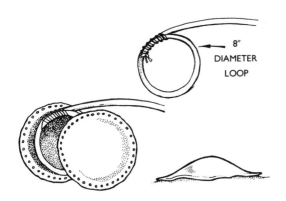

8″ DIAMETER LOOP

hill for a few weeks—the ants will do it for you.

To play:

The jawbone comes ready to play. Just run the smaller bone across the teeth.

These are just a few instruments I've used and liked. There are so many more—as many, I guess, as you can dream up.

I. S.

To make:

Bend your branch, making an 8″ diameter loop. Tie with thin lacing. Cut rawhide in a circle about 2″ larger than loop. Soak. Place on mounds of sand to get desired shape. Let dry. Place rawhide circles on each side of loop. Trim. Make punch holes. Using rawhide lacing, lace around branch. Halfway around, put 10 beans inside drum, finish lacing, and tie.

To play:

Shake or hit the rawhide end of the rattle on a hard surface.

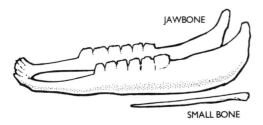

JAWBONE

SMALL BONE

Jawbone Rasp

Materials:

- jawbone of a large animal with teeth intact (bear is nicest)
- small animal bone
- paints—if you wish to add a design

To make:

Clean the jawbone if necessary. If the animal is freshly killed, place the jawbone on an ant-

 SIMPLE WINTER FOOTWEAR

Some friends told me of a design for cold weather footwear that seemed easy to make and practical. I tried one pair, and have made several other pairs since.

I took some sheepskin with fleece and cut the pattern so that the fleece was inside the boot. I modified the pattern so that I could have a higher boot. I wear these boots mostly inside or on dry snow. I wore out one pair on pavement and rough ground. Since then, I have glued soles of tougher leather onto the next pair to protect the sheepskin. These soles can be replaced if worn through.

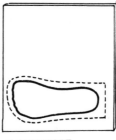

(1) TRACE FOOT, ADD MARGIN

(2) ROUND OUT PATTERN

Here's how I make the pattern: Put foot on a paper sack opened at its seams. Trace around the foot. Mark ½″ around the outline

(3) FOLD TO DOUBLE PATTERN

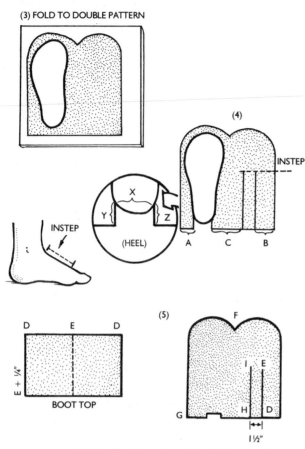

(4)

INSTEP

INSTEP

X
Y   Z
(HEEL)   A   C   B

(5)

D   E   D

E + ¼"

BOOT TOP

F

I   E

G   H   D
|←→|
1½"

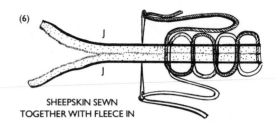

(6)

J
J

SHEEPSKIN SEWN
TOGETHER WITH FLEECE IN

ing to get thick skin for the sole. Reverse the pattern for the other shoe. Cut them out. Cut a strip the width of "DE" plus a ¼" seam and the length of "DE".

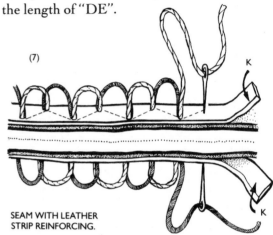

(7)

K

K

SEAM WITH LEATHER
STRIP REINFORCING.

except at the heel, where I mark 1" (Figure 1).

Round out pattern so that the top is symmetrical and the sides are parallel from the widest point to the heel (Figure 2). Fold the pattern over so that there are two identical pieces (Figure 3). Find the width of the heel on the left piece and mark it out to the edge of the pattern (Figure 4). "A" and a ¼" seam plus "B" and a ¼" seam should measure "C." "Y" and a ¼" seam plus "Z" and a ¼" seam should equal "X."

Mark the instep, find the middle of that side of the pattern, and mark a 1½" strip. For a low boot, cut out the piece. For a high boot, I cut along the sides until I get to the instep but do not cut the piece out (Figure 5).

Trace the pattern onto the sheepskin, try-

I use linen thread and two harness needles. Since sheepskin tends to tear easily, I use a strip of ⅛" soft leather to reinforce the seam. The stitch is done with two needles threaded on the ends of the same thread (Figure 6). "J" is the two layers of sheepskin with the fleece in, to be sewn together. The needles go through the same holes in opposite directions and are pulled tight after each stitch. Figure 7 shows the leather strips "K" and "K" in a side view, and Figure 8, from the top. "L" is the thread. I wax the thread with beeswax or a candle before I thread it.

(8)   TOP VIEW OF THREAD PATTERN IN REINFORCING STRIP

L

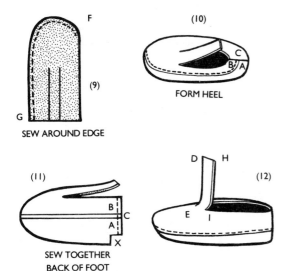

(9)

(10)

F

G

SEW AROUND EDGE

FORM HEEL

C

B A

(11)

B

A

C

X

SEW TOGETHER
BACK OF FOOT

(12)

D H

E I

This pattern is made so that the boot fits either foot. The boot will stretch with wear, so it should be tight to begin with. If the fleece mats, add a felt inner sole for warmth. For an additional outer sole, I glue on a piece of sturdy leather, larger than the foot outline, so that I won't walk on the sheepskin. I use a contact cement.

H.

To sew, fold the pieces together with the fleece in and sew from the outside from "F" to "G" (Figure 9). Trim the fleece so that the seams are bare of fleece. This facilitates sewing. If the sheepskin is too thick for the needle to go through easily, I use an awl to make the holes first.

Fold "AB" to meet "C" and sew them together (Figure 10). To sew the heel, join the "AC" piece to "X" and sew them together (Figure 11). Take the piece cut out of the front "EDHI" and sew the high boot piece onto it, starting at "DE" and ending at "HI" (Figures 12 and 13). If I want a low shoe, I cut the piece off at "EI," and the shoe is done.

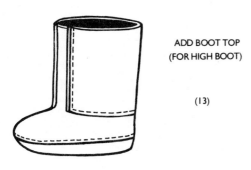

ADD BOOT TOP
(FOR HIGH BOOT)

(13)

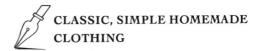

CLASSIC, SIMPLE HOMEMADE CLOTHING

Many of us country people tend to wear clothing that is different from the clothing worn in town. Our clothes have to be durable and comfortable to work in. I'm going to sketch some simple styles for clothes that have served us and that have drawn compliments.

For children's clothes, I use cloth from old clothing or buy remnants. I can't see spending a lot on clothes that are outgrown so soon. We also get stuff from thrift shops, our community free exchange box, and rummage sales. I "rebuild" jeans by putting long patches down the front legs as soon as the knees wear thin. The patches usually are gotten from the back side of the legs of rummage jeans and turned backside out.

I've also been working out designs that are simple to make and that bypass fancy cutting as well as fancy style, requiring the least amount of work necessary to make comfortable clothing. (Many of the designs I end up with are the same as traditional designs.) I'm

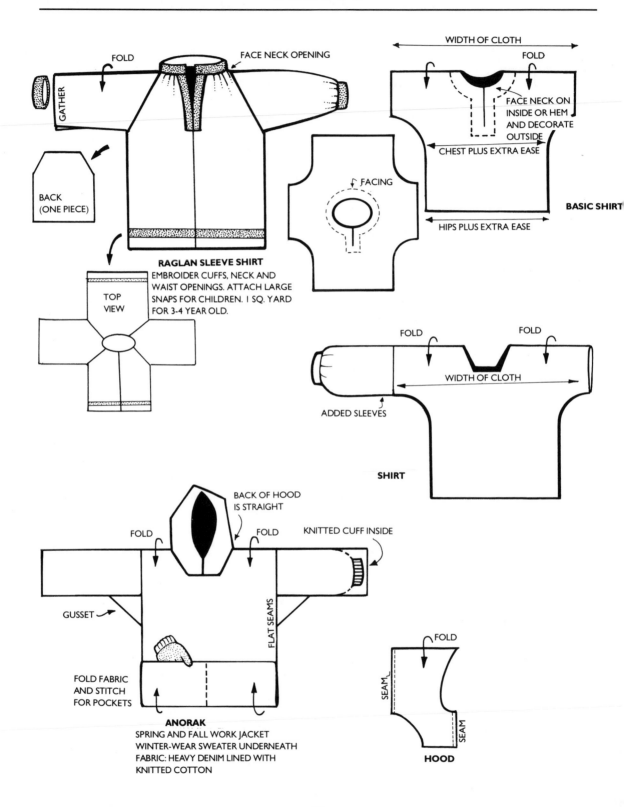

FOLD

FACE NECK OPENING

GATHER

BACK
(ONE PIECE)

RAGLAN SLEEVE SHIRT
EMBROIDER CUFFS, NECK AND
WAIST OPENINGS. ATTACH LARGE
SNAPS FOR CHILDREN. 1 SQ. YARD
FOR 3-4 YEAR OLD.

TOP
VIEW

FACING

WIDTH OF CLOTH

FOLD

FACE NECK ON
INSIDE OR HEM
AND DECORATE
OUTSIDE

CHEST PLUS EXTRA EASE

BASIC SHIRT

HIPS PLUS EXTRA EASE

FOLD   FOLD

WIDTH OF CLOTH

ADDED SLEEVES

SHIRT

BACK OF HOOD
IS STRAIGHT

FOLD   FOLD

KNITTED CUFF INSIDE

GUSSET

FLAT SEAMS

FOLD FABRIC
AND STITCH
FOR POCKETS

ANORAK
SPRING AND FALL WORK JACKET
WINTER-WEAR SWEATER UNDERNEATH
FABRIC: HEAVY DENIM LINED WITH
KNITTED COTTON

FOLD

SEAM

SEAM

HOOD

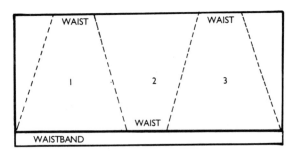

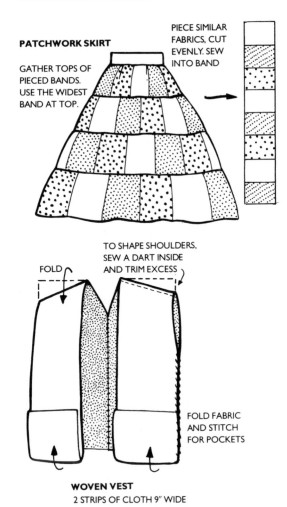

PATCHWORK SKIRT

GATHER TOPS OF PIECED BANDS. USE THE WIDEST BAND AT TOP.

PIECE SIMILAR FABRICS, CUT EVENLY. SEW INTO BAND

WAIST

WAIST

1

2

3

WAIST

WAISTBAND

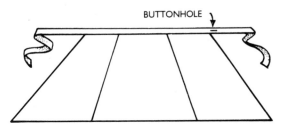

BUTTONHOLE

PASS WAISTBAND THROUGH BUTTONHOLE

TO SHAPE SHOULDERS, SEW A DART INSIDE AND TRIM EXCESS

FOLD

FOLD FABRIC AND STITCH FOR POCKETS

WOVEN VEST
2 STRIPS OF CLOTH 9″ WIDE

assuming that anyone using these ideas knows something about sewing and terms. If not, look them up in a sewing book in any library.

H. K.

WRAPAROUND SKIRT DESIGN

Thanks for the pattern ideas. Here's a simple long skirt shown to me by a friend. Take pieces 1 and 3, turn 2 up the right way, and sew two seams. Leave the third to make wraparound.

K. L. V. R.

BIRCH DOORMAT

When a friend was visiting, he made a birch doormat for us. He used baling wire for the warp and fresh birch twigs (3′ long and ½″ thick) for the weft. There were four strands of weft, which were crossed every 2″ or so.

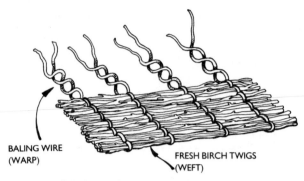

BALING WIRE
(WARP)

FRESH BIRCH TWIGS
(WEFT)

To finish it, he tied the wires together by twisting them with pliers and wove the ends back into the mat, then straightened out the ends of the twigs with a hatchet on the chopping block. This mat has lasted us all year and shows little signs of wear. It is great for cleaning off barn manure and snow. People in Norway make new mats each year.

B. T.

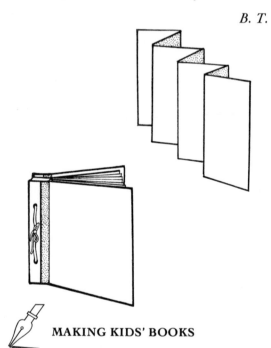

MAKING KIDS' BOOKS

When I was in the sixth grade, our class made bound books. I have since used my knowledge of bookmaking to make other similar books. Unless one intends these kids' books to last, it's not worth expending a lot of energy in making the book itself. I say this because when I spend weeks on a project, I tend to think the book itself is precious and am less eager to let the kids use it roughly. It is more important that the words be clearly printed, the pictures bold, the paper stiff, and the pages easily turned than how pretty the book is from the adult point of view. The book is for the kids. They will outgrow it soon, and new ones should be made.

When I worked in an experimental project in teaching reading, we were asked to point out to the kids that they *could* read, since they had a "reading block." We showed them they could "read" street lights, stop signs, traffic signals. In the same line, a book with just colors or animals is as much a reading book for our little kids as word books. They enjoy the recognition of familiar items. The more personalized the book, the more they enjoy it.

One of my kids' favorite books is a looseleaf folder with cardboard pages in it, with colorful pictures from magazines of everything—birds, plants, vegetables, animals, etc.

For *Akka's Book,* I made a hard cover out of thin plywood and used leather hinges. Inner pages were thin cardboard with typing paper pasted over it. Niko, my second, liked to pick apart the page that is loose from the cardboard, so poster board would make a better page.

A folding book of hard paper with text or pictures on both sides is easy. Score the folds with the back of a table knife. The book can be held together by colorful string.

H. K.

LITTLE KIDS' PACK

When our daughter was 2½ years old, I used to send her off to a play group with a pack on her back that contained her snack and indoor boots. When she was younger, we'd go for a walk and she'd carry her bottle and a change of diapers. She was eager to carry her own things and enjoyed the responsibility.

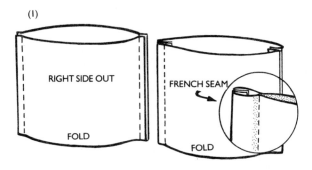

(1)

RIGHT SIDE OUT

FOLD

FRENCH SEAM

FOLD

To make a kids' pack, take a piece of strong cotton cloth, closely woven, 14″ wide and 25″ long. Fold the cloth in half with the right side out and use a French seam to sew ¼″ seam. Turn it inside out; crease the seam well. Sew a ⅜″ seam over the other seam, enclosing the ends of the threads inside it so that when the cloth is turned right side out, there is a seam with no raw edges showing (Figure 1).

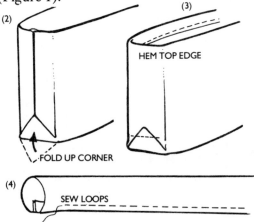

(2)

(3)

HEM TOP EDGE

FOLD UP CORNER

(4)

SEW LOOPS

Sew up the two sides so that there is a bag with the top open. Fold one side on the bottom to form a corner and sew 3″ across on both sides. This creates a rectangular bottom (Figure 2).

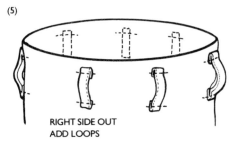

(5)

RIGHT SIDE OUT
ADD LOOPS

Fold the top down inside to make a 2½″ wide seam. Tuck the raw edge in and sew it around (Figure 3). Cut a strip 1½″ wide and 17½″–18″ long along the length of the cloth. Fold it so that the raw edges are inside and sew it (Figure 4). The strip is about ⅝″ wide now.

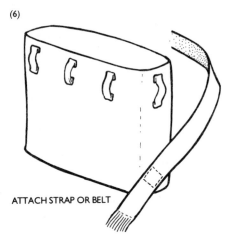

(6)

ATTACH STRAP OR BELT

Cut 2½″ pieces off the strip to get seven pieces. Turn the bag right side out and attach the cut strips, which will function as belt loops. Place the loops as shown in Figure 5. Fold the edges over ⅜″ and sew on the fold at least three times so that it will stay fastened. For the straps, I weave a 1″ belt on my inkle loom, 4′ long. This can be done on any simple belt loom.

(7)

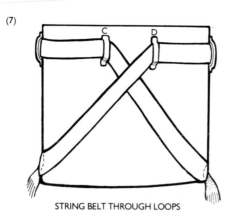

STRING BELT THROUGH LOOPS

Attach one end of the belt to the bottom of the bag with the fringes down by sewing a rectangle with diagonals in it (Figure 6). I often use the same thread that the belt is woven with to make the fastening inconspicuous. It is also easier to do this by hand than by machine because of the awkward position.

String the belt into the loops, starting between C and D (Figure 7) and ending by crossing the first end. Attach the other end, checking that the belt is not twisted.

The pack is done. You could add pockets or other innovations. To wear the pack, put the arms into the straps where they cross and tighten them with a knot on the other side. If this kind of pack is made for adults to carry any considerable weight, the straps should be made of wider, stiffer material and should be padded so that they will not cut into the shoulders.

H. K.

RESTORING SHRUNKEN SWEATERS

Instructions for restoring woolen garments that have shrunk appeared in *Grass Roots*. Dissolve three ounces of Epsom salts in boiling water. Set aside to cool. Soak shrunken garment in this solution for 30 minutes. Remove, squeeze out excess water, and restretch the garment to its correct shape. Allow to dry flat, then press under a slightly damp cloth.

B. T.

USES FOR SOCK TOPS

I'm always bugged when good work socks get worn out in the feet while the tops are still good. Here are some ways to use those tops.

Draft Stop (Worm)
Sew several sock tops together, close the bottom end, and stuff the resulting tube with sock scraps and some pebbles for weight; it needs to be full and dense. Sew the other end closed, and when the cold winds blow, throw your sock tube against the bottom of a drafty door. Eyes and tongue can be added to make it double as a worm when not in use. Kids love mine!

Liners for Leather Mitts
Lay a sock top on a table, measure where your thumb should go, and slit the sock. Cut a scrap and sew it into a thumb-sized tube,

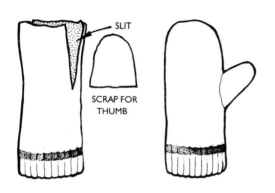

SLIT

SCRAP FOR THUMB

then stitch it in place. Gather the openings and stitch. These are good because you can have a long wrist on the liner to tuck up your sleeve. They can get dried and changed easily. A farmer who grew up in the depression showed me these. He uses fishing line to sew them.

D. P.

JOLLY JUMPER

A few simple contraptions can make mothering much easier. I find I get downright ornery if baby takes up 100 percent of my time and attention. Aside from that, so much doting doesn't seem to make happy babies, either, and no chores get done.

I recently made a "jolly jumper" for our four-month-old boy that works well. The seat is made from two layers of heavy cloth, part of it being filled with teased wool and quilted. The seat is attached to a bar by 1½" wide strips of rubber inner tube. A short piece of rope with a loop on the end hangs the swing from a hook in the ceiling over a double bed.

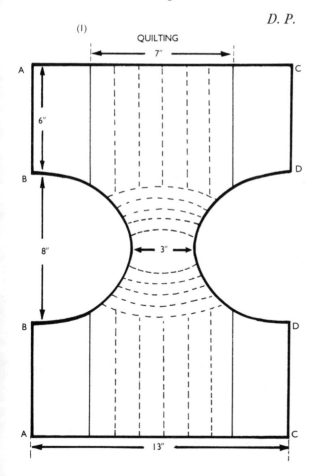

(1)

QUILTING

7"

A 6" C

B

8"

3"

B D

A 13" C

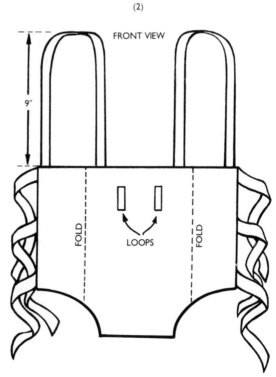

(2)

FRONT VIEW

9"

FOLD   LOOPS   FOLD

Cut out two pieces like the one shown in *Figure 1*. Quilt the center part. Dimensions are finished, so add for seams. Then sew AB to AB, CD to CD. Sew shoulder straps to the back piece (*Figure 2*).

Then sew on ties, shoulder straps, and a pair of loops for the top ties to go through to keep the ties from riding up. Put the baby in and fold over its belly and tie. The shoulder straps will then be in the right position for the arms to go through.

Y.

BABY SOAKERS

Soakers are a great alternative to rubber pants, since they breathe. For those who don't have the time or inclination to knit them, they're easy to make out of old woolen sweaters.

Wash the sweater a few times in hot water to shrink it—it will mat up. Simply cut out a soaker in the shape you want—it won't unravel. I found that an open sleeve works well.

You can buy old sweaters for very little money at thrift stores. Tell them what you want them for. They may have out-of-shape sweaters at the back that you can have for free.

If the wool is very itchy or if the baby develops a reaction to the wool, try trimming the soaker with strips of a shrunken angora sweater.

T. G.

RULE-OF-THUMB SWEATER

I thought people might be interested in my rule-of-thumb sweater instructions:

1. Figure out how many stitches you will need for desired width. (Suggestion: check pattern in store for this kind of wool and see how many stitches are cast on for *back*.)
2. Knit ribbing for *back*. Now knit as many rows as you have cast on stitches. (If knitting on round needles, knit half as many.)
3. *Decrease* for shoulder one stitch at the beginning of each row. (It is different for round needles: four every other round.) Do this ⅔ as many rows as from ribbing to armhole.
4. Measure ribbing on wrist of subject. After ribbing, increase one stitch each side of every sixth row.
5. Make sleeve longer than body by length of ribbing.
6. Decrease as for body.
7. *Neck* around should be as many stitches as cast on for back.

E. de B.

RECYCLED MUSICAL TOY

Here's a musical instrument your children can make for themselves from easily obtainable "junk."

Take a metal grating, such as an oven rack or old refrigerator rack, and tie a three-foot piece of string on each of both ends of one side. Make a loop on the other end of each string.

Put the first finger of each hand through

each loop and put your fingers in your ears. Stand up and let the grate hang in front of you in the air. Now ask a friend to bang on it with a stick, or better yet, a metal object like a large spoon.

The sound produced is full and deep, like organ music. Amazing!

B. T.

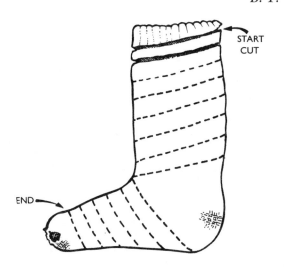

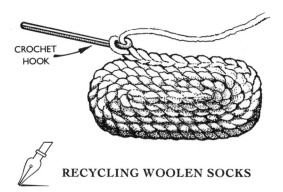

 RECYCLING WOOLEN SOCKS

Last winter I discovered I had a large bag of wool work socks that needed darning. I'm not into darning, but I am a devout recycler, so I started looking for other ways to use them.

I started cutting one from the cuff, around and around, into a strip about 1½" wide. I just kept cutting until I got to the heel, which had a hole in it, then I cut around the foot until I got to the toe, which was discarded (it had a hole too). Then I had a nice ball of woolen "yarn" to work with.

I got a large crochet hook and started to work a sole for slippers. It went very quickly with this heavy yarn, and I had a pair in no time. It took four old socks to make one pair of soles. You could continue crocheting and make complete slippers, but I just sewed my soles onto a pair of wool socks. They were very warm, cozy, and cushiony.

For someone with a lot of socks to recycle and a lot of crochet time, wonderful mats could be made for beside the bed or hearth or under the dog. For the truly ambitious, keep going and you'll have the warmest wool blanket or sleeping mat.

It also occurred to me that strips or chips of these worn-out socks could be used to stuff pillows or toys.

C. H.

DESIGNER RAGS

As I read about recycling woolen socks in a recent issue, I wondered if anyone had mentioned rag weaving. This is a really exciting sphere and by no means a new idea. Rag weaving is simply using what is on hand, making your weft from old clothes, socks, jeans, and leather coats. Rag rugs have covered floors for generations.

The article on woolen socks interested me because you can make a beautiful "bouclé" yarn from any knitted item. First you cut the article into strips about a half inch wide, making sure that you cut around the article (not up and down), starting at the ribbed edge. Now you can determine your yarn thickness. After you have cut two or three inches, stretch it—the knitting will unravel some, but don't worry; that's what you want. When all the loops are woven, you can't tell the difference between this yarn and expensive bouclé yarns. Keep on cutting around and around. If you want a finer yarn, cut your initial strip narrower than a half inch. You can go as thin as the stretching will permit. When your yarn breaks, you've gone too thin. I talk about weaving because that's what I do, but I can't see why one couldn't knit with the same yarn and get great results.

For weaving, leather can be cut in quarter-inch strips and placed carefully, with the beater. Then, using a thread (the same as your warp), make one or two shots in plain weave, then place another row of leather. This will bind the fabric and give more stability. It is best to use a wool warp—two-ply fine—about 6 to 10 ends per inch, for leather.

Fabrics can be cut in varying widths and used as weft. Just beat it like you would any other yarn.

Your designs can be a random mix of color, or you can plan out your pattern and style according to what you've accumulated. For example, remember those really good wool dress pants with wide legs that still hang in the closet but you haven't taken off the hanger for five years (because you never get out of your jeans)? Well, take them out and cut them into long, flowing strips (preferably with the straight grain). Weave them into a long piece of yardage. You'll probably need two or three pairs to get enough.

Now, to go with it, there's that sweater that your partner really liked—but you shrank it in the wash. Cut it up; stretch it; get a couple more; do the same. Now you can make a sweater, shirt, jacket, or vest. To sew these articles, be sure to stitch the outline before cutting, or you'll unravel what you've just woven. Lay out your pattern piece; chalk around it; machine-stitch a double line all around this chalk line. Cut out *between* the two lines of stitching. Zig-zag stitch or overcast your edge on each garment piece—right now; don't take the chance of its getting unraveled. Now you can assemble your article without worrying that it will disintegrate before your eyes.

Your imagination is your only limit. You can produce truly fine, elegant work with silks and soft cottons as well.

The only problem I have now is that nothing gets past the door to the trash bin, so I've got big boxes piled up in the basement waiting to be cut up into rags. This winter's project is braided rugs for my kitchen and living room, another use for rags. How many of us still have a braided mat that our grandmothers made?

Happy scrapping.

C. P.

 CHILDREN'S CLOTHING FROM OLD WORK SOCKS

On a recent visit to the Glenbow Museum in Calgary, we saw some uses for old work socks displayed in the section on the Depression. A child's sweater was cut out of wool work socks. The arms were cut and stitched,

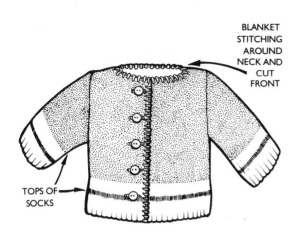

BLANKET
STITCHING
AROUND
NECK AND
CUT
FRONT

TOPS OF
SOCKS

with the top of the sock as the cuff of the sleeve. The back was the top of the sock cut in half lengthwise; then the back pattern was cut out of it. The front was similar, only it was in two pieces, with the neck cut lower. Keep in mind that the uncut edges are used to make the bottom of the body and sleeves neat. The cut edge around the neck and down the front was blanket-stitched. I couldn't tell, but the whole thing seemed stitched together on a machine. The buttonholes were cut and stitched with yarn that matched the blanket stitching. I'm not sure, but it seemed that it would fit up to an 18-month-old child.

Mittens had also been cut out and stitched. The thumb had been cut out separately (would it need to be?) and stitched on. I'm not a knitter, but I always thought something knitted unraveled when you cut into it. Perhaps the edges were stay-stitched.

If you can make baby sweaters and mitts out of old sock tops, you could probably cut out and stitch soakers for babies. I remember some time ago when a friend unraveled work sock tops and reknit them into children's socks and gave them as baby presents.

P. C.

BIRCH BARK BASKET

Is your bright orange plastic laundry basket falling irreparably to pieces after but one year of use? And what will you do now? Take it to the dump and buy a new one—perhaps a pink one this time? May I suggest an alternative? It looks good, it's made of natural materials, it will last many years, and it costs no money, but it will take some time to make. It's the birch bark basket.

1. Find the bark. The most pliable, and therefore the most desirable, bark comes from live trees cut in the spring. However, any bark will do. For a large basket, use the biggest log you can find (but again, any will do).

2. Remove the bark. If you're using whole logs, take a knife and score around the log every 18" or so, cutting all the way through the bark. If you're using firewood rounds, this step is already done. Next, score a line the length of the log. Carefully pry off the edge of a section of bark along that line. With both hands, pull off a rectangular sheet.

3. Press the bark. To get the curl out, lay the sheets in a stack and pile books, boxes, etc., on top. Leave for a couple of weeks.

4. Scrape the bark. The bark consists of many paperlike layers, the outer ones quite rough. Use a knife to scrape and peel away the outer layers until the sheet is smooth and down to more or less the same layer everywhere.

5. Cut strips. Decide which side of the bark you want showing on the basket. Having the inside showing is more common, since it's sturdier; so that's what I'll assume here. With pencil and ruler, draw parallel lines on the outside of the bark, an inch

apart, as parallel as possible to the short strips on the surface of the bark. Avoid knotholes. With scissors, cut the strips and point the ends with two 45° cuts.

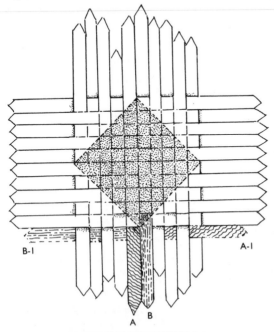

A CROSSES OVER B TO POSITION A-1
B CROSSES OVER A TO POSITION B-1
SHADED AREA IS THE BASE OF THE BASKET

6. Weave the basket.
   a) First weave the outer base. Weave strips into a square mat, envisioning a diamond placed within the square. This diamond will be the base of your basket, so weave until it's the size you want and you've used an even number of strips. Jam the strips together so that the mat is woven as tightly as possible. (That's the way I like it, anyhow.) Secure the corners with clothespins.
   b) Weave the outer sides. Find the centerpoint of each side of the square. Cross the two strips to either side of one centerpoint sharply over and continue weaving them through the others they

thus meet. This forms a corner. Be sure the inside of the bark is now facing out. Repeat with each centerpoint. Continue weaving tightly until the desired height is reached. When a strip runs out, take another and overlap it by a few squares, leaving no ends sticking out of the outside of the basket.
   c) Form the top edge. This step is accomplished by folding the strips and weaving them into the inner surface of the basket. There are two options:

SCALLOPED TOP

SCALLOPED TOP BASKET

- Scalloped top: Where two strips cross, make a neat, tight fold in the outer one so that it lies right along the path it came up, but on the inside of the basket. Take the inner strip and fold it neatly and tightly over the folded-over portion of its partner so that it also lies over its path, on the inside of the basket. Weave each strip into the previously woven sides. You know—

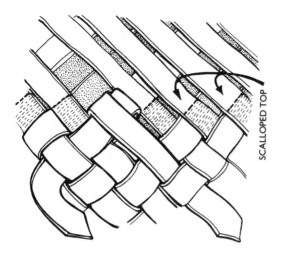

SCALLOPED TOP BASKET

However, the important thing is that you should not go *under* the square. In this case, go *between* the two strips in that square.

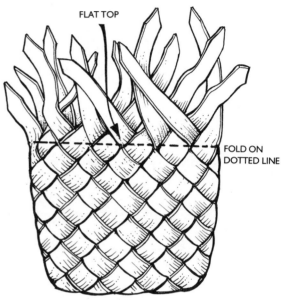

FLAT TOP BASKET

go under what strips you can and over what ones you can't. It will all be obvious, with one exception: with that second strip you bent over, you'd normally weave under the first square you come to. Instead, pass over it. Now you've dealt with one pair of strips. Repeat with all the pairs, with yet another special instruction: depending on which direction you head around the top of the basket, you'll come across one of two situations in which the strip you're using crosses a strip that's just been bent and woven in. It might be that the first strip of each pair you bend over will come to one of those second strips I wrote of that had to pass over a lot of squares. Following my instruction to weave under whatever you can, you might decide to go under it. Don't. Pin it down by going over it (and under the next one). The other situation you might come across with each second strip of a pair is a double strip in the first square you come to. Now, following my instruction for all second strips of pairs, you'd pass over this square.

- Flat top: Read directions for scalloped edge. Fold each pair diagonally, that is, so that the fold is parallel to the basket's base. Note that each folded-over strip follows the path its partner took as it came up the basket. Weave in as above. All those finicky special instructions apply here too.
  d) Double weave inside. This step is but a continuation of the weaving you did as you secured the folded-over edge. Keep weaving along the sides and bottom until, behold, two strips from opposite sides of the basket meet. Overlap them by a few squares, tucking in ends. You're done!

Here are ideas for ways to use birch bark:
- as a garden basket (for collecting and/or storing produce);

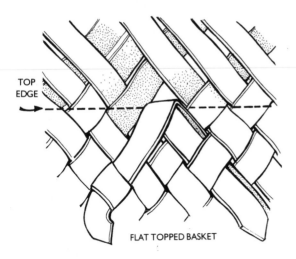

TOP
EDGE

FLAT TOPPED BASKET

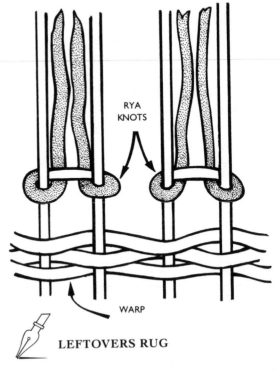

RYA
KNOTS

WARP

- as a laundry "hamper";
- as a laundry basket for wet clothes;
- as a storage basket for a variety of items, from toothbrushes to toys;
- as hot pads;
- as mats on dirt floors;
- as lampshades.

Here are some variations on the techniques I described. The appropriateness of each depends on the function the basket will serve.

- Use thicker or thinner strips.
- Scrape the bark to a thinner sheet (makes a lighter basket).
- Oil the bark (for longer-lasting flexibility).
- Leave gaps between the strips while weaving.
- Weave silver side out (beautiful, but less sturdy).
- Omit the last step of double weaving. Just make the top edge by weaving the ends in a short distance. (This makes a less sturdy basket.)
- Weave in two cloth or rope handles.

S. R.

LEFTOVERS RUG

If you have accumulated, as I had, cartons of small scraps of cloth and yarn left over from sewing and knitting or weaving projects over the years, here is a way to use them. You can also use the still-good portions of worn-out clothes.

Cut the cloth into strips. The minimum usable length is about five inches. Maximum width is about one inch for heavy wools and four inches for broadcloth. The width of a given strip can be irregular.

Sort the strips according to dominant color. This way you can plan color areas for your rug, either ahead of time or as you go along.

Yarn scraps can be as short as four inches, but you will also need lots of pieces over eight inches, including several at least three times the width of your rug, for strength.

Make a warp of strong, heavy string, with about ¼" of spacing. If you don't have a loom, you can improvise with a board somewhat larger than your rug size. Hammer in a row of small nails for each end of the rug. Space them ½" apart. They must be *firmly* into the board but stick up ½" or more. Wind the warp string back and forth between them. If you prefer, make these rows of nails semicircular, for an oval rug, or make some irregular shape.

You will need a fork or heavy comb for beating the rows of cloth or yarn firmly against each other. (With a mechanical loom, you can of course use the beater, but you can get more interesting lines if you do it by hand.)

Begin by weaving several rows with a long piece of yarn. Beat the rows firmly together (and close against the nails on the board loom) to get a good edge. Then start with the cloth strips. You will be working from the *back* of your rug. Fold a strip lengthwise so that it will be smooth (no raveling edges) on the right side. Weave as far as it will go, leaving 1½" at each end hanging toward you. Continue with another strip, overlapping ½" or more with the first. Try not to end cloth strips near the sides of the rug. Carry them around to start the next row.

Weave two rows of yarn between every one to four rows of cloth. This will help to hold the cloth in place. (As with the cloth, leave yarn ends hanging toward you.) It isn't necessary always to continue a row all the way across; you can let some areas build up ahead of others. But at least every few inches carry two or more rows of uncut yarn all the way across. This will increase strength. Your shorter pieces of yarn (four to eight inches) can be used for Rya knots, which make a fringe effect across the rug. Weave at least two rows of yarn or one of cloth between the rows of Rya knots.

With the nails-on-board loom, you can either weave right up to the nails, with the help of a crochet hook or large tapestry needle, or stop two inches earlier and cut and tie the warp ends. With a mechanical loom, cut and tie the warp as you normally would. Back the rug with heavy nonskid material, if you wish.

D. R.

 ## BASKET DESIGNS

I've been experimenting with making baskets out of local materials. Most of my efforts are usable but definitely not elegant—one assumes that comes with practice. Birch bark is easy to find, but it does mean killing a large birch tree. If you're clearing or thinning anyway, the bark is a wonderful by-product.

My one project using cedar bark was a hat that my father bravely wore for several summers. You'll have to ask him about its comfort—I do imagine it was more comfortable than, say, willow, with its cut ends digging in! At least cedar is soft and flexible, if somewhat fussy to work with. What I did was to take a four-foot length of cedar post and peel the bark off it. I tore the bark in long, thin strips, about a quarter of an inch wide (using mostly the inner bark, which is long and stringy). Then I just started in weaving— over and under, in a square mat. When it got to be head-size, I turned down the loose ends and wove them together, starting at the center point of each side. This is the same technique S. R. describes with the birch bark.

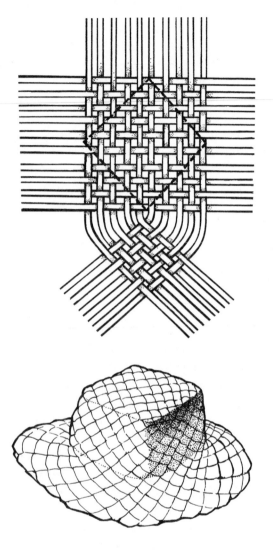

machine-stitch all round to keep them from fraying. The cedar made a very soft type of basket/hat; I couldn't imagine using it for most household purposes, where you want something sturdy.

That's where willow comes in; it's strong and sturdy. What you want is long (minimum three feet; ideally six feet) *unbranched* rods of one year's growth.

Down on the flats the beavers do the pruning for you; where they've been cutting willow, it sprouts back up every year from the stumps. This is the same principle as coppicing. We've just been starting to experiment with coppicing for firewood on a corner of our land, using mainly birch. But recently I've started attacking any willow growing around our clearing, cutting it back so it will sprout up. I know it helps for the trees to be fairly crowded, to discourage branching. We visited a willow plantation/basketry workshop in England, where they cut several acres of closely planted willow each year, of several different varieties. They grade the rods into four-foot, six-foot, and eight-foot lengths, soak (or boil?) them in vats, put them through a bark-stripping machine, and let them dry till ready for use. Then they soak them again at least overnight to make them pliable enough for weaving.

That's the way the professionals operate. What I did was go down on the flats with my pruning shears and cut an armful of three- to five-foot lengths. I've heard that the best time is fall or early spring before the sap flows, but I went in April, being too impatient to wait for next year. It definitely helps to get there before the leaves come out, though! I thought that by using the willow fresh I could avoid the soaking process—a mistake, in hindsight, as it was fairly brittle, especially

One slight problem—most heads are round, not square—but it seemed to work anyway! When I got to the brim, I pushed the loose ends out horizontally again. This turns the weaving into a diagonal weave—the strands don't cross at right angles any more, but at a shallow angle. Add in additional strands of cedar where needed. To finish I turned the strands back on themselves, pushing them in through a couple of rows of weaving. You could also leave them loose, for a fringe, and

the thicker rods. I found anything over 3/16″ too unbendable. It's fine to leave the bark on.

One note: it takes more time and material than you'd think to weave a large basket. I

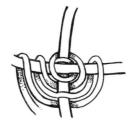

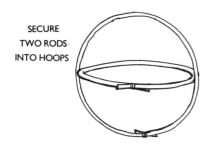

SECURE
TWO RODS
INTO HOOPS

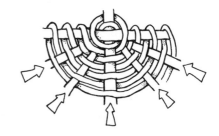

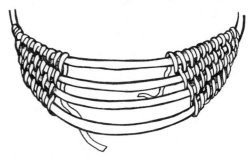

tried two different designs. Perhaps the easiest to make is the round or oval basket. Choose two long rods and make a circle of each, holding it closed with clothes pegs or twist-ties. Slip one circle inside the other, at right angles. Make sure the join of the vertical circle is at the bottom, and the join of the horizontal circle is in the middle of one side. Hold the circles in place with more pegs. Working first on one side and then the other, start to weave with a new flexible rod, round and round the crossing once or twice, then back and forth across the bottom three sticks a few more times. Now that you've secured the crossings, add in two more braces on each side of the center one (by cutting to about the right length and pushing the ends through the weaving you've just done). At some points it feels like you need about 10 hands. Persevere!

Continue the weaving back and forth, joining one weaver to the next by overlapping them for a few inches. Try to make the joins come near the middle, rather than at the edges. Do a few inches of weaving at one end, then go back to the other end of the basket. You will need to add in more bracing

pieces if your basket is sizable. You may need to do some partial back-and-forth rows across just the midsection of the weaving to compensate for the bowl shape of the bottom of the basket. Eventually you will meet yourself in the middle, and then you're done! If

WEAVE PARTIAL ROWS WHERE NECESSARY

you need a sturdier handle, push in another rod beside the existing one, twine it round and round, and push in deeply at the other edge. Finally, trim off all loose ends with your handy pruning shears. This basket will tend both to elongate and to flatten as the weaving proceeds. If you want a long, flat basket, relax, but if you want a deep, round one, you'll have to keep that goal firmly in

BASKET #1

mind as you go.

My second willow basket was a bit more difficult and turned out distinctly lopsided. But it is *very* serviceable. Want to try? Take

START FOR BASKET #2

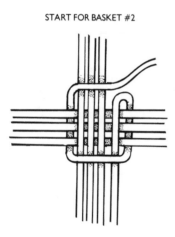

six stout pieces the diameter of the bottom of the basket. Cross three of them over the other three. Lay one end of a long rod alongside the upper three and, bending the other end back under, over, under, weave around the rods, first three at a time, then two at a time. Your second time around doing two at a time, you will be separating the rods into different pairs, because there is, of course, now an odd number of rods. (This is the function of the short end of your weaving rod.) This effectively spreads out the rods

into more or less a circle, but you will need to help the process along with brute strength. Try not to be so brutal as to crack or break the rods—you'll regret it! Weaving now over one, under one, join in another weaver when needed by overlapping it with the old one. When your circle is wide enough, secure your weaver by threading it back through the weaving. Trim the ends of the spokes to a quarter inch.

Now choose your uprights for the body of the basket. You will need 27 uprights. Cut the thick end of each to a point and push one

START FOR BASKET #2

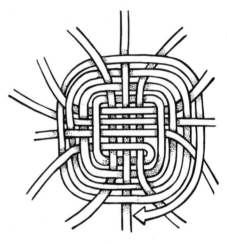

in on each side of every spoke. Place the leftover one in at random—you need an odd number. This makes a fairly large basket. For a smaller project, try a six-inch base and only one upright for each spoke (and one extra). Standing inside the basket, use the point of your pruning shears to press firmly on the turning spot, and one by one bend the uprights up. This is to prevent them from breaking at the bend. It didn't always work for me. I suspect soaking and thinner rods is the answer. Slip the ends of the uprights

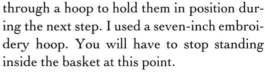

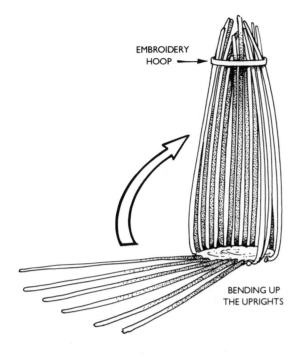

EMBROIDERY HOOP →

BENDING UP
THE UPRIGHTS

through a hoop to hold them in position during the next step. I used a seven-inch embroidery hoop. You will have to stop standing inside the basket at this point.

Weave the sides of the basket in any pattern you like. I started out with an "in front of three and behind one" pattern, using three

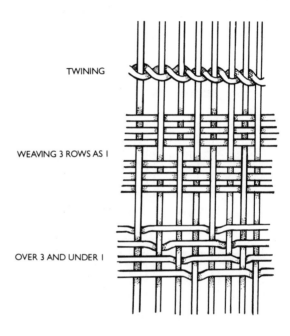

TWINING

WEAVING 3 ROWS AS I

OVER 3 AND UNDER I

weavers alternatively. This will make a firm base for the basket. Then I went on, using three rods as one, under and over each upright. This is a quick, easy way of filling in the sides, and it makes a firm basket. It's easy to join in new rods one at a time when one of the three runs out. You can take the hoop off as soon as the basket starts to hold its shape. You could make a more open basket by doing a few rows of weaving, leaving a gap of a few inches, then doing a few more rows. Twining might be an appropriate technique to use here. Using two weavers, twist them between each upright. At the top edge, fasten

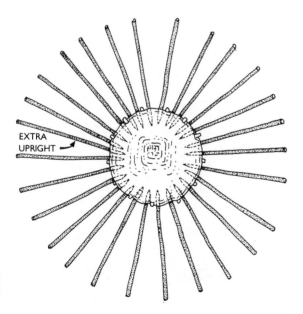

EXTRA
UPRIGHT →

UPRIGHTS IN POSITION

off your weavers. Take one upright in front of the next five, behind two, and out to the front again. Pull it down firmly into position and leave. This is another point to be careful of breakage. Take the next upright in front of five and behind two, etc., working your way around the basket. When you run out of uprights, trim the last few to a point and push them down through the weaving in the position where they would ordinarily have been left.

Trim off all the loose ends. If you've got this far, handles shouldn't deter you. On each side of the basket, push one end of a long rod down through several inches of weaving. Bend it over and pull it through the edge of the basket, six inches away. Twist it back along itself; weave around and about to secure. Make the handle stronger by fastening in a new length, twisting along the handle, and again securing. Your basket is now finished and ready for use in the laundry room or garden. It should last for years.

C. R.

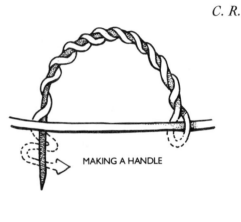

MAKING A HANDLE

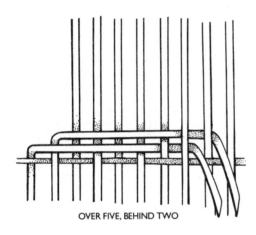

OVER FIVE, BEHIND TWO

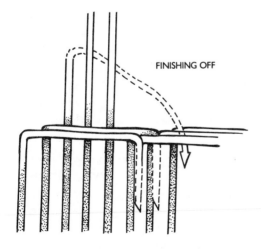

FINISHING OFF

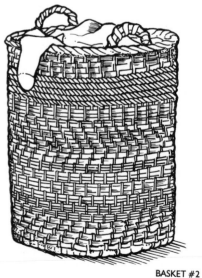

BASKET #2

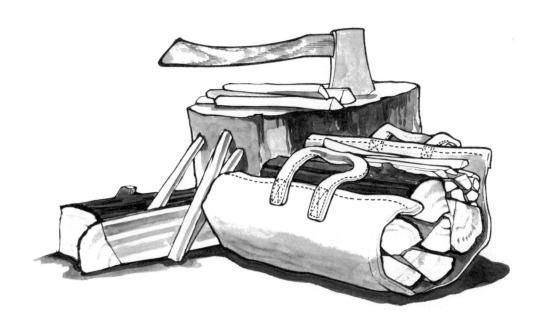

HOUSEHOLD TECHNIQUES

 COUNTRY LIVING IN A CITY

We live in a large city and have our small piece of land on which we endeavor to live as simply as possible. There seems to be a tendency for many of us to think that country living is the end-all and be-all. I would like to suggest that "smallholders" can live in the city too. We would love to be in the country, but for now, and perhaps always, to do the things that we believe in requires that we live in a city. Our free time spent in the interior and on the coast gives us the vitality to come back renewed to try again to live our way of life in a city.

At first I found it difficult moving to a large city, and I actively hated it for some time. However, I have discovered that the majority of our acquaintances here are totally clued out about simple living, and it is proving to be an enriching experience to share our skills and knowledge with city folks. Even introducing small things to these people like recycling garbage and growing sprouts is an adventure. The majority of Canadians live in cities, and we city smallholders can do much to help awaken this part of our population. It would be interesting to hear what other people have to say about this.

J. S. & D. P.

 BLACKSMITHING IS A SIMPLE SKILL

The basic tools needed for blacksmithing or forge work are few. A forge, coal, an anvil, a hammer, and tongs—that's it, basically. "Nice-to-have" items expand this list considerably but still don't make the collection unwieldy.

The Forge
The blacksmith's forge consists of a hearth, upon which soft or bituminous coal is burned, and a blower. The blower is generally connected in some manner to the body of the forge so that its air blast enters the bottom of the hearth through a pipe called the tuyere, or air nozzle. Mine is a small manufactured model probably turned out some 20 to 30 years ago. Most older farms have had forges set up at one time or another for dealing with iron and steel hardware pertinent to farming.

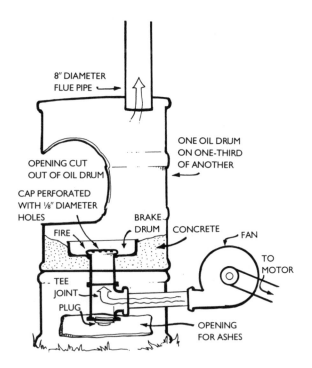

8" DIAMETER
FLUE PIPE

ONE OIL DRUM
ON ONE-THIRD
OF ANOTHER

OPENING CUT
OUT OF OIL DRUM

CAP PERFORATED
WITH ⅛" DIAMETER
HOLES

FIRE

BRAKE
DRUM

CONCRETE

FAN

TO
MOTOR

TEE
JOINT

PLUG

OPENING
FOR ASHES

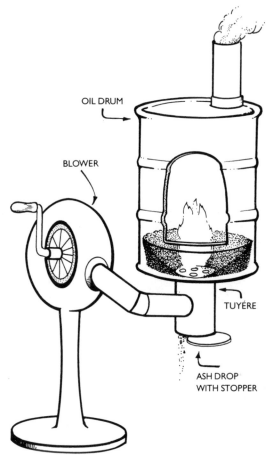

OIL DRUM

BLOWER

TUYÉRE

ASH DROP
WITH STOPPER

Old sawmills and mines generally had forges and related equipment too. So the goods are still around to be had; the problem lies in persuading owners to part with them. "Haven't used the thing for twenty years," they'll say, "but you never know ..." The forge, and particularly the anvil, is the kind of tool that one can become attached to. Old guys who have done a fair amount of blacksmithing tend to befriend these tools as a rider might a horse. If you appreciate that feeling and demonstrate some of your own, you may score an otherwise inaccessible forge setup.

I bought a forge with a blower for $10 two years ago. The tuyere is a beauty—big, with an ash drop hole in the bottom. I plan to build a stone forge eventually, using it and the blower. Mention of this impending effort leads me to point out that you can, if you have no luck finding the manufactured forge,

build your own. A 45-gallon drum with a hole cut out of the center forms a ready-made hearth and a hood for smoke dispersal. You'll still need a blower and some form of tuyere (like an old truck tire rim), but these are simple in principle. I prefer a hand crank blower to an electrically driven one with a rheostat. I find the hand crank blower saves fuel because it stops turning while I'm working over the anvil. The rheostat, in contrast, has to be flipped off each time you stop heating metal, and that becomes a hassle. Also, there is a fine rhythm developed in turning the hand crank, and blacksmithing at its best is all rhythm.

Coal

The coal, as I've said, should be soft or bituminous, the idea being to eliminate impurities. As the coal heats, impurities will combine to form a hard, glasslike substance called a clinker. Clinkers provide no heat, obstruct the air flow, and have to be removed from the fire. Blacksmith's coal (ask for it by name) is processed to a functional point of purity. Other coals will work but not as well, and clinkers will be the problem.

Anvil

Anvils are the toughest of the essentials to find. Again, old farms are your best bet.

A good anvil has a fairly sharp right angle edge plus a smooth surface plate on top. I bought one for $10 (after a year-long search) that had been badly scarred with edges chipped off and nicks in the surface plate. I had it resurfaced by an old blacksmith who had arc welding equipment. He used a self-hardening rod to build it up and then reground the surface and the edges smooth.

Anvils are becoming rare, and you won't get one cheap from anyone who knows the value of junk. If you keep your eyes open, however, you may run into someone who has an anvil and sees it only as a heavy slab of steel (which it is) and will be grateful to have you haul it away.

Hammers

I was fortunate in finding a whole set of brand new army surplus forging tools. I've added to this collection mostly from junk shops, trade for other tools, and the like. There are quite a few forging hammers (like chisels for cutting metal either hot or cold), punches of various sizes, flatters, a cross peen, a straight peen, a four- to six-pound hammer, and an eight-pound sledge. The list

could go on, but these should do you for starters.

Tongs

Tongs almost don't make it into the "basic" category. Most work can be held by the hands while one part of it is being heated and worked. When the piece being worked is small, however, tongs are essential to grip it firmly during hammering. They come in all shapes and sizes, but basically you need one for holding flat steel and one for round stock. You can make your own in the forge to fit the job at hand once you get into it.

Nice-to-Have Items

A blacksmith's vise is nice. The difference between it and a machinist's vise is that you can beat it or, preferably, beat an object being held in its jaws. It absorbs the shock via an extension that runs down and is grounded in cement, stone, or dirt. The blacksmith's vise is very useful for bending hot metal and in certain specialized forging techniques.

A drill press, a tap and die set, and a grinder are also quite handy.

Books can be quite helpful, though of course they are no substitute for direct experience. I say that because I have a tendency to collect books and to read a subject ragged without ever doing it. I've particularly enjoyed *The Village Blacksmith* by Aldren A. Watson for a general feel of the thing. For technical assistance, a lot of textbooks were written for school metal shops in the 1920s and 1930s, and some of them can still be found.

Odd Notes

Your forge can be set up anywhere that won't create a fire hazard. The immediate heat around the fire isn't extreme, but sparks do occur. A dirt or cement floor and a hood are best for this reason. The forge produces an intense heat (around 2000° F) but a very localized one.

Blacksmithing is a simple art—the grandfather of all metalwork, a teacher of mine called it—and it lends itself nicely to any number of practical tasks.

D. A.

 TEACHING YOUNG CHILDREN
AT HOME

One of the responsibilities of living simply is how to keep our children, Akka, 4, and Niko, 2, happy and busy as we bustle around. In the summer, the garden is exciting to them and they have their own little plots, but in the winter, a small space seems even smaller.

It's a challenge to educate them—not only in numbers and letters, but in attitude. We select their toys and reading material carefully. I've made several books for them. Akka's first book, before she was two, was an old, sturdy three-ring folder with cardboard (shoe box weight) cut to size for pages. I cut pictures from discarded magazines (our community center has a box for magazines and books people pass on) and pasted them on the pages, cut the cow from the baking soda box, the rooster from the cornstarch box, and saved pretty postcards. I also scanned seed catalogues and used seed packages for pictures. It's been the favorite of both kids, mostly, I think, because it's based on our lifestyle. I've added to it until it's full, and now it's time for a new one with letters and words under the pictures.

I also make other books for them—draw simple pictures with simple captions or put their photos in the book with captions, preferably using their words. (The book, *Teacher*, by Sylvia Ashton Warner has still more ideas.) They love any reference to themselves and learn to recognize their names quickly. An alphabet book has a capital letter on each page and nothing else. Pages are cards made from poster-board-weight paper gotten from the printer as edged reject paper and held together by rings. We used names of people we know for all the letters so that the symbols are connected with live, meaningful folk. The picture image is the letter. When they saw the *A*, they said, "*A* for Akka." Then we encouraged them to only name the letters, and soon they caught on. After they mastered the capitals, the small letters were put on the backs of the cards with the capitals.

Another homemade picture object is a puzzle. I cut large pictures out and paste them onto heavy cardboard, then cut them into large, simple jigsaw puzzles.

I don't like Play-doh because I don't think food should be used as a plaything. I let them help me make cookies, which they can cut out or press down, knead bread dough for rolls, cut out doughnuts, or just crack the eggs and mix the dough. Kids love to crack eggs. Or they make custards.

One thing that we do is cultivate their memories. We ask after they come back from a walk, "Where did you go? What did you see? Who did you see? What color was the bird?" These questions make them alert to their environment. They enjoy reporting what they've seen and can be encouraged to look for different things. We also attempt to identify birds, trees, flowers, mushrooms, and so on, and what we don't know, we try to find out. We ask Akka, "What does the spider eat?" And Niko asks us, "What kind of bird makes that kind of noise?" They learn as they are interested. I stop talking, often unfinished, when I see they have lost interest. We tell them as many facts as we think they can handle.

Our kids help whenever they can in real work. They like to hold the bottles for the goat kids (the bottles rest in holes in the fence, so not so much support is needed), look for duck eggs, and feed the chickens. They run little errands with great pride and enjoy breaking the news like "The goats are out!"

Of course all this doesn't keep them busy all day. They run their own lives and come to us only when they are bored. Akka cuts out pictures for her own books, which are kept where the kids can reach them, and they have access to most of their toys (except ones that need supervision), so they don't need us to change from one activity to another. Their coats and hats are hung at their level so they can dress themselves and go out when they want to.

I recommend two kids close in age for a family unless there is a communal group. They enjoy each other as playmates and companions and don't need adults for constant company. They usually play as we work around in the house or outside, so we are all aware of where everyone is. We can get a lot done even though the kids are with us all day. They are an integral part of our home, and they know it.

H. K.

HOME REMEDIES FOR INSECT BITES

An antidote for nettle stings is dock. Crush the dock leaves and rub them on the stings.

Baking soda, applied damp on blackfly bites, relieves the itch and the swelling.

For yellowjacket and honey bee stings, apply damp baking soda.

Can anyone tell us more about prevention for mosquito bites or applications? We have heard of and have used salt, soda and vinegar on bites.

B. T.

MOSQUITO BITE TALK

Mosquitoes must be some sort of heavy spiritual lesson. We are probably lucky to have them as teachers.

But I have made a homemade mosquito repellent that works! I searched my various herb books and found lists of things that make good repellents and some that are good for soothing the bites once you have them.

For Insect Bite Pain: Chamomile flowers, comfrey leaves and root, nettle seeds, plantain leaves, sorrel leaves, dock leaves, pyrola leaves, ragwort leaves.

As an Insect Repellent: Chamomile flowers, elder leaves and flowers, nettle leaves, onion bulb, oxeye daisy flowers, feverfew leaves and flowers, pennyroyal leaves and flowers.

Oxeye daisy is the prevalent wild one.

Feverfew *(Chrysanthemum parthenium)* is a shrubby member of the daisy family with masses of deeply lobed, toothed leaves and branched clusters of yellow, buttonlike flowers surrounded by small white rays. Bees particularly dislike it.

Pennyroyal *(Hedeoma pulegioides)* is used in old-fashioned "fly dopes." A member of the mint family, it has aromatic hairy oval leaves and tight clusters of small, pale violet flowers in the leaf axils. Prefers dry soil. Common from Minnesota to England and south.

The recipe I found went like this: in a small canning jar, pack the chopped leaves and flowers of pennyroyal and feverfew; add a small stick of cinnamon, crushed; cover with almond oil. (Almonds contain a small amount of sulfur, which all insects dislike.)

Now I had neither pennyroyal nor feverfew, so I just substituted mint and oxeye daisy. I added several tablespoons of powdered cinnamon and covered it with regular vegetable oil. And it worked. It works even better after it has been brewing for several hours. After five or six days the mint and daisy pieces get rather grungy, and I would recommend starting another batch. My goop seemed to soothe bites as well as keep the mosquitoes away. I then tried adding several tablespoons of strong powdered garlic and it seemed to work even better, but the garlic slightly burned the old bites I had. Also, my young daughter eventually smears whatever I put on her face into her eyes, so I use a batch without garlic for her. I would recommend experimenting with mixtures of any or all the plants on the repellent list.

Concentrated oils can be purchased from the druggist. You might also ask your druggist if he or she has a recipe for a repellent. You can get oil of citronella and pennyroyal oil. Citronella *(Cymbopogon nardus)* is a grass grown chiefly in southern Asia and has a pungent citron aroma. It is a main ingredient in many commercial repellents. Just remember that the oils you buy are very concentrated. Concentrated pennyroyal oil is supposed to be poison and should be kept away from eyes and mucous membranes. I have

also heard that it is dangerous to pregnant women and can cause contractions.

Another relatively effective repellent is a smudge pot. Smoke seems to annoy mosquitoes and keep them at a distance. I have been using mint leaves, but burning almost anything will work. Just put some dry tinder and some wet or fresh leaves in a can with holes punched in the sides or on any fireproof surface and light them. It's a good thing to do before you go to bed. Good luck.

L. E.

HOW LAPLANDERS COPE WITH MOSQUITO BITES

In Lapland there are many mosquitoes—*many.* Samer (Lapps) appear very unbothered by mosquitoes in comparison with the fair-skinned Norwegian. The reason is that at the beginning of mosquito season Samer let the mosquitoes bite and drink their fill. It hurts, but the bite won't itch as much after. You can become sick; I was quite dizzy the first few days, but you soon become immune to the mosquito's poison. It's difficult, but it is worth the trouble and better than spraying poison all over your skin.

A. K.

REUSING LETTERS AND ENVELOPES

We appreciate notes on recycled paper in recycled envelopes. We use the back of all the letters sent to us to write drafts of articles, make notes, outline copy, make copies of copy, etc. We fold letters that are written on one side of the paper and bypass the envelope. If we need to use an envelope, we reuse one you sent us.

H. K.

TWO WHITEWASH RECIPES

Enclosed are recipes for whitewash. As I look out the window, I see snow lower on the mountain. Winter's a comin'. It's been a good year.

Expensive Whitewash
Combine:

    25 lb. hydrated lime

    4 gal. hot water

    Mix into 1 gal. cold water:

    2 gal. skim milk (for sticking power—it won't flake)

    5 lb. salt

    5 lb. cement

    ½ lb. alum

    ¼ tin of lye

When both solutions are cold, mix together slowly, stirring vigorously. Thin the mix with fresh water if too thick.

Cheap Whitewash
Combine:

    50 lb. hydrated lime

    6 gal. water

    15 lb. salt, dissolved in 5 gal. water

Add lime paste to salt. Mix and stir vigorously. Thin to milklike consistency.

R. M.

FIRE: A CAUTIONARY TALE

We have always considered ourselves very careful about fires. We cleaned our stovepipes regularly, were careful about not putting items too close to the stoves, and in general were very safety conscious. And after all, fires happen to other people, right? Yet the night of November 27, our place burned to the ground. The careful accumulation of homestead tools and equipment for the way of life we love was gone in a few minutes.

We had a very charming living arrangement. This summer we built a huge platform, placed a tipi at each end, and built a kitchen room in the middle. We connected the tipis by small tunnels to the kitchen room so that we had a reallly unique three-room house. We loved it, and it bought us more time before we had to build a permanent house.

We had insulated the kitchen room and the tunnels to the tipis with standard paper-covered fiberglass insulation. We were waiting for some foil paper to arrive to cover the insulation paper. The pipes for the airtight heaters in each tipi were safely and correctly brought out through the canvas. In the kitchen we had a wood cookstove. We have no electricity and used Coleman lanterns for lighting. We had a kerosene-burning lantern because it was supposed to be safer than naphtha.

The night of the fire I had filled our lamps and lit and hung one on a hook from the ceiling after it was properly established. A few minutes later there was a pop, and flaming kerosene started pouring out of the lamp. It immediately ignited the paper covering the insulation and spilled all over the floor, making a large pool of fire there. The paper covering the insulation provides a barrier to vapor and contains tar, which is quite flammable.

I had attended a fire safety talk that very morning, and it was fresh in my mind that I should not put water on an oil or gasoline fire, since it will spread the fire. It is hard to see how anything could have made our fire spread faster than it did, and I have since learned that once the gasoline is spent, it is safe to put water on the fire. In any case, we had only a hose from a nearby spring, and the pressure was insufficient to reach the ceiling fire. Baking soda was nearby, but not enough to have any effect.

Our valuable papers were in one tipi, and after quickly debating about going in after them, I decided I would probably be trapped and went out the front door. I almost certainly would have been. Our children heard the commotion and came running, and one said as I came out the door the flames were right behind me and it looked as though I were on fire. All of this took less than five minutes. The flames were already into the tunnels to the tipis and had reached a neat stack of small, dry, split cookstove wood stacked against one whole outside wall of the kitchen. On our platform up against the outside walls of the kitchen there were also chain saw gas and oil, naphtha, and kerosene. Both tipis contained ammunition, which quickly began to explode.

Our goats were in a corral right below the platform, and we led them down to a neighbor's barn for safety. Soon all of the community had arrived, and a human-chain bucket brigade was formed from the creek nearby to the fire site. Our one hose was used to keep the fire from spreading, and someone arrived later with a pump. The heat was incredible. In an hour it was all over,

and the water hose was running quietly over the charred and blackened foundation logs.

I received two small burns on one hand from dripping tar from the insulation paper, and there were tar spots all over my shirt from those first two or three minutes when I was trying to deal with the fire at its inception. Experienced fire fighters say we could have done nothing and were wise to get away quickly.

We knew there is no fire insurance in the woods except individual care and safety consciousness. In many ways we were scrupulously careful, and in as many others our place was doomed.

We believe there is only one thing that might have saved our place, and that is a good fire extinguisher used in the first moments of the fire to encircle and contain the ceiling blaze and the floor fire. We had no other buildings on our property, so all our tools and equipment were either on or under the platform. We lost them all. It would have been much wiser to have even a simple shack located away from the main buildings so that *everything* was not stored in one place. This would have really helped to cut losses.

Please look around your own homesteads. Correct your own fire hazards so you do not experience the total loss in a fire that we did. Remember:

- *Don't* store flammable liquids near a building.
- *Don't* store ammunition in your house.
- *Don't* have everything you own in one place.
- *Don't* store good dry firewood, all split, up against a house wall.
- *Do* cover insulation paper with something less flammable.
- *Do* have a way to get water to a fire quickly

to cool it and thereby save some things. The fire department tells us that lots of water is still the best protection in a house fire.

- Your life is much more important than your possessions, and don't take unnecessary chances with it.

Fire, in its destructive form, leaves an ugly scar on the land. Our site will take a long time to heal and look beautiful again, especially when so many people's belongings were burned. I am writing this in the hope that someone will learn something from our loss. We too thought it couldn't happen to us.

M. Q.

CLEANING YOUR RUGS

If you have a dirty wool rug and there is snow on the ground, now is the time to clean it. Pick a day when it is 25°F or lower and there are powder snow conditions. Put your rug outside for a half hour or so to cool off. (This will allow any grease in the fabric to harden, and the rug will not melt the snow.) Place the rug upside down on a clean patch of snow and walk all over it so as to work the snow well into the rug. Then shake the rug—or better yet, hang it up and beat it—to remove the snow. Repeat the process until you are satisfied with the results. Children even enjoy this kind of work.

M. B.

FRAMING WINDOWS BY THE MOON

I've noticed that winter sun takes the path of summer full moon, and winter full moon takes the path of summer sun. One-quarter and three-quarter moons use the path of the sun three months from that time. This information can aid folks who move to an area and want to see where the sun will be on their to-be-constructed dwelling so that they can make the best use of solar energy and summer shade. It is a handy trick for siting that window to get all that fleeting sun on the 15th of January when you are constructing in the summer or standing on a snow bank staking out a proposed plan.

R. P.

P.S. In fact, any full moon gives you the sun in six months.

CUTTING SHEET METAL—MEXICAN STYLE

Can I offer this tip for those who would like to make a barrel stove? This is a method of cutting heavy sheet steel without a cutting torch with an ease and efficiency that almost must be seen to be believed. I learned it from some auto body workers in Mexico. Using a hammer, you strike the side of the tip of a screwdriver so that it protrudes as little as possible through the metal. The blows must be struck as close as possible to the metal. Each blow will yield over a half inch of the cleanest cut you ever saw, with little damage to the screwdriver.

R. N.

NOT THIS

THE ART OF WOOD SPLITTING

Wood is a nice thing, especially when you admire it growing, make things like houses with it, or sit by a warm wood stove with your feet in the oven on a blustery night. It doesn't just jump into your arms prepackaged, but that doesn't have to spoil your love for the stuff if you know what you're doing. Instead of beating around the bush, I will get to the point, namely cutting and splitting alder for firewood.

Alder has a reputation for killing more people than any other kind of tree. Remember that fact when you fall any alder over 6" through. When you get over 15", then look out. It's nice to split when it's freshly cut in rounds, but it would just as soon split while you are falling it. Any sizable alder with a considerable lean to it will just love to barberchair when you are making the felling cut. A barberchair is when the tree splits up the middle and hinges about 10' or 15' up instead of where you want it to. As the front part of the tree falls in the correct direction,

the back half sweeps back past the logger and takes off his or her head if he or she is in the way. This all can happen instantly. If this or anything similarly drastic happens, chuck your chain saw and haul ass along your safety route, which you have spotted before you began cutting. Naturally you will have cleared all branches up to 8' and anything on the forest floor that might trip you up. Keep an eye on where the tree is falling.

When an alder barberchairs, it is about as much fun to get down from its high hinge as a tree that gets hung up in another tree. To prevent barberchairing, don't fall in the direction of the lean the tree has. Pull the tree to the side by aiming the notch to the side and leaving more wood in the hinge on the side you want the tree to fall to when you make the felling cut. This causes the tree to pull in that direction as it falls. Also consider branches and foliage to see how the tree is weighted up above. Be exceptionally careful if the top of the tree is dead; it can fall on you as you're cutting. Don't cut with more than a slight wind blowing, and take that wind into acount for direction. On a slope, find the plumb line with an ax or string and rock so you interpret the lean of the tree correctly. If the tree comes back on the saw when you are making the felling cut, a wedge can be used to free it (from the notch side if necessary). Always stay relaxed but exceptionally aware. Use your sixth sense to avoid danger.

When the tree is down, all the branches must be trimmed off. Be wary of the trunk of the tree when you are doing this; it can drop or roll and break your leg. Pile the small branches in an out-of-the-way place; alder rots amazingly quickly. Sometimes it is useful to drop a tree across a log so that it isn't lying flat to the ground; the rounds can then

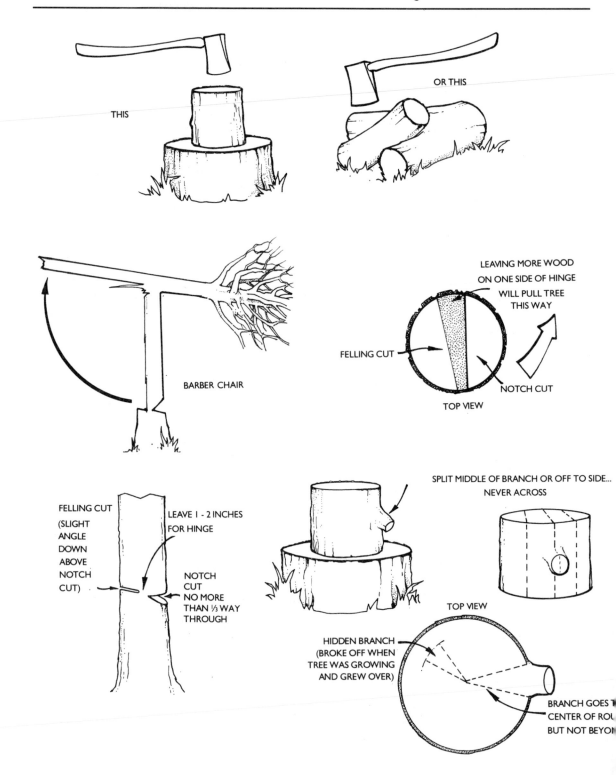

THIS

OR THIS

BARBER CHAIR

LEAVING MORE WOOD
ON ONE SIDE OF HINGE
WILL PULL TREE
THIS WAY

FELLING CUT

NOTCH CUT

TOP VIEW

FELLING CUT
(SLIGHT
ANGLE
DOWN
ABOVE
NOTCH
CUT)

LEAVE 1 - 2 INCHES
FOR HINGE

NOTCH
CUT
NO MORE
THAN 1/3 WAY
THROUGH

SPLIT MIDDLE OF BRANCH OR OFF TO SIDE...
NEVER ACROSS

TOP VIEW

HIDDEN BRANCH
(BROKE OFF WHEN
TREE WAS GROWING
AND GREW OVER)

BRANCH GOES T
CENTER OF ROU
BUT NOT BEYON

be taken off more easily. If the tree is flat to the ground, there is risk of dulling the chain on dirt or rocks. (The Stihl 041 is a lovely saw. It is light enough for women yet has 5 horsepower and is capable of holding a 25" bar with rollernose tip.) One solution is to buck the log into 10′ lengths and slide the lengths onto a branch or something so that one end is off the ground. Be very careful when cutting a 4′ piece in half. Keep your foot away from the saw and your balance steady. It's safer on the last two rounds to cut partway through without using your foot to hold the log and then to turn it over to finish the cut. Keep the saw sharp enough to cut effortlessly.

I don't like chain saws for vibes, but after cutting with a crosscut saw for a year, I decided a chain saw was worth it. Sometimes it's nice to use an ax and a Swede saw to fell trees. Then you can hear the tree and know what's happening. With a chain saw, you just keep your eye on the felling cut. If it's opening, then the tree is starting to go. By the way, side notches an inch or two deep will help prevent barberchairing. Do these after front-notching the tree. Also, don't notch a leaning tree as deeply as usual. Sometimes a leaner will go just after the felling cut is started (all the tension is in the back surface).

Split your alder as soon as possible after cutting, ideally right where you have cut the rounds. It is tough to split when it's seasoned. Alder really changes a great deal in seasoning. It is hard to season for carpentry use, but it's one of the most dimensionally stable woods that there is after seasoning (meaning it won't warp easily). When wet, it is white and heavy with moisture. Alders love water and will lose a surprising amount

of weight as they dry. Here on the coast, an alder can grow to cutting size (nine inches) in 15 years. They grow like weeds.

If a round has a branch, then split down the middle of the branch or well to the side of it. It is impossible to split across a branch. Remember, the branch goes to the center of the round, but not past the center. I find it handy to turn branches so they point down. Use a wedge if necessary. Big rounds often require a wedge to split them into halves or quarters before an ax is used. A six- or eight-pound sledge will do for a five-pound wedge. Have a second wedge in case the first gets stuck. Don't use your ax as a wedge. A chip of metal can come off the axhead and injure or blind you when you strike it with the sledge. To save handling and hassle later, split your wood right down to the size you will need. A roof over your wood is necessary for winter, but you don't need walls. If you cut your wood by September it should be quite dry by November. To dry wood in a hurry, cross-stack it in the woodshed rather than stacking it all in the same direction. If you are burning green wood through misfortune, dry it in the oven before stuffing it into the stove. If you must stack rounds outside of shelter, never leave the cut ends up, because they will absorb rather than shed rain.

Often a piece of wood won't split when you strike it with the ax. Check for branches or knots. Then hit the axhead on the chopping block rather than the piece of wood. The momentum will force the wood into the ax. Use a full swing when you do this, being sure the piece is tight on the ax so it won't fall on you during the swing. Naturally this doesn't work with a big piece, since it would be too heavy to swing over your head. Use the wedge on big pieces that get stuck. Remember to do a full-circle swing with the smaller pieces.

When swinging an ax, get in touch with its momentum. Use a circle and add force throughout the swing to the natural momentum of the axhead. Never fight the ax. Flow with it. Think of the surface of the chopping block, the ax sticking in the surface, and the alder lying split on either side. Focus of energy is important. Don't doubt your strength.

There is a scene in the original Japanese movie version of *Seven Samurai* of a samurai who trains by chopping wood. This is very instructive.

A good chopping block is essential. Often a stump trimmed to the correct height is the best. At least it's well rooted. Maple makes excellent chopping blocks too.

Red cedar is the kindling par excellence. Trim from shake cutting or shake logs that are too rotten for shakes make good starting material. Second-growth cedars are often too knotty.

Fir is more difficult to split and requires wedge work and patience. Birch and maple are great. Fir is the only firewood in many places, and it burns well when split up. But when available, alder is the best firewood. Reserve fir for carpeting the hills with green.

S. L.

 PREVENTING FIRE

Fires usually have a common cause—the stove hookup. A high percentage of the stove hookups that I've seen in people's homes have aspects that are frightening. And the building done by the back-to-the-land bunch is no exception; I see little respect or knowledge of how to handle this element in an all-wood home. But how do you get people to alter their work or attitudes? Here are some points I've noted:

1. At the top of the list! When designing your house and installing your stove, chimney, and roof jack, leave enough distance between wood and heated metal. Remember, that stovepipe could be red hot sometime. I hate to try to set a figure, but I'd say eight inches is too close to a stovepipe unless there's a workable form of insulation in between. When you have a roof jack made up, make the square sheet of metal that joins the roof large enough to allow you to cut a sufficiently large hole in the roof for the chimney to pass through. If you have a second floor, the rafters and floor joists must be lined up rather than staggered so that the chimney doesn't pass too close to a rafter on one side and a floor joist on the other. I've seen boards one and two inches from a bare stovepipe.

2. A lot of people don't realize the full function of an insulated chimney. Not only does it contain all that radiant heat in the event of a chimney fire, but it is the main factor in preventing chimney fires. Chimney fires happen because of creosote buildup in the chimney. Cook stoves burn hot, dry, and fast and don't usually leave much creosote. A heater that has been loaded with wet, green softwood and shut down for the night creates the ideal conditions for producing creosote for two reasons. One, of course, is that the fire is not going to be hot enough to burn up all those vapors and tars, which will all go up the

chimney in the smoke. The second reason is that since there is less heat going up the chimney from a slow fire, the smoke cools before reaching the top of the chimney. That is when the moisture in the smoke condenses, leaving the creosote. Once I couldn't figure out why my stove wouldn't burn, and on inspecting the stovepipe, I discovered that where it left the warm cabin and entered the cold winter air it was completely plugged solid with creosote. (No exaggeration; I had difficulty chiseling it out with a bar.) So anyway, it's very important to have the exterior portion of your chimney insulated right at the top, and the interior portion at least where it's near wood.

Creosote can do different things. It can be thin and gooey, the kind that seeps through the cracks, runs down the outside of the stove pipe, and is easy to burn out in the morning. Just get a quick fire going of kindling or newspaper, open the door of the stove, and whoosh—it's gone right to the top. (If your roof is dry, don't forget to look for sparks afterwards.) Also, creosote can build up dry and chunky in the upper sections and be hard to light—until that time you load up the stove and go out for the day.

If you can't afford an insulated chimney, it's advisable to take the shortest route through the house (keeping a good distance from the wood as you go) and out near the peak of the roof to avoid exposure to the cold outside air. In any case, you should maintain a high level of consciousness as to the condition of the inside of your chimney!

3. A lot of people staple foil or asbestos paper to the wall behind their stove and figure they've taken all the necessary precautions. This is grossly inadequate and could be making things worse. Never attach anything flat to the wall without leaving an airspace behind it. The air and heat are trapped there, and the temperature of the wall can build up until the wood starts to char. But you don't know it because you can't see or feel what's happening. The best thing to do is attach a sheet of tin, cut large enough to intercept all radiant heat from the stove. It should be mounted 1–1½" from the wall with non-burnable spacers. This can be done by cutting short lengths of pipe or conduit and driving a nail through the tin and the spacer and into the wall. Don't extend the tin all the way to the floor but leave an inch or two for the air to come in. The tin will deflect the radiant heat, and through convection, a constant flow of cool air from the floor will run up the wall, with warm air escaping out the top. It will also enable you to stick your hand back in there when the stove is burning extra hot and find out how warm the wall actually is. If you think one layer of tin won't be sufficient, add a second layer and airspace.

4. Make everything solid. Long, rickety lengths of stovepipe all haywired together are pretty risky. If you value your house, contents, life, etc., you won't take any chances. Stovepipe seams can come apart, and when that happens there is nothing to keep two sections tightly joined. Using a sharp nail for a center punch, you can drill three holes where the sections join and put in three sheet metal screws. An insulated chimney especially needs something to support its weight. Don't rely on the roof jack; it's often only soldered together, and

the natural tendency is to run the roof boards too close to gain extra support and keep things from sagging. With that metal plumber strapping with the holes in it that comes in a roll, and a variety of sheet metal screws, stove bolts, lag screws, washers, etc., you can make a hanger that supports your chimney from the bottom. If you're thinking about building—maybe you should think about building a cement-block chimney.

5. When creosote is burning, it can come out of your chimney in a range of forms from hard little sparks that bounce off and roll down the roof to flaming gooey chunks that might stick and burn. I've got a shake roof, so I keep track of my chimney even though it's insulated. Here again, if you're building, you might consider aluminum roofing, at least on either side of your chimney. If you live under or near trees, check your roof in the fall for dry leaves and tamarack needles that might have built up against the uphill side of your roof jack or in the cracks between the shakes and that might catch wayward sparks. You should also be aware of the probability that sparks may occasionally jump out of the stove through the draft vent. Take preventive measures, like laying tin on the floor or maybe fitting screen inside the vent.

6. Everybody who has a house should put some thought into how he or she would control a fire if one did break out. Some prerequisites I've thought of are: Have a good water supply to your house that will be dependable through the driest summers and coldest winters and that has enough pressure to spray water to the top of your roof. Have a hose long enough to reach anywhere in or around your house, with a nozzle and spare washers, drained, coiled, hanging out of the weather, and ready at all times. Have a good fire extinguisher. Of the dry chemical type, I know that the orange ones are rated A, B, and C. They are meant for wood fires, whereas the red ones are only rated B and C. Other good things to think about are installing a frost-proof hydrant outside the house, acquiring a secondhand fire pump if you are near a creek, or at least having some buckets around. Remember, even if you can't put the fire out, it is worth your while to keep dumping water on it. There are usually things you can salvage like kitchen utensils, books, canned fruit, etc.

7. The only other thing that I can think of is to keep aware of potential dangers: like going away and leaving a lamp burning around cats and little kids, or letting things get piled or pushed too near a stove (maybe you want to build a little wrought-iron fence around it).

These are some things I've learned from living around wood stoves all my life.

R. V.

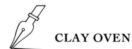

CLAY OVEN

My friends Anne and Hugo built a beautiful clay oven here, and soon after they left to hunt for land in Brazil, I forgot to protect it from the rain and it is no more. We are going to build another like it sooner or later, and this time we will cover it with something permanent and waterproof.

The oven was about four feet long by three

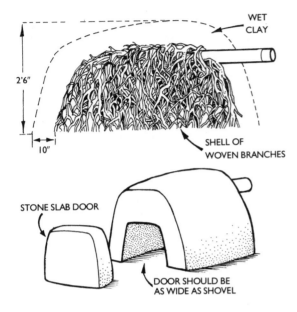

WET CLAY

2'6"

10"

SHELL OF WOVEN BRANCHES

STONE SLAB DOOR

DOOR SHOULD BE AS WIDE AS SHOVEL

will stand the weight of the first layers of clay, since it will be burned away after the oven is finished. Sturdy branches were stuck firmly into the ground, because wet clay is heavy. Before Anne and Hugo started plastering on the clay, they found a flat slab of stone to use as a door; the finished front hole needs to be quite a bit smaller than the stone, so it is just as well to find the stone first.

They found a source of clay, mixed the clay with plenty of binding material (roots, willow—the kind of things that don't rot easily in the compost heap), and just kept plastering it on layer after layer until they had built the walls up to about 10" thick. They left it to dry out in the sun, and if a crack appeared anywhere, they filled it in right away with wet clay. They mixed some lime with the final layers, but I don't know why, and I don't know whether they know either. That is also the time to do something about waterproofing the surface to avoid the kind of tragedy that befell us when it rained for several days at a stretch. It doesn't get very hot on the outside, so there are probably all kinds of ways to waterproof. When it seemed to be dried out, they lit a good, bright fire inside and kept it going steadily for several hours, burning away all the original wood framework.

The oven had been built by the side of the camp fire because at that time we were living in a tent on the site and cooking on the fire. To heat the oven for baking, Anne and Hugo shoveled all the hot ashes of a dying fire into the oven and closed it up tight, even stuffing up the chimney. (Heating up the walls of the oven takes a fair amount of time with not-too-fierce heat). Then they emptied out the ashes after they had cooled off somewhat and put in the things to be baked.

feet wide outside at ground level, shaped rather like a cross between a barn and an igloo, and about two feet and six inches high at the ridge. For a chimney, a 40-ounce juice can with both ends removed was stuck in a hole at the top of the oven. The chimney was pointing upwards, but it would be better to have it pointing outwards from the top of the back end. A can with a plastic end cover (like some of the coffee cans) would be ideal, as most of the time it is best to have the chimney sealed up.

Anne and Hugo first cleared away the sod down to mineral soil, which was only a few inches to good clean sand. If you have deep soil with humus in it (and if—horror of horrors—you live on peat), you need a good, thick layer of incombustible something under and around the oven.

They started work on the oven by making a shell of woven branches, with one end open and wide enough to take the widest shovel (because you have to allow for easy insertion of hot ashes). Any wood will do as long as it

It worked like a charm once they had learned just how hot to get it (in the early tries it was usually too hot), and I think some of the people who came to buy vegetables really came to have another look at the oven.

I would like to hear from anyone who tries to make this kind of oven and has trouble — when I try to duplicate the Anne and Hugo model, I would like to do it right. Have fun.

B. C.

CHINKLESS CONSTRUCTION

A word or two on building with logs. Select them carefully; 12–14″ in diameter is best. You have the same amount of work on a 6″ log as on a 14″ log, only you need a lot more of them. If you devise a good hoisting apparatus, the size of the log won't matter. You could roll the logs up two other logs, running from the ground to the top, but with a hoist you can lower the logs back to the ground to be worked on, once they are roughly notched. This is especially helpful with the "chinkless" construction that involves cutting a *V*-shaped groove in the underside of each log.

I recommend this chinkless method. It takes longer at first but will probably save time in the long run, and I think it looks nicer. Because of the grooves, each log fits tightly over the log below. Insulation is placed in the groove but remains unseen. A cabin of this type will settle up to three inches but gets tighter as it settles. With this method, green logs can be used more readily.

Since I didn't have time to hew my ceiling and porch joists by hand and still have them

in by winter, I took the joists to a local mill and had one flat face sawed on them. Then I squared each end of the joists to the same dimension and laid them in precut notches on the top and bottom wall logs.

P. C.

TREATING BEE STINGS

A friend told me about an article suggesting the use of meat tenderizer "to take the sting out." One day I came running in barefoot. "Let's try it! How much do you use?" I yelled to her. "About one teaspoon, I guess," she answered. Before her astonished eyes, I gulped the stuff down. When she had finished laughing, she managed to tell me I should moisten the tenderizer and put it on my foot. I did, and it does help!

B. T.

MELTING WAX SAFELY

Many of us melt down wax for making candles, doing batik, or rendering down old bee comb, but may not be aware of the potential danger of hot wax. Never attempt to render combs inside a building with anything except steam heat. Many beekeepers have burned down their homes and honey houses by rendering combs indoors using various types of burners. Once ignited, wax spreads as it burns and makes an extremely hot fire that is difficult to put out. A bucket of sand near the wood stove would be handy to smother a hot grease fire or wax fire and keep it from spreading.

M. & W. H.

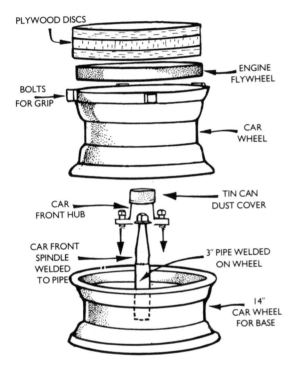

PLYWOOD DISCS

ENGINE FLYWHEEL

BOLTS FOR GRIP

CAR WHEEL

TIN CAN DUST COVER

CAR FRONT HUB

CAR FRONT SPINDLE WELDED TO PIPE

3" PIPE WELDED ON WHEEL

14" CAR WHEEL FOR BASE

POTTER'S WHEEL FROM AUTO PARTS

Here's how to build a cheap potter's wheel out of automotive parts.

Access to welding equipment is required. I've built two wheels, and they both work fine. Parts required are: two car wheels, a length of 2–3" pipe, a front spindle and hub from a car, a flywheel from a car engine, miscellaneous bolts, nails, and one tin can.

Weld the car spindle to approximately one foot of pipe. The pipe is then welded to the center of a car wheel, preferably 13" or 14". Remove the brake drum from the hub, then put the hub on the spindle. The hub and bearings have less drag if they are washed out with gasoline and lubricated with oil, not grease. Then you place the 15" car wheel upside down on the hub and bolt it on with the lug nuts. The original dust cap of the hub sticks out too far, so replace it with a tin can cut to size. I've even had to cut the end off the spindle and the nut with a hacksaw to gain clearance.

Then you have to find a flywheel that fits into the wheel and down over the end of the hub as low as possible. You may have to take the ring gear off with a torch to get the flywheel down far enough. The actual working surface is a plywood circle that is coupled to the flywheel. Use plywood at least ½" thick to prevent warping, and use exterior grade. On one wheel I made plywood circles and coupled them by driving three nails down through the plywood and into the holes in the flywheel. Another way that works better is to make three studs of 5/16 bolts and have them stick up into the plywood disks.

I also weld four square nuts around the circumference of the wheel for a traction surface until the wheel gets coated with clay. You should have three or more plywood disks so that your projects can be removed from the wheel to dry and you can replace the disks and continue working. A coat of gray paint makes your wheel look more professional. It is used just like the old Oriental wheels built into the floor. You give it a spin with one hand, and then get at it!

C. Y.

MUD: DRIVING IN—AND OUT

In our neck of the woods, almost everybody gets stuck at least a few times a year, and it's usually a Jackall, not a $20-an-hour tow truck, that gets you out.

The first thing you do is walk around the vehicle, roll a smoke, try to figure out how the hell you got into this mess, and make wild promises about never being so stupid again. Then you've got to decide how you're going to get out. Forwards or backwards? In the ruts or straddling them? Wheels straight or turned? Once you've got a plan of attack, then you start worrying about the immediate problem: how to get moving again.

I assume that you have already had your partner out pushing and that she's tired, dirty, and maybe mad. Often the man jumps out the minute the car is stuck and makes the woman drive while he pushes from the back. My policy is to let the best driver of the vehicle drive and let everyone else push.

Next thing to do is to gather up your "unstucking" equipment. This includes a block of wood to put under the jack to stop it from sinking into the mud. I mean a Jackall, not one of those ridiculous hydraulic jacks that you'd never be able to put under a vehicle that's up to the axles in mud. And get all the old boards, rocks, or logs that you can find to use as blocks. Then go around to the corner of the vehicle that has sunk deepest and jack it up high enough to put those rocks and boards under the wheel and in front of it to make a trail of boards for the wheels to drive on. If you're lucky, your vehicle will sit up on your blocks when let down, and you'll just drive away. More likely, however, it'll slide off the blocks or sink at another wheel or maybe move a few feet and sink once

again. So you repeat the whole process. If this method only seems to get you more tired and the vehicle more stuck, then obviously it is time to change tactics.

About this time it is nice if you can flag down a big truck, throw a chain around your axle, and get pulled out. But if the truck is not forthcoming, then you get your tire chains out, digging around in the mud as you put them on, and hope that you'll just drive away. However, if you have no tire chains or if you left them at home, then you get your old logging chains, which you always have stacked behind the seat!! for just such an occasion, and winch yourself out. To winch out, you'll need a tree or rock or anything else close enough to reach with your logging chain.

And what if you don't have a hand winch? Well, you can't buy a hand winch that will do half the job your good friend the Jackall will do. Attach a short piece of chain to the jacking point of the Jackall (the part that goes up and down) and the other end to the axle or frame of the vehicle—not to the bumper if it is the flimsy decorative type. Then attach another chain from the top of the Jackall to the tree or rock. Then, presto, start jacking, and as the jacking point moves up the jack, it draws the short chain with the vehicle attached out of the mud towards the tree or rock or whatever. Naturally, you'll only be able to winch the length of the Jackall, but by then you'll need a rest anyway, so you shorten the chain and repeat the process. Don't try to use nylon tow ropes, which, though great for pulling stuck vehicles by another vehicle, stretch too much to be used for a Jackall winch.

Getting stuck in the snow, besides being a lot colder, is a little different from being stuck in mud. Snow is a lot easier to shovel than mud. But only if you've got a shovel. Never be without one! Most vehicles need extra weight in the winter to get the needed traction, and when you're stuck, anything you can find to put weight over the rear wheels will help. Even all the snow you've been shovelling out from under the wheels should go up in the box of your truck. Sand, sticks, rocks, sawdust, or your logging chain placed under the wheels will increase traction, and once again you can use the Jackall to place blocks under the wheels.

Sometimes absolutely nothing seems to work. Then you must decide to go for help.

Getting stuck is murder on vehicles, especially old ones, and back-and-forth rocking, stalling, and occasional engine roaring have been the death of many an old and even not-so-old engine. Obviously, the best way to avoid hassles, strains, and oaths is not to get stuck in the first place. But as I always tell my old lady, "If we didn't get stuck so often, we wouldn't be getting so good at getting out." Pax.

T. A.

COLD SMOKEHOUSE

For people who like smoked anything but do not want to marry the smokehouse for a bite, try this self-feeding burner: a discarded 13-gallon oil can, upright, filled to the brim with 6″ × 6″ alder chunks and a scattering of branches throughout.

First, stuff some kind of wire grate in the bottom to allow ashes to fall through. I kindle it with cedar, get some coals going with small alder branches, and then stoke it up with alder chunks on top. I lay a piece of ¼″ scrap steel with an X cold-chiseled through the middle of it with the flaps bent up. Over the flaps I place a 6″ elbow connected to the smokehouse with 8′ of pipe. Then I listen to it burn, and when it sounds furious, I close up air intake by wedging a jar top over the hole with a rock. It will cold-smoke for 8 hours, and I have seen it do 10.

M. F. B.

SOD ROOFS

I would like to have a sod roof on my new cedar log cabin (16′ × 14′). Could anyone tell me how to go about it? Has anyone had experience living in a cabin all year with a sod roof? The climate here is a bit on the wet side. I heard of one case where the owner had used tar paper underneath the sod, and the paper rotted. But I don't know if he used building paper or roofing paper, which is much heavier. I am planning to use roofing paper on top of the sheathing, plastic (4 mil) on top of the roofing paper, and then sod. What do you know-how people think about that?

I.

Hi, I.:

I've done a little research into sod roofs that may help you somewhat. First, I assume you're sure that your cabin structure can support the weight. When sod is supersaturated (contains as much moisture as it can possibly hold), it weighs 150 pounds per cubic foot. This is two to three times the weight most people's houses will support. Jim B., who built a sod roof on a small eco-cabin he designed, first laid down a layer of the lightest-weight rolled roofing he could find. Over this went a layer of 6 mil black plastic. Strips of sod were then laid sod side down on the plastic, and another layer of sod was placed on this, sod side up. Jim found that the sod was a very efficient insulator in the summer (it kept the cabin very cool), but its insulating qualities were very minimal in the winter when it was exceptionally wet (the cabin is on a soggy coastal island).

Tom Bender, in his paper *Living Lightly*, recommends a layer of rolled roofing, a coating of selvage cement, a layer of 6 mil black polyethylene, and another layer of selvage cement. Normal meadow sod (bromegrass and bluegrass) goes over this, one layer down, one layer up.

The traditional sod roof was laid in two layers of sod over a layer of birch bark shingles. Birch bark is one of the most rot-proof materials available, and it formed a waterproofing layer for any water that seeped through the sod. The edges of the roof were held in place with logs to retain the soil. Traditional sod roofs were expected to last 60 years.

V.

SWEDISH SMALL FARM FENCE

To keep your flax secure from wandering animals, we would like to tell you about a nice kind of fence we saw in all the northern parts of Sweden. It looked like it would be very good for goats and other smaller animals too.

This fence takes a fair amount of material, but if you are clearing land, this would be the type of material you would have no use for otherwise. It consists of skinny stakes, rails, and binding material. Ten- to 16-foot-long rails of spruce or pine can be split, or if they are small, barked on two sides. An inch of

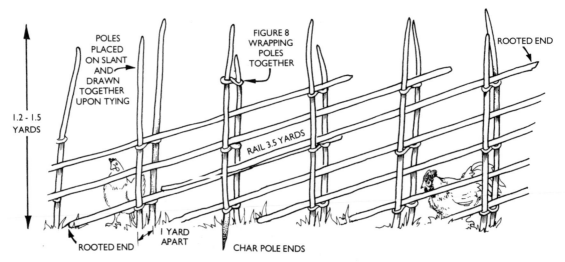

POLES PLACED ON SLANT AND DRAWN TOGETHER UPON TYING

FIGURE 8 WRAPPING POLES TOGETHER

ROOTED END

1.2 - 1.5 YARDS

RAIL 3.5 YARDS

ROOTED END

1 YARD APART

CHAR POLE ENDS

bark stripped off on each side will make the drying faster and also prevent insects from attacking. The stakes, 4 to 5 feet long, should be taken from spruce or pine bushes.

Start your fence by setting your stakes in pairs about four inches away from each other and about three feet apart. In the olden days this was done in the fall, so they could settle down well, and the rest of the work was done in the spring.

Put your stakes in slanting slightly outwards, after you have first charred the ends over a fire. This is to prevent them from rotting too quickly; the rotting process usually starts just at the point where the soil and air meet. If you make your stakes good and long, you can later just poke them down farther when they rot.

The bindings should be laced in a figure eight and can be of wire, fresh spruce branches, juniper, birch branches, spruce bark strips, etc. To get your spruce branches, for example, soft and pliable, you hold them over the fire. The water in them will then boil and soften up the fibers, and at the same time burn off the needles. You will need to have gloves on during this work.

There are three bindings on each set of stakes. The top one is placed about four feet above ground. They are set at this height on all stakes, and the distance between the stakes, about three feet, will be judged so the rails can lay on every second binding (see illustration on previous page).

When you set up the whole fence, you put the bindings on every second pair of stakes, and just three at a time. It is very hard to put the rails in if you bind up too many stakes ahead of time. Tighten your bindings so that you bring your stakes together.

If you use double rails, root to top, you don't need rails that are so long; you can simply adjust them to the length desired. This fence probably takes quite a bit of work, but it stands up a long time and looks very picturesque.

W.

QUICK 'N' EASY HOT TUB

Last year during tree planting we put a cast-iron bathtub on some rocks and put a fire under it. For temperature control, wood and water were standing within reach of the bather. A floating frame or legless chair keeps you off the hot bottom. Fire under an empty tub blisters the enamel.

D. B.

CONTINUOUS HOT WATER

Here's an easy way to have a constant supply of hot water on hand if you have a kitchen range with a water jacket in the firebox. If there are two pipes sticking out of the back of the firebox, you've got it made. Build a wooden stand behind the stove with steps leading up to it. On the stand put an open-topped 45-gallon drum connected to those two pipes, put a tap near the bottom for convenience, and fill the barrel with water. The heat of the stove will cause the water to circulate, and soon you'll have lots of hot water and probably a happy partner as well. Try not to let it run dry, though, because when fresh cold water hits that hot water jacket you'll hear the gawdarnfullest clanking sound you ever heard. The first time you'll probably grab the baby and your *Smallholder* and run for your life. It doesn't seem to hurt anything, but it's pretty scary just the same.

D. S.

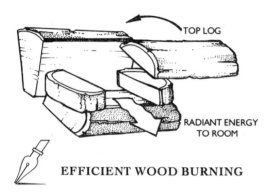

EFFICIENT WOOD BURNING

I have been experimenting with fireplace wood burning that uses radiation to keep the surface of large pieces of wood above its combustion temperature. In our small fireplace I begin by placing a fairly flat-bottomed split log on top of the ashes. Two half-split short logs are placed along the sides. I drop another split log in the back. One or more split logs on the top completes the box construction. The purpose of this design is for the inner surfaces to "see" each other. In physics this is called a "black body" radiator. With a little birch bark lit in the center, it only takes about 15 minutes for all the inner surfaces to be glowing red hot. This fire sends out about 30 percent of its energy as radiant energy for about three hours.

One nice thing about wood is that it is a good heat insulator. The outer bark can remain cold until the split log is almost burned through. This happened with a top log of birch that burst into a spectacular flame to announce the end of the fire. One should be

careful that the top log does not roll out as the sides collapse and the whole fire is reduced to glowing charcoal. You can prevent this occurrence by having the top of the bottom wood slope inward.

I would like to hear from anyone who tries this system. It may be possible to design a heater or stove with firebrick using this principle.

N. E. P.

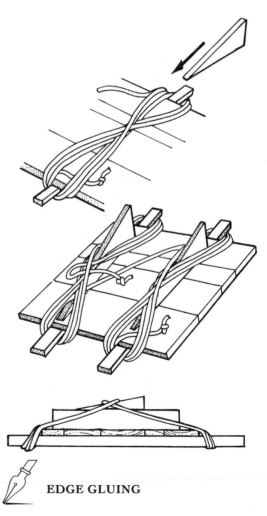

EDGE GLUING

If you ever wondered how people edge-glued

planks together before pipe and bar clamps were invented, here's a method I learned from an old guitar maker in Spain. It's simpler, better, and a whole lot cheaper! All you need is a long rope, enough wedges (with about a 15° slope) to be spaced about one foot apart along the planks to be glued, and a stout crossbar to go under each wedge. Apply glue to the edges of the planks, lay them on the crossbars, and loop three or four layers of a "figure eight" crossover point. The tight rope forces the planks together while the wedge and crossbar keeps them flat. For extra-wide jobs, another stout board placed directly under the wedge (see figure on previous page) works pretty well too.

M. D.

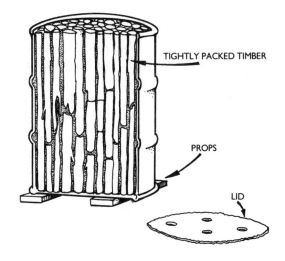

TIGHTLY PACKED TIMBER

PROPS

LID

CLEANING CEMENT FORMS

To clean forms easily as you take them down from concrete work, lay them out and use a stiff broom on them after they have been exposed to the air about five minutes. This is the best time to clean the boards. It takes just a fraction of the time it would take if the job were put off.

B. T.

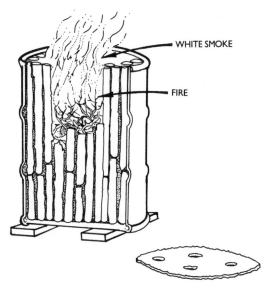

WHITE SMOKE

FIRE

MANUFACTURING WOOD CHARCOAL

Wood charcoal was used extensively in Europe before the introduction of coal and fossil fuel, and it is still a very popular cooking fuel in many parts of Africa and Asia. One important advantage charcoal has over wood is that it is much more efficient. When burned, charcoal gives from three to four times as much heat per pound as green wood and about twice the heat of air-dried wood (12,000 to 13,000 Btu/lb. versus 2,300 to 4,000 Btu/lb. and 5,200 to 6,000 Btu/lb., respectively).

In those regions of the world where forest areas are far removed from rural and urban centers where cooking fuel is needed, the cost of transporting fuel in the form of charcoal is clearly only a fraction of that for transporting an equivalent amount of fuel in the form of wood.

Charcoal offers several other advantages over wood. It is not subject to decay from fungus or insects, nor does it deteriorate when wet. It may thus be stored indefinitely regardless of weather conditions. Charcoal burns without odor or smoke, eliminating the unpleasantness of tending a wood fire and the food flavoring that arises from the tars and acids contained in the smoke, and cutting down on the buildup of tars and oils on the surface of cooking utensils. It should be mentioned, however, that the use of charcoal in an unventilated room for a long period of time could lead to the buildup of poisonous carbon monoxide gas.

Wood charcoal is obtained by heating wood with a limited supply of air. When wood attains a temperature of about 572°F, it undergoes a heat-generating reaction as a result of the breakdown of tars contained in the wood. Under these conditions, the water, acids, tars, and oils, which constitute about 70 percent of the wood's weight, are driven off as gases, leaving behind unburned carbon and ash, which make up what is called charcoal. Large quantities of charcoal are generally manufactured in brick or steel retorts or kilns; often the gases are recovered to obtain saleable by-products like acetic acid, methanol, acetone, and tar.

Smaller quantities of charcoal can be manufactured quite simply by using 44-gallon oil drums. One drum can give about 40 pounds of charcoal a day, and two workers with a minimum of training can oversee six to eight drums at a time. Any type of debarked, un-

treated wood, green or dried, hardwood or softwood, timber offcuts, or even coconut shells can be used to charge the drum. The diameter of logs or the maximum dimension in cross-section ought not to exceed 6″, nor should the pieces be longer than the height of the drum (35″).

The drum is prepared by cutting out the bottom (retain this cutout to use as a cover) and cutting one or two holes 2″ × 2″ in the top (these are in addition to the two round holes normally found on the top of oil drums). The drum is inverted and placed on two lengths of pipes or logs so that the drum is elevated off the ground. Wood is placed upright into the drum so as to pack it as tightly as possible. The center of the drum should be filled with twigs and leaves, which can be easily ignited.

Once a fire is started in the center of the drum, the operator must maintain the emission of thick white smoke. If left unattended, the fire will build up as a result of excess air or uneven distribution of heat within the drum; smoke will burn black or cease altogether and flames will shoot out, indicating that the wood is being burned wastefully. The techniques that the operator must learn to control the fire are:

1. Removing the pipes or logs upon which the drum is resting. This will be necessary 30 to 60 minutes after the start of the fire.

2. Partially covering the top opening with the cutout sheet from the drum top. Shifting the position of this cover on the drum will also help to reestablish the emission of white smoke.

3. Rocking the drum to reposition the logs in the drum. This should be done every 15 to 30 minutes throughout the run.

4. Adding shorter pieces of wood to the

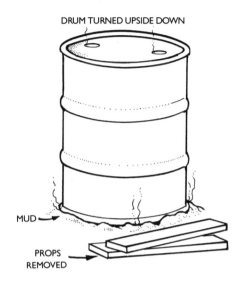

DRUM TURNED UPSIDE DOWN

MUD

PROPS
REMOVED

drum. This will first become necessary after about 90 minutes and may be required two or three times thereafter. If the first three techniques fail to reestablish the emission of smoke, this last technique should be tried.

A steady stream of white smoke maintained for about 5½ hours will give a drum filled to the top with red-hot charcoal. It is now necessary to seal off the drum so that the charcoal can cool down. This is accomplished by fitting the cover into the top rim of the drum, turning the drum upside down, and sealing off the holes in the top and the gaps between the ground and drum with mud. To invert the drum, one person can knock the drum over, first tipping it onto its side and then completely over, while a second person holds the cover in place to prevent the charcoal from falling out. Each person will require a long pipe or plank of timber and probably a heavy pair of gloves for this operation. The sealed drum, left overnight, will cool down so that it can be emptied.

After a little practice this method should result in charcoal free from ash, along with unaffected pieces of wood. Any pieces of charred wood found can of course be used in subsequent batches. Charcoal can be distinguished from charred wood by the fact that it is totally black throughout and can be broken up by hand.

N. G.

TESTING A LEVEL

You can test your level for accuracy by placing it horizontally against a wall and centering the bubble. Draw a line along the edge of the frame, then switch the ends of the level and draw another line just above the first with the bubble exactly centered again. If the two lines aren't exactly parallel, the level isn't accurate.

B. T.

NO BEARD AND NO WASTE

I'm sure I'll grow a beard again sometime, but in the meantime I like being bare in the face. When I decided I'd take up shaving again, I also decided to stop throwing away all those little metal slivers. So I bought myself a straight razor. I had thought about doing this for some time, but even after I'd bought it I let weeks go by before I declared this was my last packet of razor blades. Shaving with a straight razor has some tricks to it, which is what always happens when you take a step down the technological ladder. I'd like to pass on some of these tricks in the interests of reviving another old skill.

It's most important to have a sharp razor. It makes the difference between a clean face and one full of cuts. This means finding a blade in good condition, sharpening it, and then keeping it sharp.

I'm sure that barber supply houses have straight razors. I found mine at a swap meet and paid two dollars for it. That seems a reasonable price, since I've seen straight razors in secondhand stores for anything from eight to twelve bucks. I guess they're called antiques, along with all those other useful items country folks still think of as basic tools, like kerosene lamps and bean pots. I checked the one I bought carefully, and even though I was disappointed it didn't have a pearl handle or other such fanciness as I had seen on older razors in those stores I mentioned, it had a blade in perfect condition, and that's what matters. As far as I could tell, it was unused.

When I decided to start using it, I took a soft Arkansas stone to it. It seems that the ridge running along the blunt side of the blade is designed to be a rest for sharpening. You lay the blade on the oil stone and sharpen it with the ridge sliding along the stone.

Sharpen both sides of the blade; you'll be using both sides to shave. I'm sure any hard whetstone will do this job. Sharpen until you can't see the edge in a strong light or you draw a burr.

Keeping the razor sharp is the essence of a good shave. You need a strop to do this. A strop is a piece of heavy leather a few inches wide and 10" to a foot long. A strop is usually impregnated with jeweler's rouge to help it

sharpen. The rouge is a compound that adds to the sharpening action of the leather and actually turns it into a very fine grinding surface. It's rubbed into the leather, which is then heated to help it absorb the rouge. I bought a strop and a chunk of jeweler's rouge for less than two dollars at a guitar store. The strop will remove the burr and also put the finest possible edge on the blade. You've probably seen a barber strop a razor, even if it was only in some Western movie. I was told it's best to have the strop on a flat surface, even glued to a block of wood. Press the blade firmly against the leather surface and draw it down the strop with the blunt edge leading. Strop it several times on each side, or until it's as sharp as possible. I now strop my razor both before and after using it, and the edge has gotten to be just fine. Sometimes I strop it in the middle of a shave if it's especially tough going.

So that's what I've learned about straight-razor shaving. Hope it helps you along if you're shaving and want to switch to a non-disposable blade.

D. R.

 SIMPLE BOOT CARE

Here are a few tried and true recipes for boot polish that will give you more mileage and comfort from leather footware. They range from simple to complicated, but all are effective.

1. Render and clear animal fat. Put in a can and store in a cool, dry place. Melt a little as you need it and rub thoroughly into leather.

2. Melt together one part tallow and one part beeswax. Pour in can and use as needed.

3. Melt together equal parts of paraffin, vaseline, and neat's-foot oil. Bottle and rub on shoes as needed.

4. Melt together four parts beef tallow, one part resin, 1 part beeswax, and six parts neat's-foot oil. Warm and apply to boots with a soft cloth, rubbing in well. Be sure boots are clean and dry. Let stand in a warm place — not a hot place, since leather is easily damaged if exposed to too high a temperature — to allow the conditioner to sink in. Two applications are required to make the leather thoroughly waterproof.

B. T.

 SEASONING HARDWOODS

Wood must be seasoned and dried to a certain moisture content before it is ready for uses requiring stability. Moisture content is reduced either by letting the wood stand in a covered stack (a slow process) or kiln-drying (a speedier process). Either method requires great care if a high-quality wood is desired.

There are two types of moisture in wood: free moisture between the cells of the wood, and hygroscopic moisture within the cell walls. Free moisture dries fairly quickly in an open, well-ventilated pile. Hygroscopic moisture takes longer to evaporate.

Before hardwoods are kiln-dried, they are usually stacked in a shed with spacers between each layer for three to six months to get rid of the free moisture. Wood without free moisture has a moisture content of about 25 percent of its oven-dry weight. Kiln-drying then removes the hygroscopic moisture in three to eight weeks, depending on species and dimension.

Air-dried hardwoods rarely have a moisture content of below 15 to 20 percent in this part of B.C. To make laminated furniture for dry indoor settings, 5 to 10 percent is desirable. Outdoor uses such as toboggans, snowshoes, handles, cider presses, and flooring can tolerate 12 to 20 percent moisture. To further dry air-dry hardwood, stack it with spacers in a dry (but not too warm) environment, such as a heated basement or shop. The wood should not be in direct sunlight, since the radiant heat of the sun dries only one side, causing distortion and checking.

About six weeks before a project for which low moisture content is required is begun, the wood should be brought into the kind of atmosphere it is to be used in. To properly stack lumber, leave some space between the boards in each layer and place spacers every two feet across each layer. Keep the spacers directly above each other and the sides of the pile fairly plumb. Lengths should be separated so that boards in a pile do not differ greatly. Extremely soft woods do not make good spacers, since they crush easily, causing distortions in the lumber. Spacers should be less than 3¼" in width by 1" in thickness, and all should be of the same size. Lumber stacked in this manner will have minimum tendency to warp and twist and will dry evenly.

Wood is like a sponge. Dry lumber exposed to a moister environment will slowly take on more water until an equilibrium is reached with the surrounding air — just as wet wood loses water to a drier atmosphere. Once your wood has reached the desired moisture content, remove the spacers and loose-pile it to prevent rapid change in humidity from distorting the lumber. With kiln-dried woods it is advisable to cover the lumber and close-pile it to prevent an increase in moisture. Wood with less than 20 percent moisture content is not prone to fungus attack.

Some woods, such as ash, cherry, walnut, and maple, are relatively easy to season. Others, like beech, birch, and yew, require more attention and a more controlled environment. Experience will teach you how to handle the different woods you are using.

Kiln-drying has the advantage of being fast, but many wood workers believe that kiln-dried wood has less luster in finishing and is more prone to rot because of the absence of the natural oils and preservatives. Kiln-dried wood is also more brittle and not as tough as air-dried wood.

When handled correctly, using either kiln- or air-drying, the resulting wood can be most satisfying, and wood workers can release their creative energy with confidence. We hope the information herein will aid that creative process.

For those people wanting to know more about seasoning, kiln-drying, and properties of hardwoods, we highly recommend the following books: *Timbers for Woodwork*, edited by J. C. S. Brough (New York: Drake Publishers, 1972); *The Encyclopedia of Furniture Making*, by Joyce Ernest (New York: Drake Publishers, 1970); *Canadian Woods: Their Properties and Uses*, by the Canadian Forestry Service (Ottawa: Queen's Printer, 1969).

R., G., D.

 ## SMALLHOLDING DOWN UNDER

When I read that some of you are making a go of five acres, my hat's off to you. My two eldest boys and I (they are 16 and 17) share-farm a Friesian dairy farm. And although I make my living farming and shoeing horses, I too have been completely self-sufficient. And I would rather be poor doing something I like than getting a lot of money for something I don't like doing.

I homebake everything, spin my own wool and weave it. I shear my sheep, kill our meat, and grow all grain, hay, and vegetables. Make my own soap. Sometimes I am so tired it isn't funny. However, here are a few things I think you might be able to use.

Rennet
Take a giblet from a fowl next time you kill a chicken. Slit it around and remove all bits of gravel and grain. Peel the skin off it. Use the meat for soup. Wash the skin well, rub with salt, rinse, hang up to dry, and use the same as calf rennet. My gran told me how to find the rennet on a calf: it is the small bag beside the large pouch, and it resembles leaves of the Bible. As soon as the calf is killed, remove the bag, scour it, rub it well with salt, and stretch it out to dry. Take a piece of rennet and pour some boiling water over it and leave it for about six hours. Then use the water to turn the milk. It takes about two to three hours to curd.

Stove Black
Sift 1 lb. of charcoal (or common asphaltum) fine and melt together with ½ pint linseed oil and 1 qt. turpentine. Apply to cold stove and polish when the stove is warm.

Lamp Chimney
To clean, hold it over the spout of a boiling kettle until it is steamed up: polishes well.

Linoleum Cream

1 lb. white beeswax

3 oz. potash

1 qt. turps

6 pints boiling water

Cut the wax finely, put into a can or kero tin (the vessel you boil your soap in would do), and keep on the fire till melted. Then take off fire, add turps and potash, and stir until cool (it is important to keep stirring). Put away in tins with lids (far away from fire).

Coconut Oil

Coconut oil is good for soap making, etc. Grate as many coconuts as you want. To 6 grated coconuts, add 4 cups boiling water. When cool, squeeze out juice until very dry (in a muslin bag). Leave in a saucepan at the back of the stove to simmer. The water will evaporate and leave the clear coconut oil (usually takes eight hours for ½ pint of oil).

M. S.

 ### THE MANY USES OF TALLOW

In addition to its use in the making of soap, tallow (rendered beef or mutton fat) works well as a lubricant on threads of things you might someday want to unbolt. It is excellent as protection against rust on tools used outside or stored in damp or unheated places. My forge blower, anvil, and vise are tallowed and have not rusted this winter, although rain can blow in on them. I melt one pound of tallow and add an equal amount of kerosene for an easily spread mixture. The kerosene evaporates, leaving a coating of tallow on the steel. Plain tallow, used on the Jotul every

couple of months, works to keep off rust. Smells a bit like frying for a day or two, but it is preferable to the concoction of polish from mystical and/or poisonous ingredients.

If you have no beef (or sheep) fat to render for tallow, you can buy it in one-pound blocks already rendered white and clean, as Devon Deep Fry, Refined Beef Fat in the section of the store where lard and other refrigerated shortenings are kept. Tallow, however, appears to keep well without cooling.

D. D'A.

 ### STOVE LINING PATCH

Here is a handy cement to patch burned-out stove lining—three parts sifted wood ashes, one part salt, and enough water to make a stiff dough. We reinforce larger holes with stiff wire, old nails, or pieces of metal.

M. L.

 ### USING MOLASSES IN JANUARY

Old deep freezers make good grain storage boxes. Tear off the rubber seal around the edge so that tiny tots will not suffocate if they accidentally get in.

For frozen water pipes, wells, or outlets, pour a cup or two of molasses inside. Crazy as it sounds, this method really works. We have used it several times. It may take a few hours on a hard freeze, but it will thaw it out.

W. C.

AIRY FLOORBOARDS

A reply to S. T. about airy floorboards: become a shipwright and wedge-seam them. This is a technique for smooth plank hulls for racing vessels. Rout the grooves to an even *V* by running a router along a parallel board tacked to the surface. Cut *V* wedges, oversized, on table saw. Glue wedges into seam with high-quality glue. Plane and sand flush. This is a lot of work but promises a lasting, handsome solution. One could use contrasting wood for a decorative effect.

E. M.

UNDERSTANDING YOUR FIRE

This is in response to a letter regarding wood heat and poisonous gas. It applies to every type of fuel that we normally use (with the exception of electricity), including natural gas, propane, fuel oil, coal, and wood, and applies whether it is burned in a hot water heater, kitchen stove, box stove, Fisher, or fireplace.

Anyone who has a heating problem, whether it is a smoking unit or one that does not function properly, should first note that a smoking stove indicates a faulty chimney in almost every case. Another major cause of a smoking stove or fireplace is a house that is so airtight that the stove or fireplace is not getting enough combustion air.

All of these units take a considerable amount of air to produce their heat and the normal combustion products of carbon dioxide and water vapor. When the heater is starved for oxygen, the carbon dioxide then

becomes carbon monoxide, which is where the danger lies, since it is colorless and odorless, and when you feel it, it is usually too late.

Combustion air must come from cracks in the floor, wall, ceiling, and around the windows and doors. The location of your stove and your air leaks will affect the comfort of your house, whether or not you have drafty floors and so forth. Heating efficiency is lost because of this colder air that is coming into your house and cooling the entire interior. A simple solution to all of the above problems is to provide a short and easy supply of outside air as close to your heating unit as possible. This could mean drilling a hole through the floor right underneath or near the stove, provided that if you have a basement, it is not heated. A three-inch clothes dryer air vent with the flap valve removed and a screen inserted in its place will make an excellent, through-the-wall air supply. The inside outlet can be plugged or capped with a tin can when you are not using your heater.

A fancier way of doing it would be to use a hot-air register control with the little flap valve inside. The smallest one available would supply enough air for the largest fireplace, which requires the most amount of air. Hope this clears the air on the subject!

J. F.

FOOT-OPERATED YARD GATE

A gate that can be unlatched with the foot is a great convenience across a path where people frequently pass with both hands occupied. Pivoted to the side of the gate, near its center,

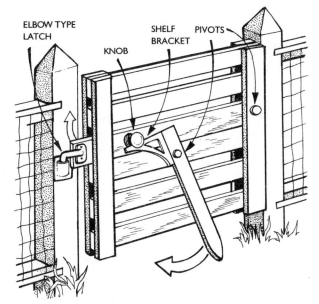

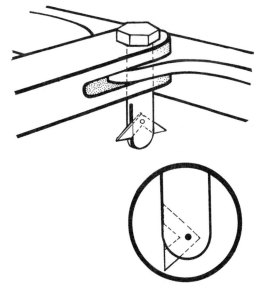

a beam, or foot lever, is hung in a vertical position, extending almost to the ground and having a shelf bracket fastened to its upper end. The horizontal arm of the bracket passes beneath a knob projecting from a pivoted bar that engages the elbow catch. If you push the vertical beam to one side with your foot, the bar is raised above the catch, allowing the gate to swing open. If the gate is properly hung, it will close by itself, the elbow catch preventing its being open again, except when the bar is raised.

B. T.

CONVENIENT TRAILER HITCH PIN

A very useful trailer hitch pin may be made with a steel bolt and a triangle key, as shown. The bolt is slotted, and the triangle key held in place by a pin.

The shape of the triangle key causes it to

hang in a horizontal position, with the ends projecting from either side of the pin to stop the bolt from bounding out of the hitch. This saves a lot of time when hooking up and un-hooking.

B. T.

PULLING UP A FENCE POST

These simple methods of pulling out fence posts cheaply and quickly are particularly useful if a line of posts has to be pulled out.

The main essentials are a timber Jackall and a stout chain, with a strong hook. The chain is looped around the foot of the post, and the loop is closed with the hook. The remainder of the chain is then lifted, and when taut, one of the links is laid in the lug of the jack, which is held erect and as close to the post as possible. The jack, which must touch the post where the chain engages it, is then wound up and the post comes up with the chain. It is important that the chain be kept taut and that the jack be as near upright as possible. When the ground is wet and sticky, the foot of the jack is inclined to sink in as the jack is wound up. This sinking can be avoided by resting the butt of the jack on another post or on a length of a 4" × 3" timber.

In all but the stickiest and tightest soil, the following method of pulling a post will usually succeed. Take a strong pole about 12–14' long and fasten a chain around the foot of the fence post and then to the pole about 2' from one end, leaving no slack chain between the pole and the post. By pulling up the far end of the pole, you can lift the post, although it usually helps to loosen the soil around the post before attempting to move the pole. The chain must be taken around the lever from the outside so that the first loop will be gripped between the lever and the post. If the direction is reversed, the pole will simply turn in the operator's hands and will not exert any lift at all.

B. T.

SAVING AND SALVAGING

Bill makes planters, cutting boards, and holders to hang potholders on. His latest creations are candle holders from roots and odd-shaped pieces of wood around here; he recycles oddments of copper piping and tubing from old commercial lawn chairs. We've given away some for gifts but hope to sell some, too. Bill has tins with nails, screws, pins, etc. We often go to the local dump and salvage any wool or string, sweaters, etc., to bring home. String I mix with crochet thread and use to knit dishcloths. I used to sell these up North for a dollar each. I use two to three strands of wool and knit up bed throws on number 8 needles or larger. I do the envelopes too, and sometimes my daughter sends me colored paper and I make colored envelopes and maybe cut a bird or butterfly and paste it on. I also make Christmas cards from them. I make Bill's shirts and knit his wool socks, since nylon poisons his feet, so they too are multicolored from odds and ends of pure wool.

We are pensioners and have been trying to get a few acres of our own, but property is sky-high hereabouts. I also keep zippers, buttons—you name it, we salvage it all. I even write my four girls letters with advertising on one side. We have phone books, and we cut pictures and glue them on the pages to make interesting scrapbooks for children. We save all postcards, birthday cards, and Christmas cards for that purpose too.

I'm allergic to doctors' medicines, so I grow a lot of herbs and also gather wild ones. Fireweed for one—the stalks are like asparagus; the leaves make a nice tea; and one can gather the soft, silky down in fall and dry it for toilet tissue or to fill cushions. Bill makes a lot of our furniture too—tables, benches, lawn chairs, etc.

M. W.

OILS AND SALVES

Easy Salves

Today I am making my winter's supply of salves. It is quite easy, and they last a long time. An easy method to make a salve is to take about eight parts of hard coconut oil and add two parts of the herb remedy you wish to use. Thus, if you were to make a sulfur salve, you would use eight ounces of coconut oil and two ounces of sulfur. Stir and mix well while hot, and when cool store in glass or porcelain jars. Zinc or iodine ointment is nice to make yourself.

Ointment of Bark, Roots, Seeds

To make an ointment with the virtues of some bark, roots, seeds, etc. boil ingredients in water until all properties are extracted. (Juniper berries and chickweed work well for burns and diaper rash.) Strain off the ingredients and add fresh herbs, seeds, or flowers to strained liquid and boil again. Add this to enough olive or coconut oil and simmer until all water has evaporated. Cool. Add enough beeswax and rosin to solidify. Spruce or pine gum works well for the rosin. Melt them together over a low fire and allow them to be thoroughly mixed. Cool and store in jars.

Herb Tinctures

Take 1 oz. of the powdered herb and add 4 oz. of water and 12 oz. of alcohol. Let stand for two weeks. A teaspoon of glycerin may be added. After standing for two weeks, pour off liquid and bottle for use. Tansy is a good one to try.

Odors of Flowers

Roses and other flowers containing perfumed oils will yield their aromatic properties if you steep the petals in a saucer of rainwater and set it in the sun. The petals should be entirely covered with the water. Leave it undisturbed for a few days, always making sure the petals are covered with rainwater. At the end of a few days, a film will be found floating on the top. This is your oil and can be taken up very carefully with a *small* eyedropper and deposited in vials, which should be allowed to remain open until all the water has evaporated. Your oil will last a long time and will always remind you of your summer garden.

Sachets and Potpourris

I always liked sachets and potpourris. My mother and aunt would put them in with the sheets and nightgowns, and they always smelled so good. To make a spicy sachet, mix 2 oz. dry rose petals, 3 oz. lavender flowers, 1 oz. orrisroot, 2 tsp. each of cloves, allspice, and cinnamon, and ½ lb. rasped sandalwood (try and find it).

I. S.

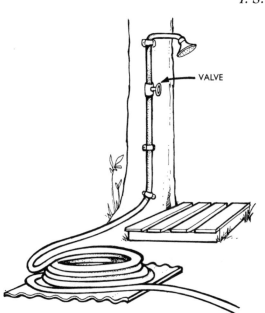

 SIMPLE SOLAR HOT WATER

A very simple and inexpensive solar water heater can be made using black plastic pipe for a heat collector. Ours consists of 300' of ½" pipe coiled on a piece of galvanized steel roofing and connected directly to a shower head hung on a tree. The coil, about 6′ in diameter, is inclined slightly to the south, and 20 minutes of direct sunlight will heat the water to a comfortable temperature for bathing. Our plumbing is very simple, with no way of mixing cold water with the heated water. Often the water is too hot, so we just run out the overheated water and the pipe retains enough heat to warm the next batch of water as it passes through.

The plastic pipe cost $4.49 per 100′, and the shower head was $3.29, so our total expense for this rather crude but effective device was less than $20. The possibilities for refinements are almost endless, but in the meantime, it is exciting how well the system works as is.

R. T.

HAND LOTION AND CHAPPED LIP OINTMENT

Here are a couple of recipes your readers might appreciate.

Hand Lotion

    1 Tbsp. almond oil
    1 tsp. liquid honey
    ½ tsp. liquid lecithin
    ¼ tsp. apple cider vinegar
    a few drops of your favorite perfume

Blend ingredients into a smooth lotion. Apply a small quantity and rub in well, until hands are almost dry. Blot excess with tissue.

Chapped Lip Ointment

    1 Tbsp. beeswax
    1 Tbsp. olive or sweet almond oil

Place ingredients in a small dish and heat over boiling water, mixing well as they melt.

Pour into a small jar before mixture cools. Rub on lips when needed.

J. G.

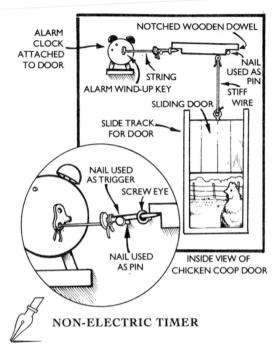

INSIDE VIEW OF CHICKEN COOP DOOR

NON-ELECTRIC TIMER

In situations where electricity may not be available, there is sometimes a need for a nonelectric timer to automatically perform simple chores, such as feeding and watering livestock or closing livestock gates. Such a timer would be especially useful if no one is planning to be present at the time the chore is usually performed.

For example, we have devised a nonelectric timer for the automatic closing of the chicken coop doors. As shown in the figure, the door closer is simplicity itself. An ordinary wind-up alarm clock is the timer; you simply set the fully wound alarm clock to go off when you want the sliding chicken door to close. We chose to build the sliding door into the main door of the coop for ease in setting the clock and trigger. When the alarm goes off, the alarm wind-up key turns, winds up the string to the trigger, and pulls the trigger so that the door drops.

· The automatic door closer as shown in the figure has been built and works beautifully. Of course many such uses of an alarm clock timer are possible, and designs other than the one shown are feasible.

D. P. G.

go up hills with much less slipping and sliding.

Doing it this way does not materially decrease the payload, since a full sheet of plywood can still be slid between the fender wells and let the tailgate close. Also, by extending the tops of the fender wells forward, it gives a place for a rider to sit.

J. E. F.

 ### GET A GRIP ON WINTER WITH BETTER TRACTION

For years when fall came I filled two gunnysacks with dry sand and put them in the rear end of my vehicle, one on each side of the rear wheels and ahead of them, if possible— to give better traction during the winter months. These weighed only about 100 pounds apiece, and often I wished I had more weight.

The last few years, I have been driving four-wheel-drive pickups, and I have discovered that I can get much better traction, which is helpful the year round, especially when I do not have a load in the rear. The method I use now is simply to enclose the space ahead of the fender well by using a vertical board that is even with the inside edge of the fender well and extends forward to the front of the truck bed. I use small pieces of angle iron on the inside to fasten this board. I then fill this enclosed space with sand packed tightly. I put a lid on this compartment at the same height as the top of the fender well. This means approximately 250 pounds of added weight on each side, for a total of 500 pounds, which makes the truck

 ### CELLULOSE FIREPROOFING

We were recently told a house owes its life to its new insulation job. The homeowner was able to save his child after the fire broke out, but when he started to re-enter the house to attempt some firefighting, he was literally blown back out the door by an explosion. He expected to lose all. However, only the interior of the house burned out. He was able to reconstruct the wall surfacing and inside walls, restoring his house to a livable condition.

The secret was that the walls and ceiling were insulated with cellulose material (basically, recycled newspapers with boric acid added as a fire retardant), which did not burn. Even the 2 × 4s in the wall were protected; they only charred some on the room side but were still sound and could be left in place.

Our informant rated this type of insulating material as much superior to other types currently in use. Foam, he said, gives off fumes when heated, and fiberglass would have burned in a similar fire.

B.

SOLAR HOT-WATER SYSTEM

The power of the sun has been harnessed in Benewah County, Idaho, with materials provided by the National Center for Appropriate Technology and labor provided by the county winterizing crew. These plans are meant as an example of a working system that can be partially or completely duplicated by any handy person.

This system heats water and will work when the sun shines, year round. It cost about $350 for materials, because most materials were purchased new and because less expensive substitutions, which would have slightly reduced efficiency, were not made. Electric water heaters consume half the electricity used in an average home (without electric heat) in this area, and year-round this solar system is presumed to cut this energy usage by 10 to 20 percent. Thus, at present utility rates, in 5 to 10 years the heater will have paid for itself.

The temperature of the water in the first of these heaters built by the winterizing crew was 116°F on the first day of its operation, but the amount of energy saved by its use will not be known for several months.

The sun heats the water in the copper-tube gridwork inside the collector box (see Figure 1). The box is insulated with 3½" fiberglass and covered with two layers of glazing to retain the sun's heat even in winter (Figure 2). The inner glazing is filon—a thin fiberglass sheeting, often used on greenhouses. The filon is protected by an outer cover of crystal-strength glass. Filon may sag under conditions of high heat and melt itself onto the copper grid. A long strip of molding ½" square attached to the walls of the collector box and running lengthwise down the center of the collector box is placed just under the filon to prevent this. In a cold climate two glazing layers are suggested, but used windows or filon alone would suffice.

The grid is made of soldered rigid (type M) copper tube (Figure 3). The horizontal tubes (called manifolds) are one inch in diameter, and the vertical connecting tubes (called risers) are a half inch. The grid is

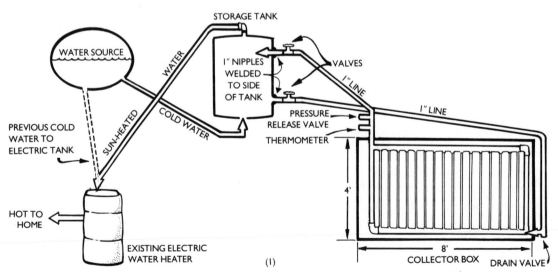

(1)

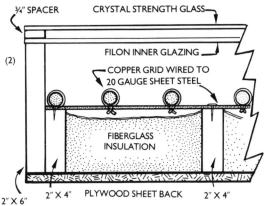

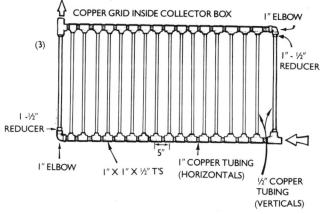

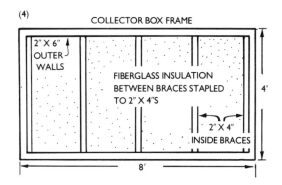

attached with copper wires to a sheet of 18-gauge hot-rolled steel. The steel sheet and copper tubing are bonded tightly to ensure good heat transfer from the steel to the tubes. The interior of the collector box, including the grid and sheet, are sprayed with flat black automotive paint, which can withstand high temperatures. The water in the grid rises upward as it is heated by the sun, circulating to the upper manifold and then through the one-inch copper tube to the storage tank. Without the use of any electricity or any type of pump, the water circulates itself through the process known as thermal convection from the grid to the storage tank and back again, so the water in the tank is as hot as that in the grid itself.

The placement of the storage tank and grid is crucial. The bottom of the tank must be placed a minimum of 18 inches higher than the top of the gridwork, or the water will not circulate properly. Also, the tubes connecting the tank to the collector box must be as short and direct as possible, because water circulation is hindered by bends in the pipe, and heat is lost as water flows through the tubes. The storage tank should be located near the home's existing water heater to further lessen heat loss. The connecting tube from the top of the collector box must enter

the storage tank a few inches below the top of the tank, and the tube from the bottom of the collector must enter the storage tank a few inches above the bottom of the tank for proper water circulation to occur.

Heated water in the storage tank will flow into the existing water heater, which remains operational. Energy usage is reduced because the water entering the electric heater has already been heated by the sun. The cold-water pipe which originally entered the water heater is rerouted through the storage tank.

To conserve heat, wrap the storage tank and the connecting tubes in fiberglass insulation. With the storage tank located in the house, there will be no danger of freezing and breaking in the winter. The collector box and the tubes must be exposed to the cold, however, and in winter these must be drained to prevent freezing. (An antifreeze solution and a heat exchanger tank is an alternative to the draining and refilling process, but this is much more difficult and expensive for the back-yard builder to construct. As well, such a system is potentially dangerous because every precaution must be taken to keep the lethal antifreeze solution from contaminating the household water.)

There are three valves in the system. To drain the grid and the connecting tubes, the two valves inside the house next to the storage tank must be shut off. The valve at the low corner of the collector box is opened to drain it all, and the process is reversed to refill it to take advantage of the next available sun. The connecting tubes and the collector box are not built level, but all are set off the horizontal pointing toward the drain valve to ensure that no pockets of water are left in the grid to freeze and break the tubes. A thermostat should be set into the tube above the grid, to monitor the performance of the system and to warn when the water is dangerously close to freezing and must be drained.

The collector box should be attached to the outside of the house and facing south (within 20 degrees of south is optimal). For best year-round use, the collector should be set at a 45° angle to the wall of the house.

The collector box could be made movable to face the sun as it rises and lowers in the sky during the different seasons, but that also is more difficult and expensive. A second set of connecting tubes from the storage tank to a coil either in the firebox of a wood stove or around the stovepipe would ensure a year-round supply of free hot water.

Utility rates can only rise as fuel sources diminish, and installing a solar or solar- and wood-powered water-heating system will make even better economic sense in the future. And it always makes sense to become as independent as possible.

B. T.

 ## POWDER YOUR FOAM FOR A BETTER FIT

Have you ever struggled to get a large foam cushion inside the slipcover you've made for it, and felt that you were wrestling an alligator? Try a dusting of talcum powder on the foam. It works.

B. T.

 ## BETTER CONCRETE

Here is some information on concrete:
Cement
Good concrete contains approximately twice as much gravel as sand. Each particle must be surrounded by a paste of cement and water.
Sand
Sand should have particles ranging from fine to ¼".
Gravel
Gravel should range from about ¼–1½" for most work. All materials should be clean. Silt clay loam is objectionable in making concrete, as it coats the particles and prevents

the cement paste from bonding to it. New concrete should be protected from drying out for at least seven days.

A fairly decent concrete mixture is:

one unit cement

two units sand

three units gravel

A one-to-six mixture is also commonly used. Here are some simple tests to see if your local materials are suitable for concrete:

Silt Test

This is for testing to find out if there are harmful amounts of silt or clay in materials to be used for cement.

1. Place 2″ of sample (sand or gravel) in a pint fruit jar.
2. Add water until the jar is almost full; put the lid on the jar and shake vigorously. Set the jar aside until the water clears.
3. Measure the layer of silt covering the sand or gravel. If this layer is more than ⅛″ thick, the material is not clean enough for concrete unless washed.

Vegetable Matter Test

1. Dissolve a heaping teaspoonful of household lye into a half pint of water in a one-pint fruit jar.
2. Pour a half pint of a representative sample of sand or gravel into the jar containing the lye water.
3. Cover the jar tightly and shake vigorously for one or two minutes.
4. Set the jar aside for 24 hours. Then inspect in good light.
5. If the water is clear or colored not darker than apple cider vinegar, the material is suitable for use in concrete. However, if the color of the water is darker than this, the material should not be used for concrete before it is washed to remove the objectionable vegetable matter.

A Bit on Footings

Footings should be twice as wide as the foundation wall and approximately half as thick as wide. The width of the footing needed is figured by the load to be carried and the support quality of the earth.

Load Capacities of Some Soil Types

Type of soil	Capacity (tons per sq. ft.)
Soft clay	1 ton
Wet sand or firm clay	2 tons
Fine, dry sand	3 tons
Hard dry clay or coarse sand	4 tons
Gravel	6 tons

J. V.

QUICK BUTTONHOLE FIX

An enlarged buttonhole in your children's clothing can be a problem, since it allows the button to slip out. Cut a bit of iron-on mending tape that is larger than the buttonhole and press it on the reverse side of the clothing item; then make a slit in the tape with a knife or razor blade.

B. T.

ACID BRUSH

A long-lasting acid brush to use in soldering jobs and other acid-using projects can be

slip-on pencil eraser to form acid-holding "bristles." Rubber is nearly acid-proof and so will last longer in this use than will ordinary brushes.

B. T.

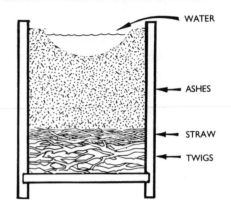

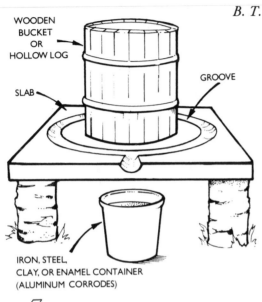

MAKING LYE AND SOAP

Ingredients for Lye

5 gal. ashes

Hardwoods yield the best lye. Ashes of burnt seaweed produce sodium-based lye, from which hard soap can be made. Lye from ashes of plant life (except seaweed) is potash or potassium carbonate (K_2CO_3), an alkali. This alkali reacts with fat to form soft soap. Ashes from other materials, such as paper, cloth, and garbage, cannot be used.

2 gal. soft or medium-hard water

Leaching the Lye

In the bottom of a wooden bucket, make a filter to trap the ashes by criss-crossing two layers of small twigs and placing a layer of straw on top. Fill the bucket with dry ashes. To keep the lye from being leached acciden-

tally, the ashes must be kept dry before they are used.

Pour warm water into the bucket, making the ashes moist and sticky. To make sure the water passes through the ashes at the correct rate for leaching the lye, move the ashes up at the sides of the bucket to form a depression in the center. Add all the remaining water in small amounts in the following manner: Fill the center depression with water; let the water be absorbed; fill the depression again. When about two-thirds of the water has been added, the lye or potash, a brown liquid, will start to flow from the bottom of the bucket. Use more water, if necessary, to start this flow. It takes about an hour to start the flow of lye.

The yield from the amounts given here is about ½ gal. of lye. Results vary according to the amount of water loss from evaporation and the kind of ashes used. If lye is of the correct strength, an egg or a potato should float in it. A chicken feather should be coated, but not eaten away. If the solution is weak, pour it through the barrel again, or through a new barrel of ashes, or concentrate it by boiling. Nine gallons of ashes is about the right amount for 4½ lb. of fat.

Recipe for Making Soap

Put ½ cup of lye in an iron kettle for every

cup of fats or oils used. Add the measured amount of fat. Boil the lye and fat together until the mixture becomes thick, rubbery and foamy. Remove the kettle from the fire and let it cool. The soap is a thick, jellylike substance that ranges in color from tan to dark brown, depending on the fats or oils used and the length of boiling time. The soap greatly improves with age. Store it in a container for at least a month before using it. A cup of fat yields a cup of soft soap.

Adapted from *Village Technology Handbook,* edited by Margaret Crouch and Leonard Doek (VITA, 1987).

B. T.

 ### TIPS FROM A HEARTY 70-YEAR-OLD

I'll be busy again this winter recycling clothes and wool for quilts, throws, cushions, wool socks, etc. During the 120°F. days here, I've made myself several more new dresses. Next I must get material and thread to make Bill more shirts; I find it cheaper than buying them, since the stitching is none too good on bought ones.

I made a batch of cherry and rhubarb wine, but there is not enough sugar in, so I have 1½ gal. of cherry-colored vinegar.—OK for cooking recipes that call for wine vinegar. Second batch—near 2 gal., same fruit—turned out like Baby Duck. Just put the right amount of sugar in. Will make cherry and apricot brandy for Xmas—very simple and good mulled if colds or flu occur.

We are renting part of an old ranch and have a southern slope for garden. It really

pays off, what with all my canning left from last fall—we can survive at least two years. The new potatoes that would have just shriveled up in storage, I scrubbed well and processed three hours with mint and a scant teaspoon of salt. Great if unexpected company arrives to open up for stew, potato salad, or just warmed in oven with butter and more dried mint sprinkled over. We live mostly on vegetables and fresh eggs and odd meals of trout that Bill catches at least once a week.

We use no Hydro or phone here. There was propane in the house, but we found it just as costly as Hydro, so we don't use it. There's a Selkirk chimney in the front room and kitchen, so we have a large cook stove in the front room. I do all my cooking meals and canning on a garbage burner outside, since there is lots of dry wood around.

I wash clothes by board and old-fashioned wringer. Guess lots think I shouldn't at my age—70 in January. I could take the laundry to town, but honest work in moderation never killed anyone. There are quite a few families in our valley, and we barter, trade vegetables, milk, and jars for canning, and are like one big happy family; it's a great lifestyle.

W. A. W.

 ### CHARCOAL COLD-WEATHER CAR STARTER

For those who cannot plug in their car in the cold, let us tell you what works well for us. If you can, get the vehicle under cover; any kind of shelter makes a big difference. Then make a cover for the hood that will reach the

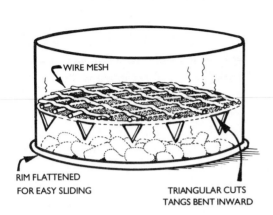

WIRE MESH

RIM FLATTENED
FOR EASY SLIDING

TRIANGULAR CUTS
TANGS BENT INWARD

HAND CLEANSER FOR CEMENT

For all you root cellar builders and other cement users, have you ever wondered what to do about your "sandpaper hands" when using cement? Logic taught me that cement, being quite alkaline, can be neutralized with an acid. So the other day when I was pouring my root cellar, I washed my hands with vinegar. Yes, it works. For good measure, I then continued with a wash with a bit of kerosene. (Read the label on a Vaseline jar sometime. It is actually "petroleum jelly.") My hands are not exactly baby-soft yet (they probably never will be, anyway), but it sure works.

N.B. I'm sure you know that a hand wash with a bit of kerosene instantly removes tree sap from your hands after wood splitting. The kerosene smell easily washes away with soap.

R. R.

ground in front and beside each front wheel—put this on while the engine is still warm. We made our cover from two old punctured air mattresses and an old blanket and sewed on hooks to keep it from sliding off. This works fine until a real cold spell comes along, perhaps 30°–40° below, then we have another gadget—a charcoal burner!

This is made from a five-gallon pail. Remove the handle, turn the pail upside down, and flatten the rim on the bottom so it will slide along the ground easily. Measure the distance from the ground to the bottom of the oil pan on your vehicle, subtract 1½", and cut the top off the pail at this height so that the pail can be slid under the oil pan. Take a heavy knife, and using a hammer to tap lightly, cut V-shaped notches around the side at the bottom with the V pointing down. Bend the resulting tangs inward, then cut a circle of wire mesh to fit inside the pail and push it down onto the tangs. On such a cold day that the heater is needed, take a small shovelful of red coals from the heater, put them in the pail, and slide it under the oil pan; 10 to 15 minutes later, our pickup starts like summer, and at 40° below.

J. P. & P. D.

IF YOU DON'T LIKE MOSQUITOES!

Last year is still in my memory, when it was impossible to work around the place without losing precious blood night and day. The only time the mosquitoes took a rest was during the hottest part of the day, and even then, it was a good idea to wear long sleeves and trousers.

The electric bug light we finally bought and hung upon the balcony that summer brought little release. Mostly, it caught moths. It seems that mosquitoes are attracted not by light alone but also by the smell of living beings. Having the choice, they prefer the latter. So for this year, we tried an experiment that we consider quite successful. As most of you who have been involved in organic gardening know already, natural methods never work 100 percent, but we certainly got rid of over 90 percent of the mosquitoes.

This is how it works: we built a 7' × 8' pond with black plastic sheeting. It is located in a prime spot, right between the house, the horse corral, and the goat pen, a heavily infested area. This was the only available breeding place for the mosquitoes; being located in a choice spot forces them to make use of it. A dozen goldfish, along with the natural enemies of mosquito larvae (like boatmen bugs, which come around to stay as soon as the pond is established), take care of the larvae with delight.

To increase the attraction to the pond even more, we hung the bug light right over the water. In combination with the location and the body of water, it is very effective. But for this system any bright ultraviolet light will do the job, because the most important ingredient for this mosquito-pie recipe is the frogs.

Some of them will come by themselves, but with the amount of food around our place, the five that came were permanently overworked, or better said, overfed. I became worried about their health and decided to catch 10 more of their friends for help.

The pond is more balanced now, but there is still room for newcomers. After all, no food should be wasted or unnecessarily left to escape.

A large board floating right under the light makes it easy for the frogs to catch a lot in a short period of time at night. What I enjoy the most is the fun that everybody has with this mosquito-catching program. Needless to say, the pond is the most pleasant spot on our land now, where one can sit for hours in

peace watching others having a good time getting fat.

Maybe this is a big disadvantage, too, as I find myself spending too much time watching, especially the tadpoles, which just turned into frogs now. The other disadvantage is that the goats are very hesitant to leave their corral for grazing and would much rather lie close to the pond to enjoy the peace, which lowers their milk production. We now bring them into their pasture and lock them there during the day. But besides that, I'm convinced of the usefulness of this experiment. I'm looking forward to building a proper pond for next year.

There's a book in the library about pond building, how to go about it, and what materials to use. No concrete work is necessary, just some digging and a bit of time. Beyond that, you can get into water gardening, growing exotic water lilies or raising fancy fish. I'm happy with the common water plants that grow in the swamps in this valley, and the 50-cent goldfish do their job like any other. But there is room left for expansion. With a small pond like ours, it is also advisable to have an aquarium for the fish for the winter.

A pail hung under the bug light catches more than enough fish food for all the fish you need, for a whole year.

You'll also find birds are attracted by the water, and other mosquito lovers, like bats, find out really fast that there is a lot of pleasant action going on around the bug light. Don't forget bats are harmless, useful creatures and are not vampires. They seem to be very shy of people, and I have never managed to have a close look at them.

If you find yourself too old to enjoy catching frogs and tadpoles, I'm sure you can persuade your children or grandchildren to give you a hand. That way, everybody will have some fun because of the mosquitoes.

Always make sure there is a possibility for the frogs and tadpoles (as soon as they turn into frogs) to leave the water. If you have water lilies growing, the large leaves are usually sufficient and will be a favorite spot in daytime for them to sit. At night, they prefer a floating board, and some even leave to explore their surroundings, so make sure it is possible for them to get in and out.

Frogs hibernate in winter, and a thick mulch spread around the pond in fall will help them to find a warm spot. This way you can ensure that your little helpers will be around again the following spring.

D. T. A.

 REMOVING STUMPS

Stumps rot away in 1½ years if kept covered with your wood ashes. The stump should be cut close to the ground so that it gets a lot of moisture. Ashes and water mix to create caustic soda, a powerful alkali. Don't add acid to hurry the process, or you will neutralize the alkali.

S. C.

 RECYCLED JAR LIDS

About jar lids: I've been reusing my canning jar lids for about three years with the same percentage of success as for new lids. The

secret, I think, is that the lid must be in perfect shape, which it can't be when pried off mechanically. I use my two thumbs to push the lid off the jar; this way, it is not bent at all. Also, lids must be completely clean. In canning, I treat these recycled lids just the same as new ones.

B.

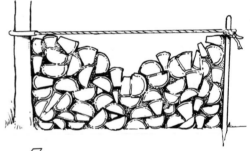

 WOOD CHOPPING HELP

Here are some smallholding techniques gleaned from "Recycle Ranch":

- A rubber tire placed on the top of a chopping block keeps the wood from falling off while being chopped and means you don't have to spend time chasing pieces of elusive firewood.
- A good free-standing woodpile can be made with a support at one end and a rope attached to a pole banged into the ground at the other end.

S.

SAUNA DOUBLES AS FOOD DRYER

For several issues now I have not been directly connected with the production, and I find it interesting to be on the receiving end. It's good to see the communications among those with similar concerns.

Being here has allowed me to practice further much of what we have discussed in the past issues. We live without electricity or running water, grow all our own vegetables (except for some soybeans) and some grain, grind our own flour by hand, and live under a taxable income.

For drying food, we use either racks suspended from the ceiling over the wood stove, or the sauna. The walls of the sauna have catches for poles to fit into. The racks (same ones used in the house) are then stacked in tiers on the pole supports. We dried our prune plums in quantity that way, as well as other fruit. One problem is that the juice tends to get the sauna benches below sticky, so we expect to move them this year and have the juice fall on the firewood below, instead. Drying green beans, which are as young as one would pick them for steaming, provides for fresh-tasting reconstituted beans in the winter. Comfrey, kale, and large leaves can be dried in quantity.

H. K.

CUTTING THROUGH GREASE

Vegetable oil can be a fine hand cleaner. It works especially well on automotive grease. It also works, but more slowly, on pitch. Just put a tablespoon or two in your palm and "wash" with the oil until the grease or pitch is well dissolved. Then dry your hands on a paper towel (a sheet of which you have cleverly made handy before oiling up). Finish with ordinary soap. Your hands will be soft and clean. No abrasives and nothing toxic.

T. Z.

COLD STARTS AND IDLING

I liked this pointer on "The Cold Start" in *Drive It Forever* by Robert Sikorsky (McGraw Hill, 1983):

Once you have started a cold engine and the oil pressure gauge or light indicates normal, place the car gently in gear and get moving. No more than fifteen seconds of engine idling should be required. *Do not* try to warm the engine by prolonged idling. Years ago this was accepted practice, but with today's engines and increased knowledge of the mechanics of engine wear and fuel economy, most engineers are in agreement that prolonged idling of a cold engine will only do harm. A cold idling engine won't warm as fast, lubricate as efficiently, or burn gasoline as completely as one that is in gear and moving—that is, one that is under load. Use slow to moderate speeds the first few miles, and don't race or gun the engine.

In general, he recommends letting the engine idle as little as possible. He says that any idling in excess of 30 seconds justifies turning the engine off. The only exception is after a long, hot trip, when he recommends one or two minutes of idling before shutting the engine down.

T. Z.

MAKING YOUR OWN HEALING SALVES

When the minor crisis happens in our house (cuts, insect stings, burns, diaper rash), I am thankful for the little brown bottle of salve that is always close at hand. The making of salves has become an enjoyable ritual for me every year. Gathering and drying the herbs that I need is all part of the process. I gather plants that are local, such as comfrey (leaves and root), chickweed, plantain, calendula flowers, as well as adding nonlocal herbs such as goldenseal. I hang the plants to dry in a dark place out of the sunlight. Once I have enough herbs to make the salve, here is how I proceed.

A few days before the full moon is a good time to make salves. The ingredients you need are oil (preferably olive), beeswax, the herbs, and brown jars to store the salve in. For each cup of oil you need 1 oz. dried root, or ½ oz. dried leaves, and ¼ cup beeswax (or less, depending on desired thickness). The herbs are put into a pot of oil and heated at a low temperature. After 30 minutes to an hour, strain the oil so that all of the plant material is removed. Add the beeswax to the hot oil. To check the thickness of your salve, put a small amount of it into a saucer and let it harden—you may want to add more wax or oil. A few drops of scented oil can be added to the warm mixture to enhance its fra-

grance. Pour the warm salve into jars, and it will harden as it cools.

You may want to make different salves, using different combinations of plants, depending on what healing properties you need.

Plantain is good for drawing out poisons, as in a bee sting, and for bruises. Chickweed is excellent for skin irritations, such as diaper rash. Calendula flowers are good for cuts, bruises, sprains, and wounds. Comfrey is good for burns, bruises, and sores.

For those who are not familiar with using herbs for healing, the making of salves may open up a whole new area of interest for you.

E.

INVISIBLE STORM DOOR

A 71-year-old man has developed a household air-conditioning system that, he says, requires no energy to operate.

Evert Carlson said the system he has constructed beside his three-room, wood-heated, 30′ × 16′ home works "just like an invisible storm door" while maintaining a constant flow of fresh air. "The beauty of it is that it's entirely automatic," he said.

He has been working for 20 years to evolve his system, which consists of a seven-foot-wide, six-foot-deep pit or "well" connected to an outside air intake pipe and another pipe leading into the house. Outside air flows into the house through the pipe—four-inch-diameter plastic drain tile—after first being "cleaned and tempered" in the well.

Air passing through the well, which is covered by two feet of earth, is warmed in cold weather and cooled in hot weather by normal ground temperature before flowing into the house. In our area, ground temperature ranges from 40–45°F.

The system "operates the same as your car" when it circulates the air in the house, Carlson says. "The air intake in your car has to be the same size as your exhaust. If the intake is smaller, it cuts down your efficiency. The air pipe has to deliver the same volume of air that's going out your chimney."

Dust, pollen, and pollution are trapped on the moist walls of the well, leaving the air fresh and cleaner than outside. The rougher the walls of the well, the better, because you then have more obstacles to trap the pollution.

"If I'd had this when Mount St. Helens blew up, most of the volcanic ash would have been left behind," Carlson said.

He said he was completely convinced that the system works well after a night when the outside temperature went down to –6°F. When he got up the next morning, he discovered that the fire in his wood stove had gone out, but the house was filled with warm air. "Now, unless it's extremely cold, I don't bother to stoke up the stove at all," he added.

Many people believe air conditioners are only needed during the summer, Carlson said, "but you need it in the winter as well. In the winter you need it more than in the summer, because you have more foul air in the house."

As well as making breathing more pleasant, the conditioner will "cut down on housecleaning" by eliminating airborne dirt. Carlson said he has not tried to patent his system because he doubts a patent would be granted for such a simple concept. Although he would like energy ministry engineers to examine his working model, no interest has been shown yet.

B. T.

ICE-SAFE YOUR SHOES

I heard recently about pulling old socks over your boots to make walking on ice less slippery. I had occasion to try it this winter, and it seems to work. I pulled a loaded sleigh into a howling wind across bared-off lake ice where in other years I had been reduced to crawling on hands and knees in a similar situation.

S.

A GOOD HOME AIR SYSTEM

We know too well of sickness brought on by oxygen starvation due to the lack of fresh air in our homes during the cold months. Lack of oxygen breaks down the body, so colds are the least of the diseases that attack us. It makes a difference when one can have doors and windows open, as we do in the warm weather. For my part, I found the more I plugged all drafts, the sicker I got, until it became serious. I then installed an air system I thought of 50 years ago. My health began improving steadily, and for 2 years now, colds haven't touched me.

This air system leads the fresh air into an underground chamber, where it is warmed and cleaned before entering the house. In the summer it is cooled, so the system works the

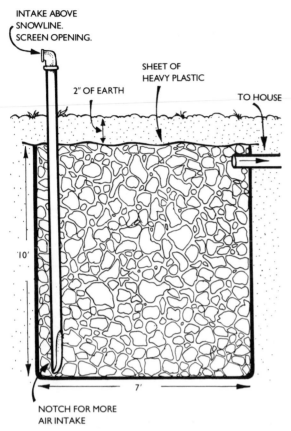

INTAKE ABOVE SNOWLINE. SCREEN OPENING.

2" OF EARTH

SHEET OF HEAVY PLASTIC

TO HOUSE

10'

7'

NOTCH FOR MORE AIR INTAKE

whole year through. The temperature of the air flow into the house is the same at all times, so the house becomes immune to outside temperatures if it is well insulated and as airtight as possible to get maximum air flow through the system. My house is old and only in fair shape; but in the three years I've had this system, the temperature has dropped to –14°F, and I've never had fire at night. When I go to bed, I shut the heat off. I act as if it were summer, and the house has never got as cold as Sacramento, California (I listen to their radio weather reports a lot).

My system needs no power or maintenance. Once it's installed, forget it. I find a four-inch air line satisfactory. I used solid plastic pipe and no concrete, so if you do the work yourself, the cost is low.

My rock pit is 7' wide and 12' deep; that seems to be right in this area. If it is not enough in other areas, you can dig another pit alongside. The pit is filled with medium-sized rocks that are easy to handle. The rocks serve to filter the air and support the earth walls. As you fill the pit, pack in small stones against the earth to prevent it from seeping into the pit.

The rocks stop two feet from the surface to allow two feet of earth to cover the pit. I covered the rock with a sheet of heavy plastic and then put on the two-foot earth cover. If the pit fills with the spring runoff, well, the cold weather has gone, and the hot spell is still to come.

When it was –14°F, the air flow stayed at 40°, so that gave 54° of clean heat at no cost. My heater then had to heat 30° to 70° where I wanted it. So the system carried about ¾ of the load. Really, my fire is used barely half the time; winter doesn't amount to much around here anymore.

The air vent in the house should be placed away from the heating unit so that the incoming air can mix well with the rest of the air. The foul air and dust settle to the floor, where the draft from the heating unit sucks it up like a large vacuum cleaner. This causes the air in the air pipe to flow into the house to replace the air that's gone up the chimney. When there is no air pipe, oxygen starvation sets in both for us and the stove. When there is a vacuum in the house and one opens the door, a rush of cold air comes in to fill the house. We have storm doors, to prevent that. In my house there is no vacuum, no storm door, and no oxygen starvation.

The air intake can be placed alongside the house, where it is protected and out of the way. To keep the snow out of the pipe, place an elbow over the top and screen it to keep the birds out. The standpipe going to the bottom of the pit has a notch about 18″ long so that it can rest on the bottom while it is being installed and let the air flow freely.

C. E. C.

HOME AIR SYSTEM: SOME DANGERS

I read with interest your article on the home air system.

It is one of a variety of systems that use the Earth's temperature to modify outside air temperature. Similar systems have been called ground pipes, earth tubes, and buried loops, but all use the phenomenon that the Earth's temperature is a constant 50–55°F. So, theoretically, all you need to do is to warm the air 15°F; this can be done with passive solar heat, wood heat, or other means.

However, I would like to point out a very real danger in using such a system, which does not seem to be airtight or watertight.

The Earth is full of decaying materials, some of which give off gases and other products of the decay process. One of the most dangerous to human beings is radon gas, given off by the decay of radium. Radium is found almost everywhere in varying amounts in the Earth's crust and rocks. Systems not sealed against infiltration of gases will accumulate them and ultimately deliver them into your living space. Radon has been shown to cause lung cancer.

The obvious solution to this problem is to make the walls of the system airtight. I would

suggest that the walls be made of metal, since some plastic pipes have a urea formaldehyde base and out-gas it, decreasing with time. Since concrete and rocks have the potential of producing radon gas, I would not use them in a tank. A loop of steel pipe would be the best solution, the length depending on wall area × volume of air × constant Earth temperature.

Another caution: in any system where dirt or moisture can penetrate and be trapped, there is a chance that fungi and similar growths can occur, with the resultant spores, etc., being carried by the airstream into the living space, where they can cause allergic reactions and other effects.

I applaud this experiment in energy conservation, and I trust that those persons who propose to build similar systems will benefit from this information.

B. T.

REFLECTIONS ON AGING

The time comes for a 70-year-old single woman to face facts—I can't forever continue to live on the ranch, two miles from the nearest neighbor, in an area where there is little or no help from neighbors and no one to hire for work. I've lived here since I retired from teaching 15 years ago.

What Are the Alternatives?

1. Continue—letting some things go (this has been happening already), using electricity instead of wood, letting others pick fruit, cutting the size of the garden.

2. Try to find a helper to live in.

3. Or (not easy—I love living alone) go live

with someone else. Much of my life was spent adapting to others: husbands, children, bosses, and I'm now selfish about time at the end of my life.

Considerations

1. I am healthy but tire sooner, so not as much gets done when it should.
2. I'm not afraid to stay in the country. Friends have moved to the city to be near doctors and hospitals. That doesn't figure in my plans.
3. California is getting crowded. I need quiet.

Possibilities

1. House- and ranch-sitting for a transition period.
2. Small place on other people's ranch as caretaker-helper.
3. Community? (One has learned much one could share.)
4. Fifth wheel to live in at homes where I help? Help others with gardens for sharing produce? Help old folks plan and sort and clean out possessions? I'm experienced!

Ideal

A place to be alone—yet it's better to be helping other old folks a little than struggling with my own place.

What to do? Have some other *Smallholder* readers faced similar problems and gained insights to share?

L. L. D.

MORE THOUGHTS ON AGING

I have just finished reading the book *Small Expectations,* by Leah Cohen (McClelland &

Stewart, 1984), which is about older women and how society treats them, especially the poorer class.

For the first time in my life I am facing the fact that I am getting older, I am a woman, and I am poor. What happens when we are old and feeble and there are no pensions accrued, no fat bank accounts, no dozen Establishment children (one hopes) to care for us? As long as our health is good, we can work and live quite happily, but *any* handicap is going to cause serious changes in our lifestyles. You can't chew coarse, raw food with no teeth; you can't carry water when your knees are too stiff to bend; you can't pick cherries when blind from cataracts.

Of course when we are young we all think good health and alert minds last forever, and there will always be somebody eager to care for us in our old age; but as a middle-aged woman with many older friends (male and female), I know that this is not always true. So what do you think your old age holds for you? I would be very interested in hearing your ideas. I know I am baffled about my own future.

W. C.

UNDERGROUND HEAT EXCHANGERS

When building a home air system, using ground heat will entail a lot of trial and error. I heard of one person who installed 300' of pipe to carry him through the winter. I'm now placing two short lines, so when one gets chilled, I'll switch over to the warm line. I believe the chilled line will recover rather soon, after the cold air flow is stopped in that section.

Last winter I used the crawl space under my house as a heat exchanger, and it worked very well indeed. The snow banks around the house melted the same as usual. So I saw then that one could have a heat exchanger in the basement to gather the basement heat, which can be flushed out from accumulated dust.

Our homes are gathering more and more articles of plastic, from radios to shopping bags; mix that with hair sprays and other chemicals, and we need an active air flow through the house. Last winter the sickness time struck us in the holiday season with flu, but as usual I was not afflicted.

I agree with Mr. T. in his letter that we must take every precaution when installing these air systems, but when done correctly, it surely pays off.

C. E. C.

 **WILDFIRES**

Although I've lived in the woods for years, I'd never given wildfires much thought. I suspect that many others are in a similar state, so here are a few things you can do to protect your homestead during a forest fire.

- Pay attention to dead and dying trees, branches, etc., that could block your passage in an escape, or block out fire fighters.
- If you don't have a creek or pond very near your house, collect rainwater. With a gas pump, you can keep your roof wet.
- It's inconvenient, but it's best to stack firewood well away from your home.
- The Forest Service people recommend putting both a primary and a secondary fuel break around your homestead.
- For a primary break, remove all dense brush, tall grass, and other fuels for 10' around structures. Prune all branches up to 8' (and *any* dead or dying branches above the roof) and thin trees with 15' between crowns. Slow-burning plants are suggested for landscaping in this area.
- For a secondary break, clean out all dead and dying fuels for 70' on the downhill side of structures and 35' on the other sides.
- It's also a good idea to make evacuation plans—for family, animals, and stuff worth saving—so that they won't be concerns while you are fire fighting.
- Should you have to give up and run for it, cover all windows (actually, you could do this well in advance) with heavy material to block heat and move overstuffed chairs, etc., to the center of the room.

Wildfires are one truly awesome experience that I hope I don't have again for a good long while.

M. C.

 LONGER LIFE FOR SHINGLE ROOFS

For years I have been raising this problem periodically in the hope of finding an easy solution that does not involve the use of poisonous chemicals. This summer we installed zinc strips, running the length of the roof, tucked a bit under the ridge cap but exposed to any rain—the theory is that the rain washes the zinc down over the roof, killing the moss that is there and preventing new moss from growing. Apparently, a very weak solution of zinc is all that it takes to kill moss.

Then I read the *Rural Delivery* article and wished that I had tried that method instead. The author noticed that the shingles below his brick and mortar chimney were in better shape than those anywhere else on the roof. Observations of his neighbors' roofs showed the same pattern. He concluded that it's the lime in the mortar, leached by rain and washed down the roof, that keeps unwanted growth off the roof.

He was able to verify this when he was shown a barn roof in Nova Scotia that had a shallow trough down the length of the peak. "They used to fill it with lime," the farmer said. Then, when rain came, the trough would overflow and send lime water down over the shingles.

One of the author's neighbors added two cups of rock salt to a five-gallon bucket of hardwood ashes and applied the mixture to a wet roof. Since the lichens and mosses that grow on roofs are acid loving, this mixture, which neutralizes the roof's acidity, makes the shingles a less advantageous place for them to grow.

Even these simple methods need to be used carefully. Hardwood ashes and water make lye, a chemical that must be handled with care. There may also be danger to plants in the ground under the eaves, although perhaps, by the time the washed-down solution reaches the plants, it is too weak to do any damage. At any rate, I think

I'd apply a bit and see what happened.

In case you're thinking that this exhausts the subject, you'll probably have another report from me next year, after my zinc strips have had time to show what they can do. I'm hoping I can tell you that all my mosses and lichens curled up and dropped off.

B.

 MIXING MORTAR

Perhaps someone has had the experience of trying to mix mortar in a cement mixer only to find the plastic mix clings to the sides instead of being spaded by the mixing blades. To help keep the mortar moving, add two or three stones about three to four inches in diameter to the mix. They tumble around and keep the mortar mixing and are easily picked out when the mortar is dumped out.

E. A.

 NOTES FROM ONE SMALLHOLDING

We continue to improve our own smallholding here and are still managing to make our living from it. For others of you who live in similar ways, we have listed some of the things that have worked for us. Bear in mind that in different climates they may not work.

We use three stoves for heat. A kitchen cook stove, always on, a basement cook stove, lit in cold weather, and a living room heater, used during extensive cold. The cookers are airtight, as is the heater. We find that three bright fires are better than one large one, which would have to be shut down during warm spells, with poor use of fuel.

We have a root cellar leading off the basement, which is in constant use as a cold room. We wouldn't have one apart from the house, since it would be a pain to go outside for access. It is below ground and has walls of used tires that are packed with earth and stacked flat. They haven't moved in five years. The vents are four-inch sewer pipe, one from the ceiling and one from the floor.

This spring we built on a 30' × 9' greenhouse, using any glass we could buy cheap and fitting it together like crazy paving. We used clear silicone to glue it together, both edgewise and flat. We installed a solar vent opener and found it first class; we wouldn't be without one now.

We made a wood heater from scrap ⅜" steel, 36" × 24". We covered it with loose stone and capped that with puddled clay. We burn trash wood in a fast, clear fire, then shut everything down. It then gives off heat for four to five hours. The water system for the house is gravity-fed from a tank in the roof. It is kept from freezing by the hot-water tank installed below it. A gravity system uses only 10 percent of the energy required for a pressure system.

Our wind power system works very well, especially since we purchased a set of deep cycle batteries from the telephone company. We went seven months this year without starting the standby generator. Raising one tower 20' higher has made a tremendous difference. We still haven't got a 32 V DC refrig-erator, and as a help we obtained an old broken unit. We stripped out the compressor and other pieces that no longer worked, then vented it top and bottom with two-inch plastic pipe through the kitchen wall. In the winter it is a refrigerator and in the summer a nice airy cupboard. We also use a broken deep-freeze as an outside storage cabinet.

We built a cabin for visitors last year. It is 20' × 25', built at a cost of $2000 complete. We found a nice level spot that sloped away gently on all sides. We marked out the corners, then removed all topsoil and roots over the whole area within the pegs. The trenches for the foundation were dug 18" deep and all water and drainpipes dug in. All fill was thrown into the center of the site. The foundation was built from stone and mortar to 1' above grade outside, and the first four logs were seated on the top. Then we dug a small "tater hole" (root cellar) under the kitchen, so it also gives access to plumbing. Once again, all fill was thrown into the center. The hole was cribbed, the fill leveled and tamped, and then the floor was covered with rubber conveyor belting (obtained free from local sawmills). This makes a very pleasant-feeling floor, upon which we put carpet (used, scrounged). The walls are log, and the ceiling is pine poles with boards on top. The roof is log purlins and pole rafters capped with 2" cull lumber and aluminum printers' plates.

The chimney is a piece of heavy 10" pipe reaching from below the ceiling to 2' above the peak. It is held up with welded brackets hanging over the purlins. A 7" tin pipe is installed inside, projecting at both ends. A plate at the bottom of the large pipe, close fitted, takes the weight of the inner pipe, and the space between the two pipes is filled with vermiculite to insulate. Then we made a cap for the top; otherwise the wind would suck it out again. We find that during a chimney fire you can hold your hand on the outside pipe quite comfortably. Windows were bought at an auction sale, and the door we made from 2 × 10 boards.

In the chicken house we continue to use deep litter with good success and find that the best material to hang over the front of the nest boxes is pieces of large inner tube. They stay clean and will last for years.

J. P & P. D.

 HOME FIRE SAFETY

Like most people who live in homes heated by wood, I observe the typical cautions about fire prevention. I clean out the creosote, stack the wood away from the stove, and keep a fairly large gap between the stove and other inflammables. But we had a fire with a fairly great potential for destruction. And it was not caused by any of the things we usually protect ourselves against.

You had to see it to believe it. More accurately, I saw it, Dottie saw it, and I still find it hard to believe. This is the story.

I had placed a box of matches on the high counter between the kitchen and the living room, halfway between the two stoves. Next to the matches was a dinner bell. Our cat made the jump from the floor to the counter, dislodging the box of matches and the bell. The matches hit the floor first and the bell landed on top of it, igniting the entire box in one or two seconds. In another two or three seconds the dust under a daybed had ignited,

which then ignited the gauzelike dustcover of the box springs. In another five seconds or so, the bed was on fire. The entire thing was then extinguished in a few seconds more with a dry powder extinguisher.

The entire fire lasted less than a minute. Cleaning up the powder from the extinguisher took days.

We used water on the fire too, but it does not work when you are directing the extinguishing substance upward from under an object like a bed.

We now keep our matches in a metal lunch box. A plastic one might do as well, or a sealed wooden one. The care that is taken with the matches is more important than the container, in my opinion.

All the cautions may not be enough. A bit of luck helps too. If I had not put an extinguisher within reach, if we had been out of the room — if, if, if.

The moral of the story: just following stove safety precautions is not enough. A general survey of causes of fires and a family discussion about fires and how to respond to them are important too.

J. R.

EDITORS' NOTE: In my own experience, I've had a package of two boxes of matches explode into flames when they hit the floor, down an aisle in a Safeway store. Apart from hiding away your matches in a fireproof box, another answer is to buy safety matches. I bought some the other day, in the usual size, big boxes, in the hardware store. I absolutely refuse to say anything about Eddylites meeting their match.

J. M.

ROCKWORK: DO-IT-YOURSELF CONSTRUCTION FOR ENERGY EFFICIENCY

Walls and floors of rock are uniquely beautiful. They display the infinite variety of shapes, sizes, colors, and textures of individual rocks, as well as their patterns of interlocking. Rockwork radiates strength and solidity, along with light and heat.

Other advantages, especially for floors: rocks are washable, they don't require sanding or coating, water doesn't hurt them, and they are a safe and heat-efficient base in front of an open wood stove. They are eminently flexible for filling or making nonsquare spaces. Limitations to keep in mind are that they make a hard surface for little bodies to fall on, they have poor insulating value, and construction takes a long time. The first

drawback can be buffered by rugs. Insulation is only a problem for walls, since little heat is lost through the floor. Exterior walls can be turned to advantage by making them interior, behind glass, as in a greenhouse. As for the time rockwork takes to complete, it's well worth it, even if only for the creative satisfaction of the work.

Heat Storage

In our house the rocks help with the heating in three ways. They soak up the heat from the wood stove, store it, and release it gradually during the night. The same is true when the sun shines onto the rockwork. In addition, we're planning a rock hot tub that will hold heat in both its walls and the water.

Eventually the 12' long, ceiling-high rock wall in the front (south) of the house will be the back wall of a greenhouse. The additional glassed-in space will prevent the heat from

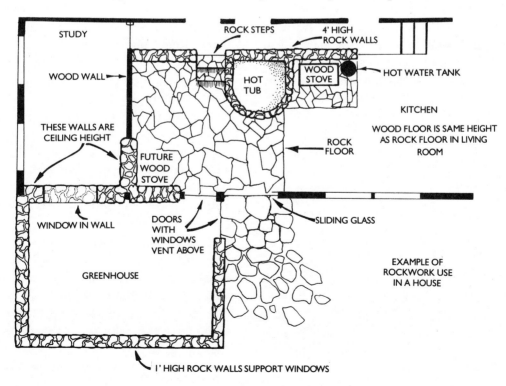

EXAMPLE OF ROCKWORK USE IN A HOUSE

that wall from escaping into the outside air. The rock floor and 4' high interior walls are designed for maximum exposure to winter sunlight—but no exposure to summer sunlight. One more note about heat storage: it took several days for the house to warm up when we first moved into the area with rockwork, as the rocks kept soaking up the heat (it was December). But once they achieved room temperature, the heating situation stabilized.

Construction Method

We didn't have to be experts to do the rockwork. But it has taken certain qualities and techniques to work well and some experienced help to get started. The qualities are patience, an eye for size and fit and pattern, and some dexterity. We learned our rock wall building from a local stonemason who was good enough to get us started with the first courses (along with his great stories). The technique we've used has the advantage of being flexible enough to fit many uses. We've built walls with both sides showing and ones with solid backing that only show the outside face. We've incorporated a vari-

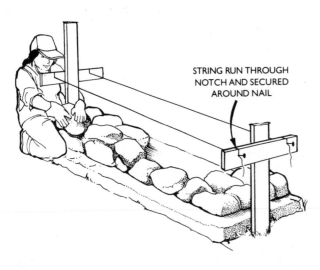

STRING RUN THROUGH NOTCH AND SECURED AROUND NAIL

ety of kinds of rock, from flat to round and anywhere in between.

Set-Up

First, start with a concrete footing. The rule of thumb is twice the width of the finished wall and to the depth of frost. The frost line in our area is 18" or so, but we went down only 4–6" because the soil is gravelly and well drained. Rebar or metal scrap (old tape measures, bent nails, bare wire) will help to reinforce the footing, especially if it's a shallow one.

Mix the concrete in a 5:1 ratio of coarse sand/gravel to cement. We've done all our mixing in a wheelbarrow, and it's not too big a chore for the amounts needed. A good way to mix it is to start with the dry ingredients, mix well, make a well in the center, add water and stir the dry ingredients in gradually. If the amount of water you start with is too much or too little, simply add whatever's needed to arrive at a porridgelike consistency. Rocks that are otherwise useless can be added into the concrete in the footing to help save on the amount of concrete needed.

With the beginning of the wall construction, you'll need a string line to give a constant reference for a line of sight to keep the wall faces plumb. For a curved wall, a level will do the job reasonably well. If using string, attach it to adjoining wood walls, posts, or stakes and batter boards (horizontal boards). Measure and mark on the batter boards the desired thickness of the wall; saw notches there and fasten the taut string line to nails at both ends of the wall. Keep the string low over the top of the wall for close reference. Set it up so you can move the string up as the wall rises. If the wall ends to show a flat surface on top, the string can be used as a level guide as well: measure down a

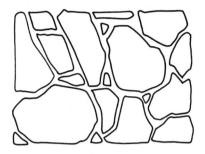

LOOKS GOOD; STRUCTURALLY WEAK

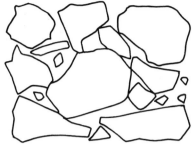

HERE THE SAME ROCKS ARE POORLY PLACED, AESTHETICALLY

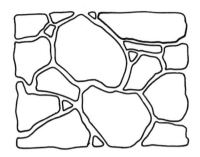

THIS IS AS GOOD AS IT GETS

constant distance (a couple of inches) to the desired wall top. If the wall ends at a wood post or has a wood backing, nails in the wood projecting into the center of the wall will help guarantee the stability of the wall. But first cover any wood surface contacting concrete with building paper or plastic to protect it from moisture.

Procedure for Walls

Start by collecting rocks—lots of them, with a variety of shapes and sizes and desired colors: light ones to reflect light (interior exposures), dark ones to absorb the heat of sunlight. It helps to keep them in piles according to size. Wash them thoroughly. Before placing each one in mortar, dampen it with a sponge so that the mortar will stick.

For mortar, use a combination of regular (Portland) and masonry cement. Regular cement alone will do, but masonry cement adds plasticity so that the mortar is much easier to work with. For mortar mix, use very fine clean sand. We got ours from the shore of the lake when the water level was low. Recommended proportions are anywhere from 2:1 to 3:1 sand to cement. The amount of masonry cement is also variable, but we like equal parts masonry and Portland cement for

a really cohesive consistency.

Mix it in the wheelbarrow as for regular concrete, but make the batches small enough to use up in a couple of hours—two to four shovelfuls of sand should be enough. Be much more sparing of water in this mortar mix—the final product should need to be packed to hold together. Mortar should be dry enough not to sag out from under a rock and wet enough not to be too crumbly. That balance is probably the trickiest and most crucial part of the whole process. If you put the mortar around a rock and tamp it tight with fingers, spoon handle, or trowel, it should stay in place, look slightly moist, and hold its shape firmly.

Choose rocks with flat faces out, unless the desired effect is round rock. The next best place for a flat surface is up, for a stable bearing surface for the next course. Try to stagger joints whenever possible when moving up the wall, for maximum strength. Work across, a row at a time. Try to keep in a plane not only the rock faces but also the mortar, which will be recessed an inch or so from the outside rock faces.

For optimum strength and appearance, the width of mortar between all rocks should be between ¼″ and 1″. Exceptions are allowed as needed, of course, but a consistent practice looks best. Try to make each rock's edges parallel to those surrounding it. Tight-fitting rocks with a minimum of mortar showing present the neatest image, but it's more painstaking to find rocks to fit so well. (In some cases you can help a rock fit better by taking a chunk or two off with a sharp hammer blow. A cold chisel can help too. But short of a real lesson from a good old-time stonemason, you can't guarantee how much of the rock will break off.) Round rock will inevitably leave large gaps between. These may be filled with pebbles stuck into the mortar. The tool to use for placing mortar is a small, stiff triangular trowel, along with fingers and occasionally a spoon handle. Be sure to wear rubber gloves. Otherwise, the fine cement particles will not only leach out moisture from your hands but will also be absorbed through the skin and enter the body's lymphatic system.

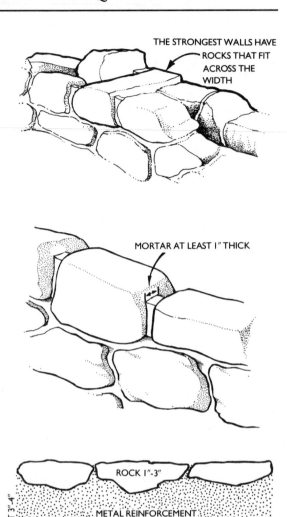

The strongest wall will have rocks fitting across the width of the wall (with a flat face on whatever sides will show). Otherwise, in a two-faced wall, up to ¾ of the wall width can be used to allow room for a thin rock to fit into the remaining space. Rocks placed vertically or on edge facing out should be a minimum of two to three inches thick. They are useful in those thin spots and can add a nice contrast in a horizontal pattern. But in general try to avoid using thin rocks on edge and facing out; place them instead either flat (horizontal or diagonal) or vertical but with only the edge showing. When a complete course is done across the length of a wall, there should be mortar between all the rocks at least one inch thick and patched right up to the top. If the rocks have been placed firmly enough to allow another layer or two while you're working, that's fine, too. Then the mortar should be allowed to set firmly for at least a couple of hours, so as to be strong enough to hold the "wet mix" that will fill the center spaces of the wall. (Again, wet or dry mix can also be used to pack small center spaces as you go.) Dump the wet mix into all the nooks and crannies; tamp gently but firmly. Build it up to the tops of the existing rocks so that a relatively uniform base is established for the next course of rocks. But be careful not to pile the wet mix in a place where a next rock will go, if the mix is going to harden first. For the wet mix, use coarse sand and Portland cement at 5:1, with a porridgelike consistency. Additional stones and rocks can be added for filler, along with metal scrap or rebar for horizontal strength. Vertical rebar is also advisable in the center of walls that are narrow or high.

Near the end of the day's work, return to the mortar joints for finishing work. The best tool for this job is an old spoon. Use either end to scrape the excess mortar away from the rocks—in effect, this will usually recess the joint a bit more, adding to the relief effect of the wall. It will also give the joints a smoother finish. The next day, a broom or brush can be used to polish the joints a bit cleaner yet. Finally, a gentle hosing and sponging of the wall will help to clean the rocks and cure the concrete. This addition of water is necessary in summer to keep the concrete from drying out too fast. All along, a wet sponge can help to keep rocks clean; but caution is needed to prevent excess water from leaching the cement out of the mortar. When work is finished, there will still be a bit of a dullness to the rocks as a result of a filmy residue of cement. We've heard that muriatic acid will take care of the final cleaning, but we're not there yet. A dose of plain water will produce a wonderful, if temporary, glow to the rocks, bringing out all the colors.

Floors

For a rock floor, you'll need lots of rocks with smooth, flat surfaces on top. The foundation for these rocks should consist of solid ground or gravel, an inch of sand, vapor barrier, three to four inches of concrete with reinforcing wire mesh embedded in it, and rock and mortar one to three inches thick. An inch of Styrofoam insulation is optional under the concrete but will only improve winter heat retention by 5 percent, whereas building without it will improve summer cooling by 10 percent. We did without. The perimeter of the floor, however, should have a footing several inches down (to frost is the standard on the exterior side); and it is important to place two inches of Styrofoam on the outside of that footing, all around, to prevent heat loss to the outside earth.

Begin in one corner. Mix a stiff "wet mix" of concrete at 5:1 coarse sand and Portland cement. Lay flat rocks in it and, using a small, triangular trowel, fill the cracks in between with a "dry mix" of mortar just like that used in walls: 2:1 or 3:1, with fine sand and a mixture of Portland and masonry cement. The masonry cement is not so important in the floor mortar, so less is required than in the wall mix. The drier mortar can also be used under the rocks, as needed. Keep rocks level, with constant reference to starting points at the perimeter. Stakes driven to the desired floor level here and there in the floor area can also be used as reference points and then removed before concrete is set.

Try to make the mortar joints level with the rock surfaces, without smearing too much on the rocks. Wipe surfaces clean with a damp sponge. Again, a gap of ¼–1" is desirable between rocks; fill larger spaces with small shards when possible. It's really a lot of fun to fit the rocks together in a tight fit: just like building a puzzle as you go. Continue adding concrete, mortar, and rocks until the floor area is covered. It's fine to stop for the day at any point, as long as the concrete is firmly enough in place not to settle out of level. Waste rock in the concrete and drier mix around the leading edge can help hold things in place while the concrete sets. After a couple of hours, finish the joints by scraping and brushing any rough mortar clean and smooth. When dry, add water to help the mortar cure. And it's done.

N. G.

CLOTHESLINE PULLEY

Our clothesline had to be fastened to a tree, and that did not work very well. When the wind blew, it got too tight or too loose. I like a natural-fiber line, and when it is wet, it gets too tight; when dry, too loose. The solution was a small-diameter pulley fastened to the tree, with a large container full of cement on the end. If rocks or sand are used, it should be waterproofed on top, because the weight should not be heavier when it rains. Natural fibers tend to unwind under such circum-

stances, so the container can be tied to the tree with some slack for vertical movement.

J. R.

BETTER MOUSE TRAPPING

I have used Havahart traps for mice for years, though they are getting to a high cost and were hard to find for a time. (They are generally available from veterinary suppliers.) Once set up, mouse removal is surely easier and more sanitary than operating an injury-type trap. And cats! The injuries a mouse suffers from a cat are probably closest to those injuries received in sword fighting (punctured lungs and spine, etc.), plus some beating and broken bones. This will not happen in my home where I have responsibility for the space. Better ways are available.

Mice apparently establish a residence and stock it with food at specific seasons, and if they are intercepted and moved in time, there are many months with no newcomers. However, if we ignore those one or two because we are too busy or don't notice, the community rapidly builds to intolerable proportions and it takes a long time to deport them all.

We keep exposed food (other than refrigerated or canned) in new garbage cans, metal breadboxes, or jars. Boxed food like cereals have somehow never been bothered by mice. But the dry dog food in the dog's dish stays out as the central attraction for the mice. Perhaps that is a help. Evenings when I hear mouse activity, I remove the dog food bowl to an inaccessible table and replace it with a Havahart trap, with dog food inside and Parmesan cheese sprinkled under the trap.

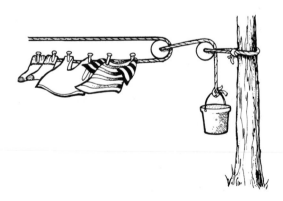

These usually produce a caged mouse within a few hours, and it can be released easily and cleanly down the road a piece away from other houses.

I noticed at one point that I seemed to be catching and removing the same mouse repeatedly. A spot of purple paint on the tail confirmed this. I carefully released it each day a little farther from home, and in a different direction. The route included a spiraling and looping path by motorcycle, with the mouse cage wrapped in a towel to prevent direction sensing. Nevertheless, the mouse returned until the distance was close to a mile. All its treasure and perhaps its family also were somewhere within my ceiling! When you travel a distance of a mile or more to release the creature, it does not return. I have never determined if they find other lodging before returning, die in attempting the journey, or finally exceed the range of homing ability. In any case, I feel I have done my part with reasonable responsibility.

Here is a great improvement on the stock Havahart trap, which applies as well to the paddle-type multiple-catch traps. We added a piece of plastic pipe to the traps, into which the mice load themselves every time to await easy transportation with no possibility of early escape. Obtain a 1' long piece of plastic pipe 1½" in diameter. Glue standard fittings on each end that adapt this pipe to threaded pipe. Onto these threads screw compression caps (the standard piece that usually connects this pipe to a metal sink drain by squeezing a rubber ring—it's a plastic threaded cap with open ends). The opening in the caps can be first fitted with metal screening, then screwed onto the pipe, creating a mouse transport capsule. Now you just cut a round hole in the side of the trap that

has no working parts, uncap one end of your tube, and stick the threaded end into the hole. At daylight, the mouse will always be hiding in the tube, ready for quick end capping and easy transport.

Be sure to use the screened fitting at *both* ends of the tube to allow quick see-through to find if it is occupied. With a second capsule available, the trap can be immediately reset for use while the first is being transported. This avoids the usual wear and damage to the trap that occurs when it is taken out in a vehicle often.

S. W.

A KINDLING SPLITTING BLOCK

One winter night Dottie awoke because she was cold. Considerate of the rest of us, she set about splitting some kindling, without taking time to wake up completely first. The result was a misdirected hatchet and a severely lacerated left thumb, which took months to heal. A few days later, our friend Bruce did the same thing at his chopping block. It was even the same part of the thumb.

So I set about to develop a better process for splitting kindling. Here is my new device. It is not foolproof, of course, but I think there may be a few more thumbs in sound condition now. The basis of the device is a way to hold the wood being split so that the other hand may be kept away from the blow of the blade, usually to hold the hatchet more firmly in both hands.

My design is based on 16 short pieces of 4" × 4" wood fastened together to form the

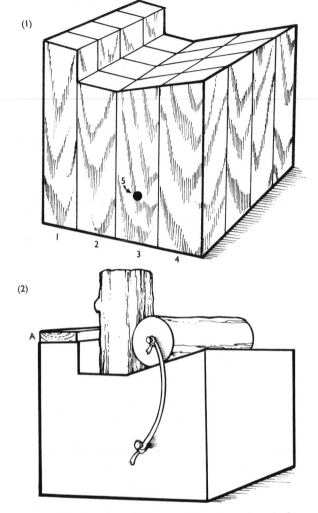

(1)

(2)

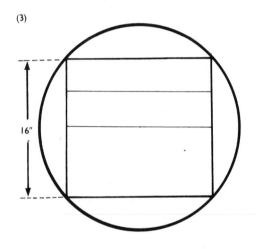

some slack but not long enough to allow the log to crush toes if it falls off.

A further refinement is a horizontal piece of 1″ × 4″ wood at (A), which takes the wear of the axe blows on cross-grain and prevents splitting the 4 × 4s. I put this on with wooden pegs to avoid nicking the blade.

My 4 × 4s were fir, which works well. Avoid cedar, which splits too easily. It might be feasible to trim a single log with a chain saw to produce a simple substitute, thus:

J. R.

(3)

16″

profile in the diagram. The length of the pieces is not important. #1 and #4 are the same length. #2 is about 4″ shorter than #1. #3 and #4 can be made from a single piece, cut on the angle shown, and then placed side by side. There are four rows of these, nailed together with 6″ Ardox nails.

At point 5 there is a protruding nail to which a rope is fastened, which connects to the center of a uniform log, about 5″ in diameter. I used birch for this. The log will roll down the slope and hold the wood in place. The rope should be long enough to allow

HOMESTEAD CEMENT

To fix leaks around chimneys, try this old-time, homemade cement. Or try it for walks. Mix together one part dry sand, two parts wood ashes, two parts dry clay. Mix in enough linseed oil to make a paste soft enough to work with. It will harden and become weatherproof.

Landward Ho!

WORK-SAVING TRICK

One of the most important things I learned in the U.S. Army was how to avoid work. It was a complex game. The officers spent a lot of time inventing unnecessary things for privates to do, and privates in turn spent their time learning to avoid them. Here's one of the work savers I learned.

One can pull a very heavy load, such as a trunk or a crate, with a common household broom. The straw provides a decrease in friction with the floor. When the broom is at the correct angle, the friction between the broom and load is higher than that between broom and floor. The load that can be pulled very easily is truly surprising. One person can manage several hundred pounds, about as much as one worker can tilt three inches off the floor at B. It won't work with loads with legs or snags at A. Adjust angle C until it works best. If you care about your floor, put a rag or small rug under load at A to prevent scratches.

A final caution. Don't let the sergeant find you doing this. He hates efficiency.

J. R.

SUGGESTIONS FOR
SELF-SUFFICIENT ELDERS

Looking back to see which letters with questions still need answers, I was caught by a letter from W. C. She discussed problems arising for older women as homesteaders, asking for others' ideas and experiences. There were not the columns of replies I would have expected.

There have been several articles about enabling tools for gardeners and tips for making certain jobs easier, one on helping an aging parent retire from active life in a nursing home, a couple of letters on an alternative way for oldsters to live in community—based on a dream but not fact yet. There was a

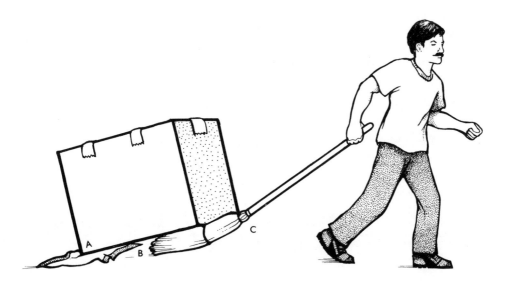

letter once about an elderly couple who attributed their good health and active life to birch syrup, which they prepared themselves and drank daily.

But I was hoping for more along these lines. I'd like to know that it's possible to continue living a rural lifestyle into old age.

My own suggestions: buy lighter-weight cookware than cast iron before your strength decreases; lower your standards of housekeeping, and learn to overlook that tall grass you used to mow so often; find a local lad or girl who can split wood for pay; use more exchanges of labor, e.g., cookies baked or shopping done in exchange for pruning a tree you can no longer climb; share tasks with a neighbor—maybe she can kneel to plant better than you can and you can dig better than she can; give work parties, where you provide food for friends who come to work with you on a project.

M. W.

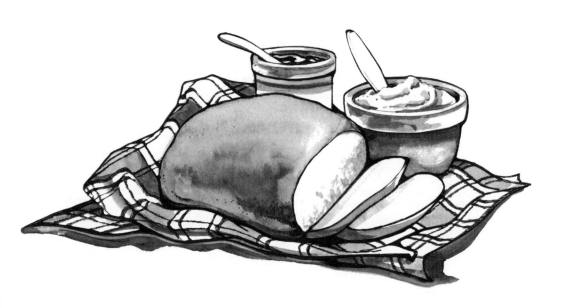

KITCHEN

 SPRING BORSCHT

I gather all the green shoots from the kale, broccoli, and cabbage stalks that were left in the garden (since we don't have any more cabbage), dig in the root cellar to find the last shriveled beets and get a few carrots and potatoes there (or the ones left in the garden over winter), steal some green onion leaves from the perennial onion, look for the dried dill in a paper sack in the rafters, get a jar of canned tomatoes, fetch the cream I separated yesterday and the butter I just made, and I'm ready to make borscht.

I boil the potatoes with the tomatoes and cut-up beets in some salted water, then cut up the kale, broccoli, cabbage stalks, and carrots and fry them in butter, and mash the cooked potatoes in cream and return them to the pot with the fried vegetables, green onion, and dill. I heat the mixture but do not boil it, adding milk for more liquid if needed.

Spring borscht is great with hot bread and butter. When summer comes, I add other vegetables and use fresh instead of canned tomatoes.

Already we start to look for signs of asparagus shoots and rhubarb. Next month will be more exciting!

H. K.

 YEAR-ROUND GREEN DRINKS

I met a naturopath who grew wheat until it was six-inch-high grass. He clipped it off, put it in the blender with fruit juice, and made a scrumptious, healthy drink. He put the extra wheat grass into baggies and popped them into the freezer.

You can have fresh wheat grass for green drinks all year round. An acquaintance told me about growing wheat grass (wheat sprouted to three to four inches high) in shallow (two-inch) flats, stacked four inches apart in front of his basement window. He seeds a flat every few days or so. There's no need for freezing, since he always has fresh grass.

B. T.

 COOKING OUTDOORS WITH A WOK STOVE

We found a simple way of cooking our meals alongside the road and on campsites with a minimum amount of fuel.

We use a stove made with our Oriental wok. Our wok is a round-bottomed, shallow pan, 13½" in diameter, with two handles. It is

When we were camping in the Sierra foothills, where large prickly pinecones are plentiful, we would use a dozen of these cones to cook a supper (like rice and vegetables). We didn't even need any kindling—a match would set the cones right on fire. We would carry an old laundry bag full of cones in the car in case there were no pines where we decided to stop for hot meals or for when it rained.

In British Columbia, I would look for long, curved white pine cones. They may smoke a little, but since they are full of pitch, they will give a quick, hot fire.

Large pieces of wood do not work well. They crowd the small space of the firebox and will smoke for lack of air. Small twigs, dry grass and weed stalks, newspaper— whatever is dry and burnable will work.

As a cover for the wok, we always use a smaller wok, which can also be used for serving food or as an extra eating bowl.

With a hot fire and a lid that does not fit too tightly, the water with the rice evaporates quickly, so to keep the rice from burning, it is necessary to add water until the rice is almost done. The water can be added without lifting the cover; just pour it around the edge. When the rice is almost done, add more oil and cut vegetables on top of the rice. Ideally, when the rice is done, the vegetables are steamed just right.

Using a wok stove is a simple, efficient way of cooking a hot meal while traveling by car. The wok stove uses little fuel, which can be picked up anywhere. The fire is contained and safe to use even during the dry season, when the hazard of forest fires is at its greatest.

J. B.

made of sheet metal, which "seasons" better and is probably healthier than stainless steel or aluminum.

To make a wok stove, I cut a five-gallon can (I have used both a square cashew nut can and a round oil can) and cut it down to about two-thirds of its original height. Then I cut an eight-inch-wide rectangular opening from the top down to about three inches from the bottom of the can. I used tin snips for cutting and smoothed off the cut edges with a file.

When using a square can, I scallop the top edges to accommodate the wok.

For fuel, we have used just about anything burnable, just as long as it is dry. When the fuel is wet, the fire will smoke, and since this primitive stove does not have a chimney, the smoke will escape through the front opening and make seeing, never mind cooking, impossible.

MAKING SOURDOUGH WITH WILD YEAST

After I lost my sourdough starter, I figured I'd make sourdough anyway. I let some warm whey with rye flour in it sit overnight, creating a sponge. (Use about 1½ cups whey to a loaf and enough flour to make it a soft dough.) After a day or so in a warm place, it bubbled a lot and smelled sour. I added wheat flour and kneaded it to make loaves and let them rise again in the pans. After they rose (they don't rise too much until after they are in the oven), I let them bake in a slow oven (about 250°F) until they were done. The loaves are done when they are browned and slip out of the pans easily. I found they had split on the sides from the rising in the oven, so I made diagonal cuts on the top of the loaves the next time, and this prevented the splitting. It's heavy bread that keeps well (two weeks, unrefrigerated, without mold). It is best sliced thin (a Chinese knife is perfect for this).

B. T.

SALT SUBSTITUTES

One plant that can be used as a salt substitute is coltsfoot. Roll the green leaves into small balls and dry in the sun for four to five days. Then place them on a flat stone and burn until ash remains. Use as salt.

Here is a recipe for a salt substitute that can be used in soups, etc.:

Grind up the following: wild carrot, goldenrod, masterwort, nettle, peppermint or spearmint, and tansy leaves; the fruits of dock, lamb's-quarters, and shepherd's purse; and the dried tops of carrots, beets, and radishes.

Next winter you'll be glad you did.

D. R.

OREGON GRAPE BERRY JAM

We find it worth picking Oregon grape (*Mahonia aquifolium*) for jam. Just boil down the berries, add honey, and can. We use the jam for pancakes, and runny jams make good syrup. Any fruit that we don't can or dry or eat raw we make into jam. A variety of fruit jams in the winter is nice, even just a jar or two of some. We had some homegrown limes from Hawaii last year and added them to cherry for jam. Just delicious.

H. K.

HORSERADISH RELISH

Don't know if anyone is interested, but here's a recipe for horseradish relish: Grate sound horseradish roots. Measure about half as much vinegar as horseradish, add ½ to 1 tsp. salt for each cup of vinegar, and pour over the grated horseradish. Pack at once into clean, hot, sterile jars. Fill jars to top and seal tightly.

R. D.

FIDDLEHEADS
RISE FROM ——►
CROWN CLOSE
TO GROUND

OSTRICH FERN

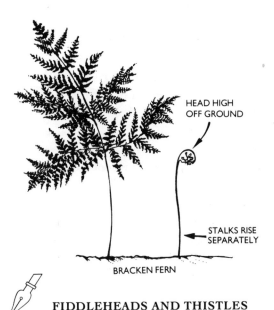

HEAD HIGH
OFF GROUND

STALKS RISE
SEPARATELY

BRACKEN FERN

not bracken (*Pteridium aquilinum*) they're eating but lady fern (*Athyrium filixfemina*), or ostrich fern (*Matteuccia struthiopteris*).

The main distinction is the "fiddlehead," so called because of its resemblance to the tuning end of the fiddle. In the lady (or maiden) fern, which is similar to the ostrich fern in the figure, the fiddlehead is close to the ground. There are many stalks coming from one cluster, which is composed of double compound leaves. The bracken form has a head off the ground and leafs out into double compound leaves on each side of each stalk. Each stalk is distinctly separate, being joined by underground roots that propagate it.

The fiddlehead is good raw in salads or cooked in stir-fries. It has an almond flavor. Some people throw away the first water. The fiddlehead is hairy, so remove the brown hair before using.

I recently visited a Doukhobor woman who grew up using wild plants, and she showed me her "garden" of edible wilds in the woods. Once my kids put peeled thistle stalks in the salad and made me guess what they were. They were tender and good, and I had no idea what I was eating, having forgotten that I had told the kids that the thistle was edible.

H. K.

FIDDLEHEADS AND THISTLES

Remember way back when we discussed eating fiddleheads? Bracken was called fiddlehead, and we discouraged people from eating it because it was poisonous to livestock. Well, recently I have heard of more and more people eating fiddleheads, and I found that it's

DRY-GRIDDLE PANCAKES

For those who don't like the smell of fried grease but love pancakes, try frying them on a dry griddle. I prefer them not too greasy, and others appreciate the lack of smoke in the kitchen. Just make sure the griddle is hot, and for nicely browned hotcakes, turn when bubbles form.

H. K.

ger each day for a week as before. Make sure to take from other plant to start third plant.

M. S.

 GINGER BEER DOWN UNDER

Cold Water Ginger Beer
2 lbs. sugar
2 oz. ground ginger
2 tsp. cream of tartar
1 tsp. tartaric acid
1 Tbsp. yeast
4 gal. water
the whites of 3 eggs
as many eggshells as you can get to clear it
1 kero bucket

Mix all ingredients in the kero bucket. When clear, siphon into bottles. Can be ready the next day.

Starting a Ginger Beer Plant
Put 8 sultanas, juice of 2 lemons, 1 tsp. lemon pulp, 4 tsp. sugar, 2 tsp. ground ginger, and 2 cups cold water into a large screw-top jar and leave for two to three days with the lid on. After that, add to the jar each day for one week 2 tsp. ground ginger and 4 tsp. sugar. Replace lid after each addition. This is the *plant*.

To make ginger beer, pour 4 cups boiling water over 3–4 cups sugar (or honey); stir to dissolve. Add juice of 4 lemons. Strain the plant from the jar into muslin and squeeze the muslin dry. Add 28 cups cold water, fill into dry bottles, seal with patent bottle tops or corks tied down. Keep three to four days.

To keep plant alive, halve the residue in the squeezed-out stuff in the muslin and re-turn to screw-top jar. Add 2 cups water and feed with 4 tsp. sugar and 2 tsp. ground gin-

 SAFE ANT REPELLENT

For an ant repellent, try mixing borax and sugar and putting it on the kitchen shelves.

M. L.

 COOKING ON AN AIRTIGHT STOVE

We cook on our airtight stove most of the winter rather than use two kinds of stoves. Of course there is no cooler side, as there is on a range. A trivet—a heavy cast-iron plat-form with decorative holes to let the heat through—is handy to keep a pot far enough away from the heat to be warm without burn-ing. But to keep something cooking for a long time without scorching (for instance, when boiling down whey for cheese), an even bet-ter device is a flat coil of medium-weight, fairly flexible wire—just make a flat circle about six to eight inches across and slip it under the pot.

J. M.

 TRADITIONAL RUSSIAN RECIPES

Here are some recipes I have compiled to-gether with Babushka (grandmother); we hope others will share the joy of cooking and eating these Doukhobor favorites:

Borscht for a six-quart pot

Fill the pot ¾ full of water or saved vegetable stock. Add quartered potatoes to cover bottom of pot, 1 large beet, a couple of whole carrots and boil until the potatoes are soft.

Meanwhile, chop 1 large onion and fry in butter for a minute then add 1 quart of tomatoes. (I use fresh tomatoes put through a blender in summer, and frozen or canned ones in winter.) Let this come to a boil and simmer. One cup of this can be added to the boiling potatoes for added flavor. Next chop 2 green peppers and grate 3 medium-size carrots, fry briefly in butter, and set aside. (A tablespoon or so of this can be added to the potato pot now.) Finely chop ½ head of medium cabbage (use a whole head in winter when you don't have as many greens); fry this in butter till it wilts, and set aside.

After the potatoes are soft, remove them, along with the whole carrots if you wish, and either blend in blender or mash, adding 1 cup thick sweet cream and 1 tablespoon of butter. Add more cream if you wish; check by the color of the borscht when you add this to the pot and by its flavor. Set aside. Dice 1 or 2 raw potatoes, 2 stalks of celery with leaves on, and add these to the pot after the cooked potatoes have been taken out. Boil until the diced potatoes are nearly done.

Now put in everything else. Be careful with the potato-cream mixture. Add it to some hot stock first before putting it into the pot or the cream may curdle.

As it comes to a boil chop any greens available—kale, spinach, parsley, rhubarb leaves (young curly ones blanched in boiling water first), and more cabbage in winter. Depending on how thick you want your borscht, put

in 1 to 2 cups of these greens, bring to a boil, add sea salt to taste and remove from heat.

Sprinkle on top some chopped dill, green onions, spinach, or green peppers. Do not mix. Let the borscht sit for an hour without mixing, if you can wait, with the lid half off.

Serve hot with homemade bread. Dedushka (grandfather) liked it with a little hot dried red pepper squeezed into the bowl!

Kartoshnik: Vegetable Tarts

Filling

Mix ½ cup milk, 4 beaten eggs, and ¼ tsp. salt with 2 cups mashed potatoes. Bake well in a buttered pan at 400°F for 20 minutes, until it is browned. For extra height you can separate the eggs, beat the whites until stiff, or add 1 tsp. baking powder, but it's not necessary.

Pastry

This recipe uses yeast and takes about a half day to prepare.

To 2 Tbsp. dry yeast add 1 cup lukewarm water and 1 Tbsp. honey. Let sit only until it just rises.

Mix ¾ cup oil, 2 beaten eggs, and 1 tsp. salt. Add 1 tsp. honey to 1 cup hot water. Pour oil and egg mixture into hot water. Mix and add yeast. Mixing with a spoon, slowly add approximately 3 cups flour, half whole wheat and half white (unbleached)—the dough must be soft. Let rise for about ½ hour. If it is cool in the kitchen, place over a bowl of steaming water.

Turn out onto a floured board and dust well with flour so it will handle well, as it will be very soft. Cut off pieces of dough the size of a walnut, lightly roll in palm of hand into a ball, and roll out into an oval circle with a rolling pin. Put about 1 Tbsp. of filling in the center, lift sides, and press down into the center.

Place on cookie sheet, cover with cloth, and let rise for 15 minutes, then bake at 350–400°F. for about 15 minutes, until lightly browned. You have to check a few times. Serve with hot melted butter or yogurt.

You may freeze the Kartoshnik; just reheat in oven in a roaster with a cover, watching that they don't burn or dry out. The energy spent is well worth it when you sit down to eat.

Other Fillings

1. Mix cottage cheese with egg and salt.
2. Mix mashed potatoes with egg, onion, garlic, and salt.
3. Grate beets and cook in water until soft, and water has disappeared.
4. Cook and mash beans; add salt.
5. Cook and mash dried peas, or fresh peas in summer; add salt.
6. Cook and mash pumpkin or squash; add salt.
7. Fry sauerkraut till tender (the sauerkraut we make is just grated raw cabbage salted and pressed into a crock and left to sit for a couple of days).
8. Experiment with other vegetable fillings!

Fruit Tarts

Use the same pastry as above, but keep it in a circle shape and fold sides up to hold the fruit. Try raspberries, sliced strawberries, apples, peaches, or huckleberries, drizzling a bit of honey on top before you put them in the oven. When you put them in the oven, watch carefully to make sure the fruit does not run out. If it does, there may be too much fruit, the oven may be too hot, or the dough may not be folded tightly enough. Serve hot or cold with cream.

Vinaigrette

A delicious salad. When Babushka cooked in the communal kitchen, she used to add freshly pressed linseed oil.

Mix 2 beets, cooked and chopped fine; 2 carrots, cooked and chopped fine or grated; 2 apples, chopped fine; 1 cup cooked beans or peas; 2 large salted or pickled cucumbers, chopped fine. These other ingredients can also be added—cooked chopped potatoes, raw onions, celery, sauerkraut.

E. B.

ALL ABOUT ROSE HIPS

Rose hips are a very rich source of vitamin C and are free for the picking. Three average-sized rose hips have as much vitamin C as a medium-sized orange and will supply your minimum daily requirement of vitamin C. Three teaspoons of rose hip and crabapple jelly will supply the daily requirement of vitamin C for one person, and one-third teaspoon of dried rose hip powder supplies enough vitamin C for one person for one day. Rose hips also contain an ample supply of vitamin A.

Collecting Rose Hips

Pick only ripe berries that are vivid red and slightly soft. They have a much better flavor if picked after the first frost—preferably in late August, September, or October. There is some loss of vitamin C if there is a lengthy delay between picking and bottling the product, although one of the important advantages of rose hips as a source of vitamin C is that vitamin C is unusually stable in rose hips compared with other vitamin C foods.

Using Rose Hips

Hips can be used fresh in making jelly, jam, pickles, juice, and so on, or they can be dried or canned to use in the winter. Or serve hips raw, shredded or halved, in salads, sandwich fillings, and desserts. The hair and seeds of the hip should be removed, since the fine hairs associated with the seeds are unpleasant in the mouth and have an irritating action.

There are four methods of removing the hairs and seeds:

1. Seed and hull first—this method takes the longest time.
2. Cover hips with water and simmer, then rub through a sieve, using the purée.
3. Simmer whole hips in more than enough water to cover, then merely strain. Bottle the juice, adding sugar if desired, and process 45 minutes. This juice contains vitamin C and may be added to sauces, soups (not cream soup), puddings, beverages, and many other foods.
4. Cut hips in half, dry (see directions below), and shake out seeds.

Recipes for Fresh Hips
Wild Roseberry Jam
Gather the berries after the first frost. Remove seeds and hull. Wash. Add water to just barely cover the berries. Cook berries until soft. If mixture is too thick, add water as needed. Set aside to cool. Mash and put through sieve. To 2 cups purée, add 1 cup sugar and cook slowly until thick, stirring frequently. A better consistency is obtained if commercial pectin is used. Pour into sterilized jars and seal. The jam may be used on bread and as a filling for cakes.

Note: If desired, lemon juice may be added and used either as jam or meat sauce.

Roseberry Catsup
4 qt. ripe berries (red and ripe)
2 medium-sized onions
1 clove garlic
1 cup water (or more if necessary)

Boil these ingredients until they are soft. Strain. Add ¾ cup brown sugar. Tie in a bag and add:

½ Tbsp. whole allspice
½ Tbsp. whole mace
½ Tbsp. whole cloves
½ Tbsp. celery seed
2″ cinnamon stick

Boil these ingredients quickly. Add 1 cup vinegar, and a little cayenne and salt, if desired. Boil catsup 10 minutes longer. Bottle it at once. Seal the bottles with wax. The flavor of this catsup is excellent.

Rose Hips Canned with Salt
Wash the hips and hull. Cut the halves and remove the seeds. Place in sterilized jars and cover with boiling water to which 1 tsp. salt for every quart has been added. Partially seal and process for a half hour. Rose hips preserved in this way are very acceptable in winter salads, desserts, and so on.

Rose Hips Canned in Syrup
Use medium-sized hips, since the seeds are very difficult to remove from the small ones. Remove calyxes and seeds. Make a thin syrup by mixing 1 cup sugar and 3 cups water and boiling together for 1 minute. Add the hips and boil for 10 minutes. Place in hot sterilized jars and process for 45 minutes. Hips retain shape, flavor, and color and lose only 10 percent of vitamin C content.

Drying Hip Berries
Cut hips in half lengthwise. These half hips should be spread on a clean surface and dried near a fire. In a damp atmosphere, they should be warmed, not heated, in the oven. Heat should be avoided because hips will lose part of their aroma and vitamin content. Properly dried, they are a distinct red color. If overheated, they become dark in color or brown. When they are dry, shake vigorously

in a jar or closed wire container (e.g., two wire sieves firmly held together) to remove seeds and hairs. Store in a dry place.

Recipes for Dried Hip Berries

Dried Hip Jam

Put 4 oz. dried hips into ¾ pint boiling water, bring quickly to boil, and simmer for 15 minutes. Rub through sieve. Boil 2 oz. sugar with 1 or 2 Tbsp. water until it forms a thread when dropped from a spoon. Mix this syrup with 5 oz. of mash and boil for 10 minutes.

Savory Soup

Boil 6 oz. dried hips (soaked beforehand in water) with 3 pints water, 3 cloves, and some cinnamon until soft (about 15 minutes). Rub through sieve. Melt 2 Tbsp. fat, add 2 Tbsp. flour, and cook 1 minute, then slowly add hip purée. Boil the soup for 5 minutes and season with 3 Tbsp. sugar, salt, and lemon flavoring. Add some milk and parsley before serving, if desired.

Sweet Sauce for Puddings

Boil 3 to 4 oz. fresh hip jam or the mash made from dried hips with 3 to 4 cups of grape or apple juice or lemon-flavored water and add sugar according to taste. If the mash is made from dried hips and is unsweetened, double the amount of sugar. Add lemon flavoring and cinnamon during boiling.

Roseberry and Crabapple Jelly

Use ½ crabapple juice and ½ rose hip purée. To 1 cup of this mixture add ¾ cup sugar. This jelly retains its vitamin C content for as long as nine months without loss. Note: Rosehip purée may be combined in chokecherry jelly or other similar fruit jelly.

Canned Rose Hip Purée

Wash hips and hull, cover with boiling water, and simmer until very tender. Rub through a fine sieve, pour into sterilized jar, and process for one hour, then seal. Use in soups and sauces, or make into jams or catsup later.

Rose Hip Honey

To 1 pint of purée, add ¾ lb. sugar and simmer until volume is reduced about 50 percent. Pour into sterilized jars and cover with wax. This product is the consistency of bees' honey and is excellent served with waffles, hot biscuits, muffins, and so on.

Pickled Rose Hips

Cook the hips in water until tender, then remove the seeds. Make a syrup of equal parts of water, vinegar, and sugar syrup, adding any desired spices. Add the seeded hips and simmer for 20 minutes. Place in sterilized jars and seal. This product was voted the best from the standpoint of flavor and attractiveness and also retained the vitamin C content better than any other. It is good with fish and meat dishes.

Rose Hip Cocktail

Dilute purée with water, using 1 part purée to 10 parts water; add any desired seasoning. Pour into sterilized jars and process for a half hour. It is difficult to distinguish this product from tomato juice cocktail, and the vitamin C content is much higher.

Rose Hip Soup

Dilute purée with meat stock, using 1 part purée to 2½ parts stock. Season to taste.

Rose Hip Aspic

Mix 2 cups rose hips, ¼ cup finely chopped celery, a few drops lemon juice, 3 cups boiling water, ¼ tsp. salt, and other seasonings as desired. Boil for a half hour. Put the mixture through a purée sieve and reheat. Put the mixture over 4 Tbsp. soaked gelatin and stir until the gelatin is completely dissolved. Pour into wet molds and chill. This product cannot easily be distinguished from tomato aspic.

U.S. Dept. of Agriculture

NATURAL FROZEN YOGURT

On any silent, brittle cold night, take out your yogurt, beat it with the eggbeater, and quickly shuffle it out the door! Now, next time you want THE TREAT, go get the yogurt (soft frozen is the best), scoop it into your bowl, and dribble some wildflower honey on it. Yummy! Fruit in it is nice too.

K. H.

BANNOCK

(for one person)
  1 cup flour
  1 tsp. baking powder
  ¼ tsp. salt

Thoroughly mix these ingredients dry. Have your hands floured and everything ready to go before you add water. If you are going to use a frying pan, make sure it's warm and greased. Working quickly from now on, stir in enough cold water to make a firm dough. Shape it with as little handling as possible to make a cake about an inch thick. Dust it lightly with flour so that it is easier to handle. Lay the bannock in the warm pan and hold it over the heat so a bottom crust forms, rotating the pan a little so that the loaf will shift and not become stuck. When the dough has hardened enough that it will hold together, flip it over.

I have tried this recipe many times and always like it. Often I wrap the dough around a stick and roast it the way you roast wieners (only it takes a little longer). Apparently the old-timers mixed the dough in a flour sack. They made a hollow in the flour and dropped baking powder and salt into it. Then they stirred with the finger while they added water until all the flour was absorbed.

L. C.

HOME CORNED BEEF

In delinquent response to a letter some months ago, I'm submitting my recipe (reliable!) for Home Corned Beef. Combine and boil together for eight minutes: 16 cups cold water, 1½ lb. pickling salt, 1 Tbsp. honey, ½ Tbsp. mixed pickling spices, 10 bay leaves, 5–8 garlic cloves.

Let the mixture cool. Tie 5–6 lb. lean beef securely into shape and place in a 5-gal. crock. Pour cool solution over the meat and weight it down with a heavy plate or rock to keep the meat submerged. Cover crock and place a clean cloth over it (to keep out dust and molds) and store in a cool place for two weeks, at least. Do not reuse the brine. (Beef tongues weighing 2½ lb. can be corned as well as other beef cuts, and they are delicious.)

I hope that this can be of use to others, and I suggest experimentation with more garlic—it only improves the flavor.

W. & N. M.

HERBAL RENNET FOR CHEESEMAKNG

Someone wanted the exact recipe for herbal rennet, or thistle-head cheese:

1. Gather flowerets of giant purple thistle when flowers have turned brown but before thistledown appears.
2. Air-dry flowerets in shallow baskets and store in a jar.
3. Use a mortar and pestle to pound the flowerets until they are very well crushed.
4. Add warm water or whey to cover and let soak for five minutes. Pound again for five minutes and then soak for five minutes. Repeat three times, or until a dark brown fluid forms.
5. Strain and add to warm milk. For every gallon of milk, use 5 small heaped teaspoons of the herbal liquid.

C. M.

POTATO CHEESE

I found the following interesting old article while I was doing historical research. It comes from the River Press, Fort Berton, Montana, 1881.

A foreign paper says that cheese is made from potatoes in Thuringia and Saxony in the manner below: After having collected a quantity of potatoes of good quality, giving the preference to a large white kind, they are boiled in a cauldron, and after becoming cool, reduced to a pulp either by means of a grater or mortar. To five pounds of this pulp is added one pound of sour milk and the necessary quantity of salt. The whole is kneaded together, and the mixture covered up and allowed to lie for three or four days, according to the season.

At the end of this time it is kneaded anew, and the cheeses are placed in little baskets when the superfluous moisture escapes. They are then allowed to dry in the shade and placed in layers in large vessels where they must remain for 15 days. The older these cheeses are, the more their quality improves. The first and most common is made as detailed above, the second with four parts of potatoes and two parts of curdled milk, the third with two parts of potatoes and four parts of cow or ewe milk.

These cheeses have this advantage over other kinds—that they do not engender worms, and keep fresh for a number of years, provided they are placed in a dry situation, and in well closed vessels.

M. S.

DANDELION WINE

Around these parts spring is not officially here until we have gone along the roadside and picked dandelions for wine. The children anxiously await the day when, with sun shining brightly overhead, we take our bread bags in hand and head off down the driveway toward those nodding yellow buttons. They pick them with gleeful delight, as if each new find might be the last. There is always the family goat following close behind, munching on rejects, and the dog dipping and splashing through spring's little puddles that glisten in the ditches along the road. For me, this annual ritual of joy comes alive with the opening of each bottle of dandelion wine later in the year.

Ingredients

1 gal. dandelion petals

3½ qt. boiling water

2 or 3 oranges cut into ¼" slices

2 or 3 lemons cut into ¼" slices

5 lb. honey or 8 cups sugar

2 tsp. dry granulated yeast

It takes approximately a gallon of flower petals to create a gallon of wine, although I usually cheat a little. Separating petals from stem can be a tedious chore unless you can find a pleasant atmosphere. I find it easiest to slip a paring knife between petals and petal head while the flowers are fully opened, although several authors recommend washing first. This seems to have the same effect as a spring shower, and once closed, the flowers will not reopen. If too much green is left, the wine will be bitter, so be thorough. Wash the petals by placing them in a sieve and swishing them through a pan of water to remove all dust and insects. Then put them into crock or gallon jars.

For wine made with sugar, boil water, cool slightly, and pour over petals. Cover with a clean cloth and let stand one week. Strain liquid through a piece of cheesecloth or fabric, squeezing out all the juice possible — for this is the essence of the flavor. Return liquid to a clean vessel and add the oranges, lemons, sugar, and yeast. Cover again for two weeks of fermentation. Strain once more and leave it to settle two days longer, or until it becomes fairly clear. Siphon the finished product into sterilized bottles to within about two inches from the top. Cork the bottles lightly for a few days to be sure fermentation has stopped, then finish the seal and dip in paraffin.

For wine made with honey (or mead, as it is known); the water and honey should be boiled together for 10 minutes. Remove the froth and pour over the petals, saving enough to soak the lemon and orange slices overnight. Add the slices and remaining liquid the next day along with the yeast. Cover with a clean cloth for a week. Strain well and proceed as for the sugar recipe.

To be sure bottles are ready to be corked, place a balloon on top of the uncorked bottles. If there is any fermentation, the balloons will expand. If they do, simply allow the fermentation to finish. Store the bottled wine in a cool place, and although the temptation to sample a bottle may be strong, try to store it for at least six months. The longer you wait, the smoother the wine will be. Our best results were aged over a year.

If you prefer a dry wine, use less sweetener. For a deep flavor, use more fruit. Pineapple may be added for a nice flavor. Other creative touches include coloring the paraffin and making original labels. I believe that wine, like any other creation, will evolve from the feelings within the maker, rather than from any set rules, and become a creation to take personal pride in.

L. W.

DRYING GREEN VEGETABLES

Now that summer is upon us and gardens are reaching their fullest bloom, it's time to fill the drying racks with garden greens, herbs, and fruits.

Have you realized that many greens can be dried and therefore used at a later date? Well, it's true. Here are some names of the more common vegetable greens that can grow in most temperate areas and can be dried: Swiss chard, mustard greens, kale, spinach, chives, and parsley, just to name a few. Beans, peas, and common garden herbs can also be added to this list.

Drying is an easy process in which most of the effort involves just picking the extra chard or kale leaves from the garden and placing them on drying racks. Drying racks can easily be made from lath strips about two inches wide with screening sandwiched between them. Old screen doors or windows make excellent racks as well. If the old screen is a bit rusty, just cover it with a layer of cheesecloth. The racks can be hung just about anywhere but preferably indoors and not in direct sunlight. I have my drying racks suspended from the ceiling in the kitchen, above my wood stove.

Drying time depends on the temperature within the drying area and the outside temperature. An important factor is whether any additional heat source is used in the drying area. If you hang drying racks in an outdoor shed, the drying time might be a little longer, but one should watch the drying material more carefully because any cold or dampness might blacken the leaves of whatever you are drying. In hot and dry weather, it is very easy to dry most greens and herbs within 4 days. However, most things should dry within a week to 10 days regardless of the weather.

It's amazing how easy it is to put away all these extra greens from the garden, just through the process of dehydration. I usually put away bagfuls of chard, kale, and spinach, to name a few. All you have to do to reconstitute any dried green is add to soups, stews, or casseroles, and there you have it! Dried greens provide a nice healthy green in the middle of winter, a feast for the eyes.

Another nice thing about dried greens is that they are easy to store in plastic bags and weigh virtually nothing. Dried vegetable greens are one of the best things to take while camping. Another tip is to pick the leaves to be dried after a sunny day, because more of the concentrated energy will be in the leaves then.

For those people who have never tried drying their garden greens, I hope I have provided a little information and a lot of inspiration. Once you try drying as a method of preserving food energy, it's hard to give it up. Happy drying times!

A. P.

SUGAR-BEET SYRUP

Cut beets into half-inch cubes and fill a canner two-thirds full, cover with water, and boil until soft (several hours). Press as much juice out as possible. Mix the pulp with water and put it back on the stove for several hours to get as much sugar out as possible. Put the juice on the back of the stove and let it evaporate until it has the thickness you want. You can wait until it is so thick you can smear it on bread. Make sure it doesn't boil too hard, or it will burn, and then it will taste bitter. Slow and easy does it.

B. T.

MALTED BARLEY COFFEE

Sprout barley, dry the sprouts, then roast them and grind them, and you are ready to make the brew. If you just want barley coffee, roast the barley, grind it, and make the brew.

J. & A. H.

PECTIN RECIPE

Here is another recipe for homemade apple pectin. This one is from the *Settlement Cookbook*, 1930, an oldy.

    4 lb. apples, skin and cores
    4 pints water for first extraction

Select tart, hard ripe apples. Remove bruised spots. Cut into thin slices. Place in a large granite kettle and bring quickly to boiling point. Cover and let boil rapidly 20 minutes. Strain through four thicknesses of cheesecloth. When juice stops dripping, press pulp lightly with a spoon but do not squeeze bag. Weigh and measure and add to it an equal quantity of water. Boil again 20 minutes and strain. Mix the two liquids (extractions): it should measure about 3 qt. Place in a wide granite pan (or dishpan) so that liquid is not more than 2" deep. Heat rapidly 30 to 45 minutes, or until liquid is ½" deep or reduced to 1½ pints. If pectin is not wanted for immediate use, pour at once into hot, clean bottles that have been standing in boiling water and seal. Bottle should not hold more than ½ cup.

D. L.

HOMINY

For those who wanted to know about hominy, the pioneer and Indian method is to boil about 1 cup of clean wood ashes in 2 qt. water, then strain out the ashes and boil 1 qt. dried white corn kernels in this lye water until the hulls come off easily (about three hours). The liquid is drained off and the corn rinsed and the hulls rubbed off between the palms of the hands. The hominy is then boiled in fresh water until tender. The modern method is to use 2 Tbsp. baking soda in place of the wood ashes.

I prefer the flavor of the corn cooked with the ashes. It comes out very sweet. To make delicious fresh masa for tortillas, put the cooked, drained corn (I don't bother to hull it) twice through the fine blade of the meat grinder. It can then be pressed or rolled into tortillas and browned in oil.

B. F. B.

FAVORITE FALL RECIPES

Here are a few of my tried-and-true favorite fall recipes:

Lamb's Wool

    1 qt. hot ale
    1 cup applesauce
    dash of ginger and cinnamon

This is an old recipe from my Nova Scotia home. Some called it Apple Ale. Stir briskly and serve just off the boil.

Brandied Fruits

Half-fill a crock or jar with good apricot brandy. Begin in the early summer with the season's first fruit, and as each fruit comes into season, toss a cupful of the washed and chopped fruit into the brandy—rhubarb, strawberries, raspberries, cherries, plums, peaches, melon, quince—all work well. Spoon the fruit over ice cream for a special treat, or add to Jell-O for an unusual jellied salad. (The crock should have a lid on it but not a screw-down or bale-top affair.)

Marjoram Vinegar

1 pint marjoram leaves and stems
1 qt. white or cider vinegar

Pour the vinegar over the marjoram in a glass container with a tight-fitting lid. Each day for three days bruise the leaves with a wooden spoon. Strain off the vinegar through the cloth. Bottle and cork. Store in a cool, dry place. Mix marjoram vinegar with melted butter and spoon over baking fish. Use it as a base for salad dressings or to marinate onions or any other vegetable.

Rowanberry Wine

3 qt. ripe rowanberries
1 gal. boiling water
1 qt. apple juice (optional)
3 lb. sugar
1 tsp. yeast

Wash and stem the berries. Pour boiling water over them into a crock. Let them stand for 10 days, stirring and bruising daily (with wooden spoon), strain off the liquid, and add the apple juice, sugar, and yeast to the liquid, which should be 98.6°F. Leave the ferment jar in a warm place for two weeks, then set away to work for three to five months. Bottle in strong bottles with a lump of sugar in each one. Wire down the corks. Store for a year. This is a very solid basic recipe. I have used it with excellent results for elderberries, blueberries, saskatoons, and chokecherries.

Chow Chow

This is a greenish-brown tart relish, excellent with roasts or cold meat sandwiches. My grandmother made gallons of it. Chop fine 4 qt. fresh green tomatoes (about 30) and sprinkle them with ¼ cup salt. Let them stand overnight. Next morning drain and add: 1 qt. chopped onion, 1 small head cabbage, chopped, 3 large red peppers, chopped, 2 tsp. dry mustard, 1 tsp. ground cloves, ½ cup honey, and 1 qt. vinegar. Boil gently for an hour till it plops off the spoon, stirring frequently. Bottle and process for 10 minutes in a boiling water bath. You should leave it a month before eating.

I. S.

ANGELICA

Angelica can be used to cut acid in rhubarb so that the sugar can be reduced by half.

B. T.

BASIC BROTH FOR COLDS AND FLU

If you are sick with a cold, flu, or whatever and don't feel like eating, yet you need something healthful, here's what I've lived on through my last bout with the flu (coupled with fresh fruits, herbal teas—sage, mint, elder flowers, rosehips—and vitamin C).

Boil some water (a quart) in a kettle. Chop up 2 onions. Put in pot with water, bring to a boil again, and turn to medium low. Add a head of garlic (as many as you can—garlic has marvelous qualities as an antibiotic and also brings up mucus and cleanses the system). Add thyme, 3 Tbsp. dry engevita nutritional yeast (not the baking kind), 1 Tbsp. kelp, 2 Tbsp. safflower or soybean oil. Now, if you have some chard, spinach, or any greens that can be chopped up, add a minute or so before you are ready to eat. This takes about five minutes in all to cook. I take it off the heat when the onion has softened.

As I get well each day, I make basic broth, then add more vegetables and rice or mashed potatoes—even leftover porridge would be good. It is a sustaining broth, open to all sorts of inventive touches from what is at hand.

Take care. And remember that food can be medicine too.

L.

DRYING MEAT AND FISH

In response to the letter about drying food, I'd like to add my experience with drying meat and fish. There are many complicated ways of doing it, but I like the easy way, which tastes just fine, uses little equipment, and stores well. All you need is a sharp kitchen knife or long sheath knife and a place to handle the fish or meat. In summer, make a pole rack outside with a tarp roof overhead (Figure 1). In cool or damp weather, food dries better in the house, if your stove is going. Meat and fish usually take about one week to dry.

Meat

Since we don't use any salt, smoke, or spices, our moose tastes like moose, which is a beauty unto itself. I've never had any trouble with flies when not using smoke. Even in the height of fly season, they rarely lay eggs, and if they do, the eggs never hatch, because the surface of the meat or fish dries too quickly. Just be sure to avoid leaving pockets and crevices that would dry too slowly. If you're hanging the meat outside, you can make a smudge below the rack, though, if you wish. I have had trouble with yellow jackets eating fish in August. Warmth and ventilation speed the drying process.

When cutting dried meat, don't pay too much attention to the grain. Take a chunk of meat about the size of your fist and cut around and around, making strips as long as you want (6' if you have room to hang them). (See Figure 2.) Aim for about ¼" thickness. If some part is too thick, score it to open it up more. You can dry the fat on the meat or in

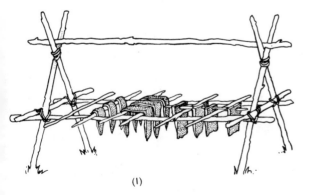

(1)

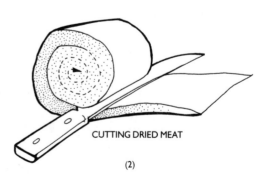

CUTTING DRIED MEAT

(2)

separate slabs for most meat, except horse (which is good meat!) and bear, both of which have soft fat that goes rancid easily.

The tenderness of your dried meat depends on the cutter, how long the meat has been hung, and what part of the animal it is from, aside from how the grain happens to fall. Cut across the grain whenever it is convenient to do so. We eat the tender pieces raw and save any tough ones along with the fat for cooking.

To cook the meat, just break or cut it into small pieces and boil with rice, beans, stews, or cracked wheat, or by itself. You can soak it first if you want to. Another excellent way is to soak the pieces overnight in a small amount of water so that almost all the juice gets absorbed. Then grind them in a meat grinder, and you have fresh hamburger! Dried meat that is not too tough can be ground in a steel grain grinder in dry pieces and then boiled a few minutes to make an all-meat gruel, delicious with grated turnips and carrots thrown in.

Fish

How to cut fish for drying depends on the size and kind of fish. For a trout or salmon, slit up the belly, clean, and hang up by the gills for a day, or a few hours if it is hot weather. This slight drying makes the fish easier to handle. Remove the head and tail. For a fish the size of a salmon, cut about six inches of the tail meat and do it separately. Cut along one side of the backbone, then turn your knife at right angles, going under the backbone to one edge, then going the opposite way to the other edge (Figure 3). Cut along the other side of the backbone so it is separated from the ribs, yet still attached. The end result is an opened-up slab of fish with the skin and bone still on (Figure 4). Score any thick parts, cutting to the skin to hasten drying. For a smaller fish, like trout or kokanee, carefully cut out the backbone, tak-

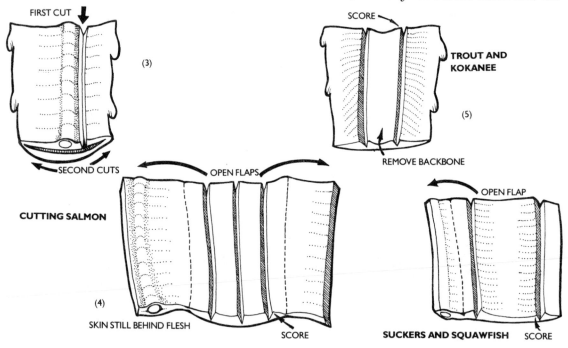

FIRST CUT

(3)

SECOND CUTS

CUTTING SALMON

OPEN FLAPS

(4)

SKIN STILL BEHIND FLESH

SCORE

SCORE

TROUT AND KOKANEE

(5)

REMOVE BACKBONE

OPEN FLAP

SUCKERS AND SQUAWFISH

SCORE

(6

ing little meat, then make two vertical scores to separate the thick meats from the ends of the ribs (Figure 5).

Most people don't realize that suckers and squawfish are good eating too. To enjoy them fresh, just skin the halves and backbone and keep them for a day or two before eating to firm up their texture. To skin, cut off the fins from a half fish, make a small cut to start the skin peeling, grab the skin in your teeth, and use your fingers to work downward, easing the meat from the skin. To clean these large-boned fish, it is easiest for me to set the whole fish on its belly, slit down one side of the backbone, and then chop off the head and tail. Scrape out the guts but save the eggs, which are real good steamed like rice. To cut suckers and squawfish for drying, leave the backbone on (it will be at one side), cut along the other side of it to the skin to lay it open, and score as for trout (Figure 6).

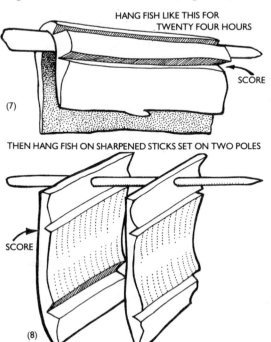

HANG FISH LIKE THIS FOR TWENTY FOUR HOURS

SCORE

(7)

THEN HANG FISH ON SHARPENED STICKS SET ON TWO POLES

SCORE

(8)

I like to sprinkle some salt on fish, since it's wetter than meat and I like the taste. Don't sprinkle any more salt than if you were eating the fish fresh, and fold the fish up for about half an hour to give the salt a chance to dissolve and soak in. Drape the fish skin side down over a thin pole for 24 hours (Figure 7). By then it will be dry enough to put on sticks and hang to finish drying (Figure 8).

Dried fish is good to eat raw, boiled, or roasted. To roast, just put it flesh side down over a slow fire (small fish just fit over a stove hole) and toast for a few minutes, peeling from the skin while still hot. Be careful not to burn it. If you do it right, the bones will crunch up when eaten, which is especially good for suckers.

All dried meat and fish should be stored in a dry, cool, ventilated place, such as feed bags under your bed or outside in a shed.

Y.

BAY LEAF BUG REPELLENT

I've found that a bay leaf in the flour barrel or drawer keeps all the creepy crawlers out and does not affect the taste of the flour.

I. S.

TORTILLA PRESS

Here's a tortilla press that uses scrap hard wood lumber: For the press itself, use any unwarped pieces of ¾"–1" thick wood that will fit together evenly. Cut the paddle-

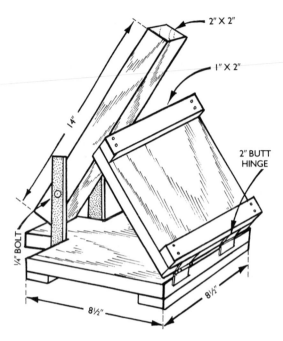

shaped bottom from an 8½″ × 12½″ piece, leaving a handle on one end, where you attach the 2″ × 2″ pressure arm. Glue and nail four 1″ × 2″ crosspieces to the top and bottom boards to help prevent warping when the press is washed. Locate the arm's ¼″ bolt at a height where the arm can lever down (not completely horizontally) over the top of the press. (My press is 7″ × 7″ with a 4″ paddle. It works as well.)

V. Y.

ALMOND "CHEESE"

If anyone feels like trying something really different, here is a recipe for almond cheese:

Take 3 cups of good hard spring wheat and place in a jar with cheesecloth over it with about 4 to 5 cups warm water. (The soaked wheat can also be used on cereal, in bread, in cookies, etc.) Let stand overnight, and in the morning strain water from the wheat. Let this wheat water stand another 12 hours. In the meantime, have ready about 2 cups of peeled almonds. (These can also be soaked overnight in warm water, making them easy to peel.) Then blend water and almonds in your blender to a creamy consistency. Place this creamy mix in a jar with a cheesecloth over its top and keep in a warm area for about 6 hours, or until mixture smells "cheesy." I use my electric food dehydrator, taking out the bottom trays to allow room for the jar to fit inside. Some people like their mixture not too cheesy and some very cheesy, and this means you have to check your timing to get the taste you want.

Sometimes a little water separates from the solid material in the jar as it "cooks," staying in the bottom of the jar. It can be drained off and put in the refrigerator to keep as a starter for the next batch. Other nuts and soy beans are also recommended, but I have not tried anything except almonds, as it seems to taste so good.

E. F.

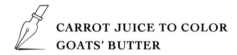

CARROT JUICE TO COLOR GOATS' BUTTER

A few drops of carrot juice added to goats' butter after the final washing will color it, I have heard. We eat ours white, although it takes a bit of getting used to at first, since it looks so much like lard.

S. D.

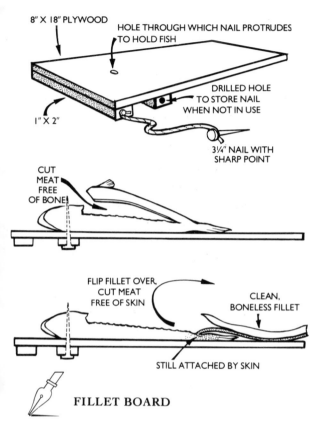

8" X 18" PLYWOOD

HOLE THROUGH WHICH NAIL PROTRUDES TO HOLD FISH

1" X 2"

DRILLED HOLE TO STORE NAIL WHEN NOT IN USE

3¼" NAIL WITH SHARP POINT

CUT MEAT FREE OF BONE

FLIP FILLET OVER, CUT MEAT FREE OF SKIN

CLEAN, BONELESS FILLET

STILL ATTACHED BY SKIN

FILLET BOARD

This is useful for all fish, but particularly the spiny varieties of rockfish and cod we catch here on the coast.

Lay the fish on the board. Nail through head to hold the slippery little devil. Knife-cut flat parallel to the board, cutting half of the fish. Travel the knife along the spine, stopping just before the tail, leaving the fillet still attached by the skin near the tail. To complete the fillet, hold knife blade at about a 45° angle against skin and cut between the flesh and the skin down the length of the skin. Voilá! Clean, boneless fillet. Now turn the fish over and do the other side. That's it. It is not necessary to clean the fish. Just take the fillets and freeze the carcass for crab bait.

C. S.

HOME-DRIED BEEF

Last fall we tried drying beef. It has turned out well, so I will give you the recipe.

Dried Beef

Brown salt like coffee. While the salt is still hot, roll each piece of beef in it thoroughly. Pack in a crock and let remain five days. Take out, wash well, and hang up to dry. Now that was the recipe.

Here is how we did it. I trimmed all visible fat from a nice chunk of roast. Using a sharp knife, my father sliced it thin *with the grain*. I placed a pie plate on the stove and added about a cup of salt. Our salt is dairy salt, without the cornstarch and iodine contained in regular table salt. I waited for the salt to "brown like coffee," and when it did not, I very foolishly poked my fingers into the salt. Wow! Talk about hurt! That salt was *hot!* So after a horsetail-vinegar soak of the injured fingers, I took a fork and laid the slices of beef on the salt. There was a sizzling sound, then I turned it over, and the other side was coated.

Since we had such a small amount, the salted pieces were placed in a small plastic bowl and a tightly woven cotton cloth placed over the top with a heavy rubber band around the whole works to deter flies. After five days the brownish-colored pieces were taken out, rinsed in cool water, and hung on strings. We hung them from the edge of a shelf near the stovepipe, encased in a cotton bag.

I cannot say exactly how long it took to cure, since we do not have much fire in the heater at any time and none at night. But when the pieces were completely brittle, we pounded them into coarse pieces and put them in a pint jar. Several months have gone by, and the meat is still good. We have used a pinch now and again for soup. The pint jar is not sealed airtight.

W. C.

SOY MILK AND ICE CREAM

Some recipes for alternatives to animal milk:
Soy Milk
  ½ cup soy flour
  1 pint water
Mix flour into a smooth paste with a little water and add the rest slowly, making sure there are no lumps. Bring to boil and simmer for five minutes, stirring constantly. Strain through fine cloth. Can be flavored with carob or honey. Will store for a couple of days in the refrigerator.
Soy Ice Cream
  2½ cups soy milk
  ¼ cup oil (soy or corn)
  ¼ cup honey
  dash of vanilla essence
Blend well and freeeze until firm. Cut into small pieces and beat or put through blender again. Refreeze. For a creamier mixture, add soy flour. (I've tried the milk recipe myself, and it works; I haven't tried the ice cream yet.)

O.

SMALL DAIRY SYSTEM

After several years of experimentation, we are proud of how efficiently our dairy depart-ment, one Jersey cow and one alpine goat, fills our needs. From Lucy Cow, the heavy cream goes to butter, the lighter cream to sour cream or butter (whichever is required). The skim milk makes a simple pressed cheese. Clot the milk with buttermilk and rennet, heat the lot till the curds mass on top, press while hot in a cloth, and tie tight to cool. Cut into fist-sized pieces and store in brine (1 cup salt per quart of water) in the refrigerator. This cheese is used, grated, on all bean, noodle, or grain dishes, which are made without salt. When we have a good store of pickled cheese, the skim milk feeds our 50 laying hens.

We drink the goat milk, and any extra be-comes cheese spread, either savory or sweet. Clot the fresh warm milk with buttermilk and rennet, then hang in a cloth bag over-night. You may heat the clotted milk to luke-warm before hanging to give a smoother tex-ture to the cheese. Add herbs for savory spreads, carob and honey or fruit purées for sweet. This works well for children who love icing!

J. & A. K.

STOVE-TOP YOGURT MAKER

Supplies
- pie plate lid
- quart canning jar
- 100 oz. billy can with water enough to im-merse jar
- pot holder pad
- pie plate lid
- aluminum pot with boiling water
Once water in the billy can is warmed up on

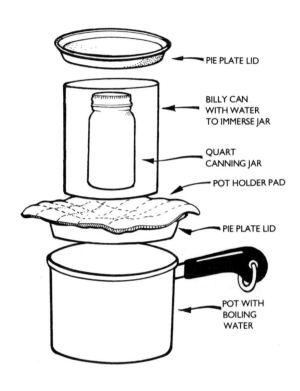

PIE PLATE LID

BILLY CAN
WITH WATER
TO IMMERSE JAR

QUART
CANNING JAR

POT HOLDER PAD

PIE PLATE LID

POT WITH
BOILING
WATER

phlet put out by the Fleischmann's Yeast Company. It is delicious, and kids are wild over it. When served cold, it tastes like root beer and vanilla ice cream.

"This delightful beverage is highly recommended by modern food experts. It combines the rich, nourishing qualities of sweet milk with the healthful action of buttermilk. Kumiss is a form of fermented milk enjoyed by children and adults alike and especially recommended for those who have difficulty in assimilating milk in its natural state. It is easily prepared as follows:

"Heat 2 qts. milk to 100°F. Add ½ cake yeast and 2 Tbsp. sugar dissolved in a little warm water. Let stand for two hours, then bottle and stand for six hours in a moderately warm room; then place on ice. Kumiss will keep four or five days if kept cold, but it is better if it is made fresh every day or two."

The way I make it is to warm 2 qts. of skim milk (cream rises on whole milk, but is OK, too), dissolve the sugar or honey in the milk, and add about ½ tsp. granular yeast making sure not to put in too much, as the bottles will explode from the pressure. I've had several do that, and now I am very stingy with the yeast.

Then, after letting it stand about four hours, or until the yeast is working well, stir, pour into beer bottles, cap. It doesn't keep very long; I've tried to make it stay good for a week, but about six days in the bottle finds it wrecked—the milk separates. Whole milk is OK and tastes good, though the cream rises to the top and isn't as nice as skim milk. I find other people either hate it or love it, and most kids will drink kumiss until ready to bust.

the stove and water in the aluminum pot is boiling, put the jar of milk and starter into the billy can and assemble apparatus as shown.

Keep water boiling in the lower pot but not too hot—keep checking the temperature in the billy can, which can be fairly hot.

The process takes three to four hours, depending on the temperature.

S. B.

RECIPE FOR KUMISS

I don't know how the Asian nomads make it, but the following recipe is from a 1917 pam-

W. C.

MEAT CANNING

I do a lot of meat canning so that we'll have summer meat. Here are a few observations.

- We like our meat browned first so that it has a better taste; I'm not that fond of just boiled canned meat.
- Moose is good just cut into cubes, browned, and packed in jars with water or stock.
- Bear is too soft to cube—it goes mushy. So I prefer to make it all into hamburger meat and brown it and pack it in jars. This canned ground meat is *very* good.
- Pork is also mushy meat, and we like it best ground up and made into sausage meat, spiced with salt, pepper, sage, and cloves and packed raw in jars. It's great warmed up in a pan with fried eggs for breakfast. It's also a good way to use an old pig.
- In the past I've added salt, pepper, and onions to canned meat, but over the years I have found that it's quite unnecessary and just adds more work at canning time.
- I also can pinto and kidney beans, so in an emergency I open a can of meat, beans, and tomatoes, add onion and chili powder and tomato paste, and presto—instant chili!

J. L.

RE-JELLING JELLY

Have you ever made grape jelly and ended up with grape syrup? Don't throw the syrup out, advise U.S. Department of Agriculture Extension Service home economists. They

say the "jelly" may not have become firm because of an improper balance of pectin, acid, and sugar. Add a half tablespoon of lemon juice per cup of syrup and cook it again until the jelling point is reached.

B. T.

HOT BLACK CURRANT JUICE

It is my turn to organize the community Christmas bazaar this year. With lots of help from my husband and a good committee, we are gathering resources for the big day.

This winter, as a change from mint and clover tea, our constant beverage, warm from the wood heater, is black currant juice. I freeze the freshly picked berries dry (no syrup) and whole. When we need some juice, I put a bagful of berries into a large enamel or steel pot, cover with water, and bring to a boil. Pour off the juice (carefully; it stains everything in sight); and repeat the cooking process after again filling the pot with water. This juice is highly concentrated. We find that one tablespoon per cup, topped with water, is good. Most people need a bit of honey with this drink.

A. K.

STOVE-TOP BAKING

"The pile in the shed is getting real small, Mom," said my six-year-old son, Noah, as he was carrying in wood to fill up the box the other day.

"We must have burned more wood than last winter because of those cold, cold days we had—or was it weeks—months? Remember when the water lines froze?" I answered. "But now it's been a lot warmer. I guess spring is waiting around the corner."

So lately, instead of lighting the wood stove and the airtight, which makes it quite hot in our small log cabin, I've just been lighting the airtight. But how are we still getting baked goodies?

Well, I just follow any muffin or sweet bread recipe and pour the batter into a deep cake pan, mold, casserole dish, or whatever, which I set into a pot half filled with water. I cover the pan and the pot and let it steam for a little over an hour or till done.

Nobody has complained yet! And I am still thankful for the wood.

Another method of stove-top baking I've used is to fill the bottom of the outer pot with 2 inches of gravel, put a piece of foil on top of the gravel, then place the cake pan full of batter on the foil and cover the whole thing with the pot lid. This way is more like real baking.

B. M.

IMPROVE YOUR YOGURT

Here's a novel way to get a firmer yogurt: add a teaspoon of carrot or tomato juice to every eight ounces of milk. Add the juice to the pre-warmed milk when you add the yogurt starter.

B. T.

UNLEAVENED BREAD

The children were making unleavened bread with me one day. As we were taking turns grinding the sprouted wheat berries—4 cups had been soaked in 12 cups of water for 24 to 36 hours (less in the summer), changing the water once; then they were sprouted for three days, till the little sprout was just about as long as the seed itself—we were talking about how much better for our health, body and mind, all the unleavened breads are.

We look at it as a family: chapatis, pita breads, tortillas, made out of all kinds of ground-up grains and seeds, are the children, who are the simple and straightforward nutrition of a great percentage of the population of our planet. This bread is the mother who has been around for many centuries!

After all the sprouts were ground up, we proceeded to the next step, which is oiling our hands a little to prevent the dough from sticking all over our fingers, and shaping it into round patties about the size and thickness of our palms. While we were doing that, we were reminded how naturally sweet the sprouted wheat is. If we want it to be even more special, or simply as a little variation, we can add a couple of handfuls of soaked raisins to the dough. It is also fun to make, especially because it is something that everybody can be part of.

Then we placed the buns on a lightly oiled cookie sheet and left them for at least two hours in a very low oven. If you use a wood cook stove, as we do, it is a good idea to keep a pan of hot water in there for some extra moisture. On a sunny summer day we let the sun be the baker!

While we were waiting for the most exciting part of it all, the tasting of them, we made sure to wash all our utensils right away under cold water; otherwise, the doughy parts dry out and stick like glue.

By the way: the first soaking water of the wheat berries (make sure they are organically grown) can be made into a drink called "rejuvelac" by letting it ferment in a warm place for 36 to 72 hours; then put it in the refrigerator or a cool place. Its high enzyme activity acts as a digestive aid. Otherwise, use the water for your plants or wheat grass; they appreciate it too.

B.

FREEZING ELDERBERRIES

If you freeze elderberries on the stem, then it is simple to strip the frozen berries off later since they won't mash in your hands. (Caution: be sure you pick elderberries—or any berries—in an area that has not been sprayed by pesticides.)

J. G.

NO SAFE MUSHROOM TEST

There is *no* test for poisonous mushrooms.

From *Mushroom Pocket Field Guide* by Howard Bigelow (Macmillan, 1974): "There are no general rules for determining an edible from a poisonous fungus. The saying that a silver coin will turn black if placed in with a poisonous fungus that is cooking, or remain silver if the species is edible, *is not true;* and

anyone who swears by this test has only been extremely lucky."

From *A Color Treasury of Mushrooms and Toadstools* (a meaningless distinction, by the way) by Uberto Tosco (N.Y.: Crescent Books, 1972): "Many traditional methods for testing fungus are unreliable.... The test of the breadcrumb, of the clove of garlic, of the coin or the small silver spoon are utterly worthless."

And finally, from perhaps the latest and best mushroom book available, *The Audubon Society Field Guide to North American Mushrooms*, 1981, by Gary Lincoff (Knopf): "No simple test can determine whether a mushroom is edible or poisonous. The only way to be certain is to know exactly what species you have found."

P. L.

QUICK PEA SHELLER

In reply to a letter asking about pea shellers, here's a method I have used often and found to be a very quick way of shelling peas. It will do the job for you if you are unable to find a proper pea sheller. Any washing machine with a wringer, hand operated or electric, works very well as a pea sheller. Set the wringer in motion, then feed handfuls of pea pods through it as you would wet clothes. The shells go through, and the peas fall back on the side from which you are feeding. As the peas are inclined to bounce around a bit, arrange a sheet or other cloth to catch them.

M. L.

ANIMALS

THE NOISE OF BLASTING

If you are planning to do some blasting, maybe you should consider waiting a while. An acquaintance of mine who is an old hand at both blasting and farming told me that if you blast while a hen is sitting on a batch of eggs, the eggs will not hatch. Guess the embryo gets killed by the shock. Even if you don't have a hen on eggs, your neighbours might, and what about the robins?

B. T.

EARTHWORMS AS CHICKEN FEED

Neighbors of ours have been raising a few earthworms on the side for several years. Their "worm farm" consists of two 15" long, 3' high board walls, set parallel to each other about 2½ to 3' apart. The food for the worms consists mostly of household garbage. In the fall, some apple pulp left from cider pressing, and occasionally some manure are added.

The garbage is piled daily in the same spot, until it reaches the top of the box, then the following day's garbage is dumped next to the completed pile. This way the worms are concentrated where their food is most readily available. Ideally, each new batch of garbage is covered by a thin layer of soil to reduce fly and odor problems. To keep the free-roaming chickens from scratching in the pile, old boards are placed on top.

During the winter, the worms migrate to the bottom of the pile for warmth. Especially now that the prices of feed are higher than ever, it makes sense to raise protein food for livestock. Our neighbors feed the earthworms both to the chicks that their bantams hatch in the barn and to their layers. They feel that it is advisable to hatch chicks early in the spring. This way the chicks stay in the barn for a month, fed on earthworms and other goodies, and then when the snow has melted and the first greens appear in the yard, the chicks are large enough to take advantage of this new food source. Also, they will start laying that much earlier in the fall.

The worms are fed from an inverted garbage can lid; this way there is no chance of the worms disappearing in the litter, where they would dry out and die.

When I started our wormpit, I got a honey bucket full of compost and worms from our neighbors as a starter. When they first built theirs, they just waited for the worms to come by themselves.

J. B.

ABOUT EGG PRODUCTION

If your egg production is going down, it may be your own fault rather than that of your chickens. In winter, you may tend to cut back on the number of times you visit your chicken coop to collect eggs. K. K. says, however, that "regular removal of eggs promotes higher production, especially in very hot or very cold weather." Also, frequent gathering of eggs makes for cleaner eggs, with fewer broken ones. She also cautions against washing soiled eggs, since they have a natural protective "cuticle" (coating) that increases their life in storage. Water will remove this coating. She suggests that if your eggs are very dirty, you buff off the dirt or manure with a piece of fine steel wool.

B. T.

COW VERSUS GOAT

Regarding the question whether to keep cows or goats, here is a personal comparison. We live on a back road and have raised goats for about a dozen years. Our nearest neighbor is a half mile away and also has goats; we have no electricity with its attendant refrigerators, etc., and our cleared land for hay and pasture is limited. Under these conditions, I can say unequivocally that goats are the best choice. Cows gain the advantage as you come closer to civilization, with neighbors, transportation, electricity, and cleared and level grassland.

Both goats and cows must be dried up for the last two months before their young are born. It is quite feasible to keep two goats and stagger their breeding so that both are not dry at the same time. But keeping two cows can be out of the question for a small homesteader, not to mention the veritable flood of milk that comes when both are yielding at once, especially in early summer. With a near neighbor who also has a cow, a milk swap in dry periods can be arranged.

However, you can keep only one cow, whereas a goat is miserable without company—though the company can be a sheep or even a horse, rather than another goat.

The dairy cow usually gives too much milk for her calf—the wee one can actually get sick from the excess, so it is impractical for the cow to raise her own; the calf must be hand-fed. Goats, however, can raise their own quite handily, and it helps stem the flood of early spring milk. The little ones can stay with mama all day and be penned separately at night, giving the owner half or more of the milk; as the yield drops in the fall, the males can be butchered and the does sold off, leaving only a few for herd replacement and keeping the household milk supply closer to even through the year, while the work of raising the kids is reduced to the nightly penning up.

Since a goat is much smaller than a cow, your investment is much less. If one goat from your herd of say two to four succumbs to some problem, you are set back much less than if you lost your only cow. And I would rather have my bare foot trampled by a goat's hoof than a cow's hoof. Also, when you have only old-fashioned methods available for keeping the meat, or if you consume only small and occasional amounts of meat anyway, it is much easier to deal with the carcass of a kid than that of a calf. However, a calf carcass is much more saleable than a goat carcass if you are within reach of markets.

In our circumstances, we need to fence only our garden, our orchard, and other homestead areas we want to protect; the goats forage freely on the nearby power line and bother no one. If our neighbors were nearer, we would be faced with a much more extensive and expensive fencing job. A cow can be confined with a lower and looser fence. A cow is also more likely to be contented on a tether. But goats almost invariably come home at night without fetching. Some cows do; some don't.

A cow doesn't mind standing out in the rain, but goats come pelting home as soon as the showers get heavy. This can make free-ranging them frustrating or downright difficult in a very rainy area. But at least goats are not likely to muddy your pond or creek by placidly meditating knee-deep in the muck!

A cow takes about three tons of hay over winter, and she definitely prefers grass pasture. Goats eat brush and all kinds of garden leftovers; you can winter three or four of them on a ton of good hay and supplement it with cedar branches in the winter. A previous article mentions the difficulty of keeping goat milk truly clean. This is not much of a problem in the goat barn of a small homestead where you are handling a little bit of goat milk and can do it quickly. We strain our milk immediately into clean jars and store it in the creek, unless we want to sour it for cheese. The reason for the difficulty is the dry, pelleted nature of the goat dung, which can make the air and surroundings dusty. This can be overcome by using a separate room for milking if necessary. But we find

the form of goat manure an advantage. For one thing, goats needn't be sloshed down before milking; a mild brushing is enough. And you needn't clean the stalls every day; just add more bedding—straw or picked-over hay or sawdust—every day until the doors won't open. Clean-out time can wait until you are ready to expand the compost heap. Meanwhile, the ever-renewed bedding keeps the animals warm, dry, and clean. Deep-littering a cow, though, must take prodigious mountains of bedding—not to mention the well-known cow pies all over the yard and pasture.

Also, goats aren't prone to the milk-transmitted diseases—brucellosis and TB, which cows must usually be checked for and inoculated against and on account of which their milk is usually pasteurized.

In paradoxical contradiction of the usual stereotype of goats, we have never had a goat bother our laundry, which is usually hung over the fence rails, easily within their reach. But a cow who once lived here went straight from a contemplative crunch out of the ash bucket to an experimental meal of a newly washed sheet!

There are, however, two factors clearly in favor of cows. Their milk can be skimmed easily without a separator. With only a couple of goats and no refrigerator, there just isn't enough milk to justify cleaning all those separator parts. And if handled carelessly or improperly, goat milk can easily develop off-flavor as it ages, sooner in warm weather than in winter. (This is not a problem with cows.) Some people can taste an unpleasant flavor in fresh, well-handled goat milk, which is delightful to most people. I am convinced that this taste is a hereditary factor, as it is said to be regarding the taste of spinach.

So whether goats or cows are better suited to the small homestead really depends on your circumstances. If you are more fond of the one animal than the other, you will prefer to live with the one you like better and you will do whatever is necessary to fit your lives to each other. But if you like them equally well, or are interested mainly in the economic benefits and practical aspects, you are likely to find that cows fit in better the more closely you are surrounded by civilization, whereas goats gain the advantage with distance from civilization.

J. M.

TRICKS FOR BEARS AND COUGARS

The best long-term protection against bears and cougars is a well-built barn for your live-stock. In the meantime, however, here are two fairly workable tricks to discourage the big fellas.

Bear: Mix 5 lb. honey, some rotten fruit and fish heads, and 2 lb. cayenne pepper, and set it on Brer Bear's favorite trail leading onto your property. He'll have heartburn, a sore mouth, and indigestion for two or three days. And since bears are smarter than smart dogs, he'll remember. Study all tracks on your land and figure out how many bears are visiting and increase your mix accordingly.

Cougar: All cats respect other cats' territorial markings—a scratched-up mound of earth with urine on top. Use a rake to scratch up a mound about one foot high at each of the four corners of your property and pour bleach on top of each one. Your cougar will

likely pee on himself while getting away from the mark of this "supercougar"!

If tended regularly, these gimmicks should keep the predators away until you get your barn built.

S. L.

HEALTHY CHICKENS

Unlike other years, this year we've been able to keep our chickens' egg production up through the winter so far by sprinkling hot pepper seeds over their food each day. It's supposed to make them feel warm (or hot) inside. We've also added a couple of cloves of garlic to their drinking water (we replace the cloves monthly). The flock is in wonderful shape, so something is working.

L. A.

CHICKENS IN THE COLD

Although we don't live in the Yukon, many of our conditions are the same or at least similar. We had a very long and snowy winter this year; still had snow mid-May. However, our chickens have survived their first winter, despite everything we were warned against.

If anyone is interested in keeping chickens in a cold climate, these are, in my opinion, a good choice: the Harco is a hybrid bird, a mix of the Rhode Island Red and New Hampshire. They sex out by color, so buying unsexed chicks is no problem. The roosters are a gray/white/black mix, whereas the smaller hens are a red/brown/black mix. They are listed as meat and egg birds, and the roosters we dressed out last fall at six months proved to be good roosters.

We kept a small flock of 10 hens and a rooster over the winter in a part of our A-frame barn. The barn is built of poles, covered in rough lumber and hand-split spruce shakes. It has no insulation, no heat, and no light. We were warned that there would be no eggs and that the birds would freeze but decided to try because it is hard to pack eggs in here in the winter.

There was a lot of snow early in the year before it got really cold, and this insulated the henhouse to a certain degree. I kept a temperature record and an egg record. During January, the coldest month, we got 6 to 8 eggs a day when the temperature was –10°F. On one 30°-below-zero morning I collected 10 eggs! This good laying continued all winter with only one problem: what does a small family of three do with an average of four dozen eggs a week? We learned lots of new egg recipes!

The hens were fed regular laying mash and some wheat and bran. They got fresh water every day, sometimes twice a day, since we regarded water as the most important part of keeping them alive. Oyster shells for calcium as well as their own eggshells and kitchen scraps were also fed to them.

I think part of the success lay in the fact that they were not confined. The henhouse door was closed, but a small door big enough only for them was open, and so every day except for the windiest and rainiest, they all trooped out. Watching a flock of hens marching over a crust of four-foot snow in the dead of winter is quite a sight! Being able to get out, they got exercise (which probably prevented cannibalism) and light, and they took any bugs they could pick up from the snow. They also pecked at bark from trees and at the needles from spruce and balsam trees.

They suffered a bit, though. The rooster's comb turned gray with frostbite, and several of the hens had frostbite on their feet. However, it has now cleared and their combs and feet are back to their regular color. Now (May) they are running around the yard and into the bush, pecking at all the new greens and still laying eight eggs a day, though some are under the trees and behind the bushes.

L. P.

 FARMYARD REMEDIES

I've had experience in giving one garlic cap to a duck and chicken daily, and they recovered from respiratory problems. Garlic is also good for chickens with intestinal problems.

It has been known that if horses are given brewer's yeast two or three times a week, they will be bothered very little by flies, if at all.

Giving cider vinegar to chickens is known to cut down on lice and help produce more eggs. It aids milk production in cows and prevents milk fever and mastitis.

We have a goat with horns on, and she would bunt our ewes. So my husband cut a piece of rubber hose and put it on her horns. This took the spirit of bunting out of our goat.

S. R.

HAPPY HENS

We have found chickens to be the simplest homestead animal to care for, and even through several years of a relatively mobile existence, our girls have kept us supplied with delicious eggs summer and winter.

We have a flock of 25 hens, Harco Sex Links and Golden Comets with a Rhode Island rooster named Bilbo. We get about 18 eggs a day, the surplus of which we trade for fresh milk. Our girls are not penned up but are free to scratch and chase bugs and dust themselves in the sun. They are much healthier for this, not to mention happier (happy hens lay more). True, we do lose a clutch of eggs to some wily biddy laying out under a fence or bush somewhere, but just when we figure she's lost to a fox, she will show up one morning with 8 to 12 fluffy chicks, this winter's chicken stew and next spring's pullets. We initially started our flock with 15 pullets (20-week-old hens, ready to lay) and keep our flock producing by culling out the 3-year-olds every fall. This keeps us with about a dozen young pullets to start laying in the spring.

Feed: Using a tobacco can as a measure, we feed the following to the chickens every morning: two parts oats, two parts corn, four parts wheat, one part oyster shell. In the winter we add to this four parts lay mash (although we may stop giving it anymore). In the evening, they get a bucket of all our table scraps, plus some cabbage leaves, turnip tops, or whatever from the garden. We save the eggshells in a bucket behind the stove and crush them to feed back to the hens. They must have fresh, clean water at all times. I've also heard that cider vinegar added to the water is beneficial.

Housing: Chickens need about 4 square feet per hen, although this is not too important if your hens have free range. You should have one laying box for every three hens. Our coop is a log building with a dirt floor, about 10' × 12'. We keep clean hay on the floor and throw the feed on it—they like to scratch, and the exercise is good for them, especially in winter. If they don't clean up their feed daily, you are giving them too much. Clean the bedding out twice a year and put it on your garden. Keep clean hay in the nesting boxes too.

Winter: If you have Hydro, you've got it made. A heat lamp will keep the water from freezing and give the girls the light they need to lay. (Chickens need about 12 hours of daylight to produce).

If you don't have Hydro, keeping the water warm helps. We put a dash or two of cayenne in their water to help create heat. Sometimes we cook them up a stew of whole wheat and table scraps. We also get fat scraps, and they really love them.

We have no problem with illness in our flock. By raising our own replacement hens, naturally, with a mother, no "outside" hens, possibly diseased, are introduced. This, and a diet that is as natural as possible, keeps them healthy.

Chickens are not as stupid as their reputation would have them. Watch a biddy hen one afternoon teaching her chicks to scratch for bugs or how to have a dust bath. Be friends with your girls, give them treats of sunflower seeds or cheese when they come to the porch, and they will pay you back many times over.

R. & M.

POWER FREE CHICKEN BROODER

A power free chicken brooder can easily be made to house 50 to 100 baby chicks and keep them mother-warm. It's a frame slatted with strips of wool stapled to hang down. The chicks huddle between the wool strips free of drafts.

To make the strips, get real wool from old coats at rummage sales. Staple two-inch-wide strips over the slats, leaving an inch between the floor and the dangling wool strips. Cover the frame with a piece of fiber-glass insulation lid.

M. L.

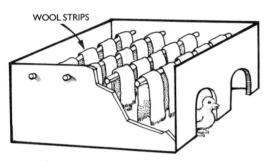

WOOL STRIPS

CHICKEN CAUTIONS

A word of caution when raising pullets is to watch their grain consumption. Ours were free-ranging and liked to scrounge near our calf, who spilt her rolled barley quite a bit. As the hens started to lay, they died, and an autopsy showed excess fat around their ovaries. It was halted immediately by controlling their grain intake and giving them a drug, Zoomycetin (which meant not eating their eggs for a while). So I hope to save others from having their pullets go the same route. We lost some beautiful young hens.

Chicks often seem to grow up with deformed feet, called "curled toe paralysis," caused by a riboflavin deficiency. As soon as I noticed our chicks showing signs of this condition, I gave them gleanings from whole wheat flour, bran, etc., and it stopped. Our rooster was one of those first chicks, and he is "Mr. Crooked Toes" to this day, but none developed the mangled-looking feet I have seen in other flocks.

Our 10 hens and rooster passed this last winter without a heater or light bulb (we don't have electricity) in a 6' × 10' insulated coop with a south-facing 3' × 3' double-pane window. The temperature was down to –35°F., at least, and they laid eggs the whole time. (This area is good for scrounging, and my only expense for the coop was four dollars for the window at a demolition sale.) Hurray for solar power!

D. P.

FRESHNESS TEST FOR EGGS

Here is a test for the freshness of eggs from *The Craft of the Country Cook* by Pat Katz (Vancouver, B.C.: Hartley & Marks, 1988): "To check eggs for freshness, put them in a container of water. The freshest ones stay on the bottom. Less fresh eggs will start to rise. If they float on top, chances are they are no good. This is a useful test if you find a clutch of eggs a hen has hidden."

S. T.

CHICKEN HOUSE COMPOST

In the chicken house we use two methods to make compost. Start with a well-ventilated building. Under the roost we make an enclosed area the chickens cannot enter and scratch in. The top is covered with an old bedspring or chicken wire so that droppings can fall through and chickens cannot. To control odor and absorb moisture, wood ashes and sawdust or dirt are sprinkled regularly. This can be allowed to build up quite deep and in winter will supply some heat to the henhouse.

On the open floor area, we use a deep litter. Almost anything can be used here: trashed hay, sawdust, moss, shredded paper feed bags, cardboard boxes, dirt and kitchen scraps or garden waste, as long as it is not wet. The trick is to keep the litter fluffed up with a pitchfork or potato rake and to keep adding more so that it stays deep. If it becomes compacted and overly damp, it should be removed and fresh litter started. It also benefits from sprinklings of wood ashes.

S. & F. M.

IN PRAISE OF DUCKS

Ducks! Why ducks? Well, originally we were looking for a solution to our slug problem. One summer we had hundreds of thousands of slugs. They ate everything, even the tops of the carrots. Without a "slug solution," it was obvious we would have no garden. Friends introduced us to their solution—ducks—and it has been fun ever since.

We got three 2-week-old ducklings. Every day we would take the little fellas and a yo-gurt container full of water to the garden. Evening was best, when the slugs were active. Ducks eat almost anything small that moves, so it was hard to convince them that slugs were food. But after they got their first taste, they figured it out. As we weeded, we would call them when we found a cache of slugs, and they would come running. The slugs were almost too much for their little bills and throats. After 10 minutes of slugging, their bills would be stuck shut. So we always brought some water so they could clean their bills and drink. Then they would go back to work.

The first year we noticed a difference. But the second year, when they were adults getting an early start, they really cleaned up. This last spring we had 10 ducklings, so with 13 ducks cruising the orchard and garden, one is hard pressed to find a slug. I think I've seen a couple dozen, total, skulking under boards. They have been quickly gobbled.

After a summer of evenings spent hand slugging, it is rewarding to watch the ducks cruise for slugs. They put their eyes to the ground and run, eating as they go. This year, with the slugs almost eliminated, we turned the ducklings on to dandelion flowers. The kids fed the flowers to them by the handful. When they cruise, they gobble dandelion flowers. The flowers are gone as soon as they bloom.

What else do ducks eat? Grasshoppers, lettuce (fence it in), caterpillars, earthworms, beetles, grass, clover, and much more. They are messy. We try to keep them in the orchard and garden, but they like to be with us. They are pets, so a lot of the mess is around the outside of the house. The grass can be sprayed regularly with a hose, and the mess disappears into the grass. The droppings in their house are powerful, slightly stronger than chicken manure.

Ducks versus Chickens

Now that I've brought up chickens, let's compare them with ducks. We have both. Ducks don't damage the garden nearly as much as chickens. They don't scratch. The damage usually comes from an occasional nip where they shouldn't. They also don't care where they put their big feet. I have weeded alongside a duck. We were both after the same stuff, chickweed. She nipped the spinach only occasionally—I'm sure it was accidental. Ducks need to be trained. Feed them what you want them to eat when they are ducklings, before they are turned loose to develop their own tastes. Take them to the garden with you so that you can watch them. They like your company, and you will probably enjoy theirs. But they may end up with dietary preferences you may not appreciate. Watch out for your lettuce!

Ducks eat more than chickens, but if you can free-range them, they forage a lot, with less damaging consequences than chickens.

Duck houses don't need heat or insulation, since ducks are wrapped in down. They need good, deep bedding, however. Ducks' feet get cold. Ours spend a lot of the time in the water in the winter, since the water keeps their feet warmer than the air. Ducks need their bedding changed more often than chickens. They get it wet, and they need dry bedding—they are prone to arthritis. I use sawdust and I change their bedding every two weeks; straw is also good. In that two weeks when the bedding gets wet, I top it up until change day, when I clear the whole house out.

Ducks will lay their eggs on the floor. It's best to keep the bedding clean for that reason. Duck eggs are more porous than chicken eggs, and bacteria can more easily get through the shell. But it is no problem if they stay clean. Don't wash your eggs, as there is a protective layer that keeps the egg fresher that will be washed off. If you want clean eggs, keep the nesting area clean. The same goes for chicken eggs. I clean out and replace chicken nesting material at least once, usually twice, a week. My egg customers comment on our clean eggs, thinking we wash them. Not so.

I find duck eggs rubbery, so I use them to bake. They contain more protein, more yolk, and less water than chicken eggs.

Ducks are also easier to herd than chickens. What I like most about ducks as compared with chickens is their attitude to each other. When a chicken is wounded, all the other chickens will peck it to death. So you must separate it and nurse it. We've had hurt ducks, and both times the flock took care of them. They made sure someone was with the duck all the time. One was temporarily blind in one eye and would wander off. The other ducks would find him and call to him so that he could stay with the group. I feel good about ducks for that reason. I suspect they are less removed from their "roots" than most highly bred chickens. But that is only my theory.

Ducks are natural comics. They look funny, they sound funny, and they move funnily. It is no accident that Donald Duck is Disney's silliest character. We have had endless laughs over their antics. The kids have really enjoyed them. However, we have two aggressive drakes that will attack in the spring. Although it is nothing serious, it is annoying to be weeding in the garden and have them jump at you. They can knock a small child down. Our youngest learned to go among the ducks with a stick and never turn her back on the drakes.

All ducks deserve water. They love it. They can be raised without it, but it makes them so happy. They bob, play, clean, preen, and mate in water.

Ours have a bathtub dug into a bank. They jump in and out from the bank side. The drain end is exposed, so we can pull the plug to clean it and refill it. We would like to make them a pond some day so they can all swim together. We have a Canada goose who takes up the whole tub herself. We always have a trickle of water running into the tub to keep it cleaner and the water fresher for the ducks to drink.

Breeds

In choosing a breed of ducks you must decide on your needs or priorities. If you want ducks for pets, maybe the prettiest ducks are a good choice. Rouens (domestic mallards) are beautiful. They are good meat birds, but don't expect many eggs. Other common meat birds are Pekins, Cayugas, and Muscovies. Indian Runners are good layers, and Khaki Campbells are about the best; they are also quite attractive. The ducks are brown, whereas the drakes are khaki with a bronze-green head and neck. They make poor mothers, but I've read claims of 340–364 eggs per duck a year. I've not had our Khakis long enough to substantiate that claim.

Acquiring Your Ducks

You can sometimes get ducks from a duck keeper. Good layers seem difficult to find. Many feed suppliers deal in ducklings, but most have Rouens and Pekins.

Incubation

I wanted Khaki Campbells last spring, so I got fertile eggs from local duck owners and incubated them. Four of six Khaki eggs hatched.

If you decide to incubate eggs and have an incubator, instructions for duck eggs usually come with the incubator. Incubating has its rewards. I followed instructions, and after the eggs were in the incubator 8 days, I candled them by putting a light inside a cardboard box that had an oval hole slightly smaller than the eggs cut out of it. The light should be adjusted so you can see through the egg. When the egg is seven or eight days old, if it is fertile, there should be a dark red spot in it that has small spidery veins radiating from it. If the egg is clear, it is infertile and should be removed. After an experience I had, I hesitate to say if it is cloudy it was fertile but the embryo died. I acquired six good eggs already a week old. Of the six, five were clear and one I could not see into. I hesitated to chuck it because I was concerned that there might be an embryo; but all the information I had said infertile eggs with dead embryos decompose quickly and would contaminate the good ones. I never saw the dark spot or veins in this egg. It must have been older than I thought. I finally took the plunge and disposed of the egg. Much to my anguish, it was indeed fertile and growing. Eggs need to be candled at 7 and 14 days and the infertile and cloudy ones removed. As I learned, as the embryo grows, at some point the inside is filled and dark.

I didn't successfully incubate duck and goose eggs together, because only one of the goose eggs was fertile, and through my ignorance I lost that one. However, I think it is entirely possible to incubate them together.

Goose eggs need to be turned three times a day rather than twice, as duck eggs are. Both duck and goose eggs need to be sprayed with water, and the necessary temperature is approximately the same. Incubating is a great deal of work, but the greatest concern is power outages. I had a night light close by my bed at night. Being a parent, I have developed the training necessary for undertaking incubation. When the light went out, I was awake and down in the basement to the incubator before the temperature had dropped significantly. If the outage is short, a hot water bottle wrapped in a towel on top of the eggs and the entire incubator wrapped in a down sleeping bag will work to keep the eggs warm. For longer outages, I put them with the hot water bottle in front of the wood stove. They must be watched so they don't get too hot.

There were three power outages in the month I was incubating eggs. I was on pins and needles the last week, afraid the power would go out while we weren't home! A day or two before they hatched, they would peep inside the shell. I could hold the egg close and peep at it and get an answering peep in my ear. It was so exciting. One time, in the excitement, the cord got knocked, and the incubator was quite cold when I checked later. It was unplugged for at least 2 hours, and I was sure I'd killed them all. Someone has since told me that the eggs can go without heat for up to 12 hours.

Ten of the 12 duck eggs hatched, an 83 percent hatch, when 65 percent is considered good and 50 percent is usual. Supposedly those that don't hatch are probably deformed or weak. One is never supposed to "help" a baby out of its shell. You will probably hurt it or bring a weak duckling into the world.

The ducklings start pipping 24 to 48 hours before hatching. They finally chip the shell until it is chipped in a circle, when the shell breaks in two. The ducklings should stay in the warm incubator for 12 to 36 hours, when they should be dry and fluffy. Then they should be put under a light that keeps them at 85–90°F for a few days. After that, you can gradually keep them at a cooler temperature by raising the light.

There are many more details, which are included in the incubator instructions. The process is not too time-consuming, but you have to be there or have a very trustworthy substitute. I have an order in for a Muscovy duck for next spring, as I suspect she will find it less of an emotional strain than I, and I would appreciate a more restful sleep.

P. C.

FLY RELIEF FOR LIVESTOCK

When we lived in the Cariboo, the flies in summer were pure torture for animals. We learned that by washing the horses and cows with plain warm water, we could relieve a lot of their misery. The wildest bronc soon learned to stand quietly while we rubbed the rag on chest, belly, ears, and any other badly bitten area. Blackflies leave a poison in their bites that retards healing and causes pain. Washing the bloody scabs off allowed new skin to form very quickly, and the flies seemed to dislike the clean pink skin.

We also made a "fly shed" for the animals—an old log building with a large opening covered with a burlap curtain. Inside it was dark and cool, and the flies were nonexistent. You'd be surprised at the extra weight gained by stock that are protected from flies. I have often wondered why more stock owners did not use this idea. Ever since that experience, we have put our stock inside a barn or shed during the day.

W. C.

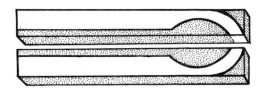

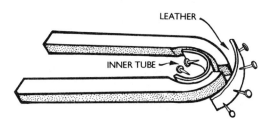

LEATHER

INNER TUBE

OATS FOR CHICKENS

I have read that giving chickens constant access to oats prevents pecking and cannibalism within the flock. We don't have this problem with our birds, but we have oats in front of them at all times to prevent it. Ample grass range and room for scratching should also help prevent this problem.

M. & W. H.

WHO'S LAYING NOW?

Here's a simple way to tell which of your hens are laying and which aren't. Pick them off the roost at night and feel the pelvic bones just above the anus. If the bones are thin and two or more fingers apart, she's laying. If they are thick and close together, she's not. Fat chickens don't lay eggs. If this test is done in the dark, they won't get upset.

D. S.

Take two pieces of lumber 1" × 4", about 18" long. Cut each piece as shown in the figure, or use half a jar lid as a pattern.

Tack a piece of inner tube on the curve (inside). Place the two pieces of lumber with points facing each other, and tack a hinge of leather to the outside of the curves, across the top of both, along the 1" side. You now have a giant pair of tweezers. Place the curved edges around a jar lid, squeeze handles together, and unscrew lid.

While I'm on the subject of bees, I used sage in sugar water and the bees loved it.

W. C.

WOOD ASH FOR LICE-FREE CHICKENS

FEEDING BEES

My father made a handy jar opener for gallon jars when we had bees. We fed the hives with a gallon jar turned upside down and holes punched in the lid.

We did an extensive lice treatment on our flock after acquiring a new rooster who infected our birds. Wood ashes rubbed into every part of every bird every evening (when they're easy to catch) for a month did it. The lice are suffocated by the wood ashes.

All summer they roosted outdoors in a place we made snug in the chicken yard— that was so we could completely clean out the coop, which we did several times with an ash/water slurry. Now, we have insulated and painted the interior of our lice-free coop and reintroduced our lice-free chickens.

We are all very happy with the results of our intensive ash treatment. And to continue the treatment on a less intensive level, we've put a large box (which we keep filled with wood ashes) next to the hatch door. Every time the chickens want to go in or out, they must walk through the ashes, stirring a little ash dust into their feathers. Also, we notice that all the birds enjoy taking their "dust baths" in the ashbox, which certainly gives them a daily lice treatment.

B. T.

FLEA-PROOFING YOUR HOME

A simple and natural plan for flea-proofing homes:

1. Vacuum often, especially in areas where your pet sleeps.
2. Wash your pet's bedding frequently in hot water.
3. Use a flea comb daily.
4. Sprinkle brewer's yeast on your pet's coat, or use a herbal flea powder.
5. Add garlic and brewer's yeast to your pet's daily diet.
6. Rub a drop or two of a natural flea-repellent oil on your hands and then rub just the legs of your dog or cat before taking the pet outdoors. Eucalyptus, pennyroyal, and tree tea oils are all excellent for this purpose.

B. T.

WHOLE WHEAT DOG BISCUITS

A dog we know has been fed these dog biscuits all the 14 years of his life, along with other home-prepared food. Tuck's owner says these biscuits taste delicious and are nutritious for people, too. Her family always hung around, waiting for them to come out of the oven.

Mix:

    3½ cups whole wheat flour (use a brand with no preservatives)
    1 pint warm water
    1 Tbsp. honey
    1 Tbsp. molasses
    1 tsp. sea salt

Leave in warm place to rest for 15 minutes. Then mix 1 Tbsp. olive or corn oil into center of dough. Leave to rest another 15 minutes. The dough will be very sticky, so use a wooden spoon rather than your hands to form small flat cakes—use the spoon to cut off small sections, and drop them into a bowl of flour. Toss in flour till each cake is completely covered. Bake on trays oiled with olive or corn oil in a hot oven—425°F—for 20 to 30 minutes. Cakes should be brown on top, not too light.

The biscuits, or any other cookies, will be crisper if spread out to cool on brown paper, such as a cut-open grocery bag.

E. M.

TOOLS

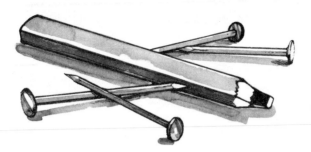

REINFORCING GARDEN TROWELS

Have you ever tried this simple idea: reinforcing your gardening trowels by driving a short nail in each? I thought of this after many broken-off handles, and it works.

M. L.

QUICK HOMEMADE BRUSH

A serviceable and cheap homemade brush can be made from a bunch of horse hair, a short length of copper pipe and a piece of wire. Follow the figures above to make the brush. Such brushes are extremely useful for countless jobs on the farm and in the milking shed.

B. T.

SOME FAVORITE TOOLS

Some people might be interested in hand tools we've found especially useful. Some are almost impossible to obtain in a hardware store in this power age, but if you know what to look for, you might happen on them at an old-time store or farm sale.

Even though we heat entirely by wood, we have no power saw. A good two-man crosscut saw (an aging female will do for one end of it!) is a must in this case. We wore one out, but a neighbor gave us a replacement he'd acquired along with his farm and never used.

A machete is also a mighty handy tool. In case you've never had one, it consists of a long blade about 2¼″ × 22″, with a 5″ handle. It is heavier than what we called a corn knife when I was a child. It is great for hacking brush, trimming small limbs off trees, even beheading a chicken if your aim with an ax isn't trustworthy. You'll discover your own uses once you have one.

One of my favorite tools is the grubbing hoe. Some might call it a mattock, but I like the more descriptive term. Ours has a 4″ blade on the grubbing end, and I think a mattock is smaller. With just a little assist from the ax, we used it to clear young trees from an area about 20′ × 25′ for a garage-storage-space structure, taking out roots and all. It is excellent for loosening and stirring rocky garden soil where a spading fork is an aggravation. It hacks through tough burdock that an ordinary hoe bounces off. There's no hand tool like it for excavating in rocky soil.

An iron crowbar is great too. We have two, a light one ⅝″ in diameter and a heavy one about 1¼″ across and about 4′ long. Not only are they good for prying, but the heavy one is my husband's favorite tool for setting fence posts or making holes for pole construction—the sharp end for loosening stubborn rocks that stop any type of digger (except a power-driven one) and the blunt end for tamping, once the post is in the hole. When a log is partly split with wedges and a sledgehammer, these two bars inserted in the crack and levered in opposite directions will often finish the split in a hurry.

We have other "pets," but these are some a beginner might not know to look for.

E. M.

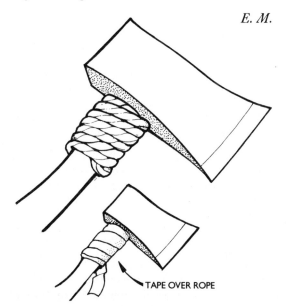

TAPE OVER ROPE

 STRENGTHEN AX HANDLES

To protect ax and maul or sledgehammer handles, wrap a double layer of half-inch-thick rope around the handle next to the head, extending it six to eight inches up. Tuck the end of the rope under the wrapped rope and cover all with several layers of duct tape.

C. S.

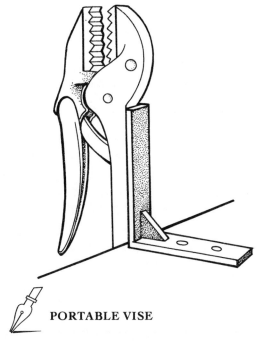

 PORTABLE VISE

This handy vise (see figure) was made from a locking plier-wrench. Bend a piece of ¼″ flat iron as shown, drill the necessary holes, and weld it to the wrench. Now you have a small but handy portable vise that can be bolted to any workbench in your shop.

B. T.

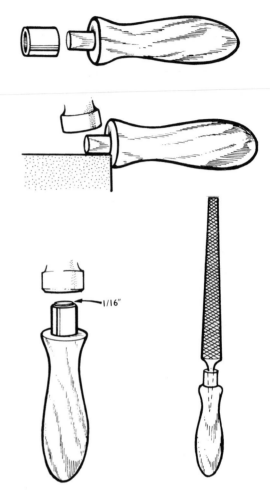

PIPE FIRE KINDLER

The Chinese and Filipinos (and probably other peoples) have been using bamboo blowers for years, and our modified version, given to us by a friend, is indispensable. We have a copper pipe, which is 20″ long and about ½″ in diameter on the inside of the pipe. A cap was put on one end, and a tiny hole was drilled into it. By inserting this pipe into coals and blowing, we can rekindle a fire in no time. A tool well worth making.

B. T.

MADE-TO-FIT TOOL HANDLES

These tool handles are best made of seasoned hardwood—suitable varieties that grow here are birch and vine maple. The wood, which must be dry, can be whittled into shape with a sharp knife; however, I am fortunate enough to have a wood lathe, which makes the job somewhat easier.

First, a copper ring is cut from either ½″ or ¾″ copper tube about ½″ long, and the handle is shaped to fit your hand, leaving a round part on the end where the copper tube will be. This round part should be pared down until it is slightly larger than the inside diameter of the copper tube.

To fit the copper ferrule onto the handle, simply tap the side of the rounded end while rotating the handle. This will compress the wood enough to tap on the copper ferrule; try for a tight fit. Now that the ferrule is in place, there should be about 1/16″ of wood past its end. Pound, striking quite hard, onto this end; this will expand the wood up against the inside of the copper tube to hold it tight. Once the handle is oiled with linseed oil and kept in a warm place overnight, one needs only to drill a hole to accept a tool; the hole should be somewhat undersized to get a tight fit.

I usually use these on my files in my shop; but last winter one of my kitchen tools got left on the hot stove, and the plastic handle melted off and dribbled down the side of the stove. I have replaced the handle with one of my own, and nothing could be better.

D. M.

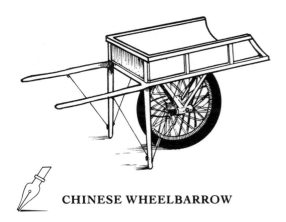

CHINESE WHEELBARROW

The wheelbarrow was invented in China about 2000 years ago and came to Europe in the Middle Ages. There the Chinese design seems to have been wedded to the traditional two-man barrow by replacing the front man with a wheel. However, this version missed the important feature of the original design, which is that a larger-diameter wheel is located not at the front but rather under the middle of the load platform, where it supports most of the weight. In the European version, only half the load is supported by wheel; the other half of the weight is on the handlebars.

The large-diameter wheel of the Chinese design is easier to push over rough or soft ground. The contemporary wheel is usually a pneumatic-tired, wire-spoked wheel like a bicycle wheel.

This wheelbarrow should be loaded so that there is still enough weight on the handles to prevent jerking on the handles when the wheel hits a bump or pothole. For heavy loads, some of the weight on the handles can be taken by a shoulder strap. If there is a following wind, it is a common practice to hoist a small, square sail.

Up to six people or an equivalent weight in goods can be transported on a wheelbarrow

of this type.

In China such wheelbarrows as well as handcarts are an essential part of construction equipment with which thousands of laborers literally move mountains of earth in mammoth canal- and dam-building projects.

H. T.

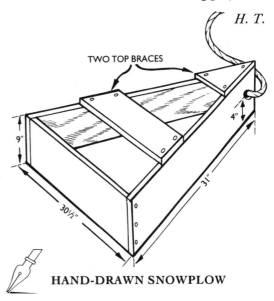

TWO TOP BRACES

9"

4"

31"

30½"

HAND-DRAWN SNOWPLOW

Enclosed is a sketch of a small, hand-drawn snowplow, which can be constructed from one-inch scrap lumber. It is generally easier to make a path in the snow with it than shovelling or sweeping.

D. & P. M

FRUIT PICKING LADDER

From *The Canadian Horticulturist*, 1899, comes a great idea for making a picking ladder.

Says the article, "Its manufacture is so simple that a glance at the illustration will suffice to show how it is done."

FRUIT PICKING LADDER

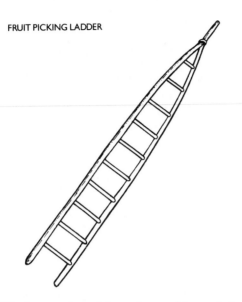

PIECE OF PIPE

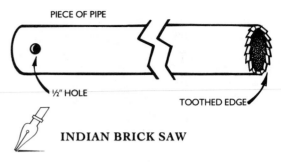

½" HOLE

TOOTHED EDGE

INDIAN BRICK SAW

I so much enjoy receiving each issue, and occasionally while at work I think of something I should share but then never get around to writing it down. Here are a few ideas that might help someone.

On several occasions I have needed to make a hole in brick walls. While working in India, I found a way to drill a neat hole. You take a short length of pipe of the same size as the required hole—anything from ½"–3" diameter. Using a hack saw, make a toothed edge in one end. At the other end, drill a ½" hole through the pipe to insert a large screwdriver or piece of rod with which to rotate the "drill." It is surprising how quickly this will cut its way through ordinary bricks. Hole saws are available here, but usually they will cut through only an inch or so of thickness. Recently I needed to cut a drain hole through the kitchen cupboard base and through the floor 4" below. I made up a drill in the manner described and made a neat hole through two thicknesses of ¾" plywood in about 15 minutes using this makeshift hole saw.

E. A.

Find a good straight pole, peel it, and ring it near the small end, bolt it, or wrap it with strong galvanized wire. Mark it off with a chalk line where you want rungs to be. Bore holes for rungs through the pole. Then carefully rip it down to the ring.

Fit in rungs of some very tough wood. The article suggests white oak, but perhaps in the West another, more readily available wood can be found. Give the whole ladder a soaking coat of linseed oil and paint, if desired.

A cedar pole will make the lightest ladder, with spruce as a second choice. Or you could use two strips, 1½" × 2", of good hard wood, bound and screwed together at the top, to make the ladder—with edges rounded off to prevent injury to limbs of trees against which the ladder may rest.

"This will make a light ladder which can be inserted between the limbs of fruit trees and poked up under the trees where an ordinary ladder would be useless or would greatly injure the branches," says the article.

B. T.

ENGINE BLOCK ANVIL

The block from an old auto engine fastened top up makes a handy addition to the farm repair shop. The flat surface can be used for straightening rods and iron, the sharp edges are good for cutting wire or tin, and the holes can be used for bending and drilling, etc. A good vise for holding pipes and rods can be made by using two capscrews and a bar of iron.

J. G.

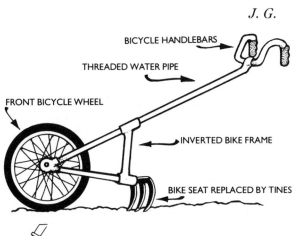

BIKE INTO CULTIVATOR

Here's an idea for converting an ordinary bicycle to a cultivator. The tines are sometimes available in yard sales or second-hand stores.

J. G.

QUICK SAWBUCK

To make a sawbuck, take two good-sized forked sticks and bore holes above each fork. Insert strong sticks through the holes, making each part a tripod that will stand up

alone. They are convenient for sawing long or heavy pieces of wood and can easily fit any length of stick.

E. F.

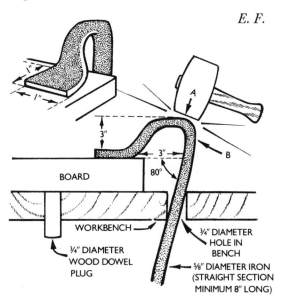

HOMEMADE HOLDFAST

A friend of mine just gave me a thing for clamping wood to my workbench, and it gives me such joy I have to pass it on! It's called a holdfast, and it is simple to make if you have access to a forge. Take an iron rod that is 13″ long and 5/8″ in diameter, heat it bright red, and hammer one end until you have a flattened area about 1″ square and about 3/16″ thick. Then put a bend in the rod to the dimensions shown in the diagram, setting the flattened area about 80 degrees to the straight part of the rod. And that's it! If you bore a 3/4″ diameter hole in your workbench, you can wedge the holdfast into it with a mallet (point A), holding the wood you're working on under the flattened end. The holdfast is released by hitting the back of it (point B) or the end under the bench. You do need a thick bench for this, but then a good workbench is thick anyway. Very thick blocks of wood can be held by a holdfast with a longer shaft.

I use two holdfasts, actually, and I've bored holes 8″ apart around three sides of my workbench so that I can hold any size board. So you end up with a lot of holes in your bench. I plugged them with 3″ long dowels, flush with the surface, that I can pop out when I need that hole and pop up to use as a bench stop for planing boards, etc. It's a joy for sure!

M. D.

How to Remove a Nut
To remove a nut from a bolt that has stripped threads, try screwing another nut down on top of the first. Fastening vise grips on the two nuts will usually remove the nut.

Nail Puller
You can make a handy nail puller by welding a ¾″ steel rod to the face of an old claw hammer, as shown in the figure. It's especially handy for pulling nails from a frieze board under the eaves of a roof where a regular bar can't work.

B. T.

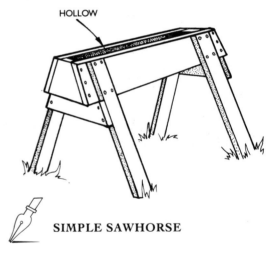

SIMPLE SAWHORSE

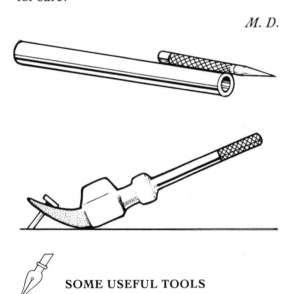

SOME USEFUL TOOLS

If you weld a center punch to a piece of pipe (see figure), it can come in handy for putting on metal roofing. Then you can punch holes in the roofing where you want to start a nail. The pipe is heavy enough to push the punch through the metal, and it can save you time and may even prevent several "black nails."

This hollowed-out sawhorse is both sturdy and easy to build and is especially useful for sawing small pieces. Just rest the pieces on the side rails and saw between them. You can make a toolbox in the hollow by nailing a board half the length of the rails to the bottom.

B. T.

GARDENING
In and Out of Doors

FREE GLASS FOR GREENHOUSES

If you're interested in free glass for cold frames or greenhouses, try car windshields. The shop here discards about 50 cracked windshields a week. That's a lot of glass.

E. & C. A.

HARDY BABY'S TEAR

We have found baby's tear to thrive through temperature extremes. Ours did fine last winter, even though the house got pretty cool some nights. If we plan to be gone for a couple of days, however, we put it in the root cellar to prevent freezing. It does better out of direct sunlight.

M. & W. H.

GROWING YOUR OWN SEED

Only vigorous, disease-free plants will give a satisfactory seed crop. There are several steps to achieve this:

1. *Have sufficient fertility in the soil.* In most soils this means adding manure each spring and often some commercial fertilizer that is reasonably high in phosphorus and potash (like 6:30:15).

Fertilizers are always quoted in three numbers, which give the percentages of the three active ingredients in 100 pounds of fertilizer. They are always in the same order: nitrogen (N), phosphorus (P), and potash (K). In 100 pounds of 6:30:15, you would have 6 pounds of nitrogen, 30 pounds of available phosphoric acid, and 15 pounds of soluble potash. Leafy crops use more nitrogen, but seed and root crops require more phosphorus and potash than nitrogen. 6:30:15, 4:10:10, 13:16:10, or similar mixes are useful. Some of these may be available from organic sources.

One pound of fertilizer will usually be enough for about 40 feet of row, cultivated into the row or in a band three to four inches away from seed before sowing.

2. *Provide sufficient water.* A thorough soaking once every five days or as needed, in the early part of the day, is better than many light sprinklings. If the ground is cultivated about once a week, there will be less loss of water through transpiration and weed growth.

3. *Sow plants thinly.* Peas, beans, broad beans, squash, cucumbers, and corn should be planted in the desired spacing for the final crop. Corn, beans, and peas

are often grown in rows, with the plants six inches apart. Bush beans should be planted from four to six inches apart. Broad beans and dwarf peas can be planted in a double row, with six inches between the rows.

Small seeds, such as those for carrots, lettuce, turnips, beets, and kohlrabi, should be thinned to one inch apart as soon as possible after the first mature leaves appear. Then they can be thinned for eating, by taking every other plant, until the crop is harvested. This gives a better crop of good roots than thinning when the plants are older.

Onions can be started in a pot and then planted outdoors with four to six inches between plants. There seems to be less problem with maggots if seed is used rather than small bulbs from the store.

Seed: Seed should be taken from plants taken out for this purpose. Since next year's crop will closely resemble the plants selected from seed, you pick the type of plant you want. Look for vigor, even shape, and freedom from disease in your seed plants.

Peas, Beans, and Broad Beans: For these plants, it is best to leave a small marked section of a row for seed and leave all pods for seed, except possibly the latest to form if they are small or immature near harvest time. Three to 4 feet of row saved will probably plant at least 100 feet of row the next year. Let the pods mature on the plant until they are brown and dry. Harvest before the fall rains. Later pods in August may get some mildew on the outside, but the seed will be unharmed and good.

Spinach, Lettuce, and Dill: Pick out three or four of your best plants. Spinach plants will have large, deeply curled dark green leaves and will show no signs of going to seed. (The plants with diamond-shaped leaves go to seed early and produce very little spinach for use.) Stake the plants you want for seed and don't cut. They will grow 2 to 3 feet high and should be tied to the stake. Four plants would probably sow about 200 to 300 feet of row. For lettuce, let several good, vigorous heads bolt and go to seed. It might be better if the lettuce had been started early and planted out in early spring, since the plant takes a long time to mature seed. For dill, let a few plants mature seed. It is usually plentiful.

Swiss Chard and Parsnips: If a plant overwinters, it will set seed. It should be staked. Occasionally a Swiss chard will bolt the first season. Two or three plants will provide seed for 200 to 300 feet of row. Parsnips left in the ground over winter will go to seed fairly early in the spring, providing plenty of seed. The seed can be planted in late October, before the first snowfall, and will come up very early in the spring, giving large parsnips in the fall. Parsnips do not transplant readily — they often fork when transplanted. Parsnip seed keeps only about two years. It is better to let one plant go to seed each year and have fresh seed.

Carrots, Beets, and Onions: All of these will set seed if good roots, large and well shaped, kept over winter in the root cellar or somewhere similar, are planted 1 to 2 feet apart. They should be hilled and staked to support the top growth (about 3 feet). Onion bulbs can be set out about six inches apart to go to seed. Three to four plants of the root crops will give enough seed for 300 to 400 feet of row. Remove seed when dry and mature, before fall rains and mildew set in.

Corn (Not Hybrids): Tie markers around six to eight of the best cobs and leave on the plants until dry. This should provide enough seed for 300 to 400 feet of row.

Squash, Marrows, and Cucumbers: These crops may cross with each other if planted close together, but if the squash is planted 30 feet or so from the cucumbers and marrows, crossing should not occur. Save seed from one or two squash that have the deepest flesh and good size and flavor. Wash off the adhering strings and dry. Marrows and cucumbers can be treated the same way. Cucumbers must be well matured and cannot be of a hybrid variety.

Tomatoes (Not Hybrids): Put seeds or a mature, almost soft tomato into water for half a day, clean pulp off, and dry on paper.

Plants of the Cruciferous Family: Cruciferous plants (cabbages, cauliflower, sprouts, turnips, radishes, kohlrabi) cross over readily with each other and with wild mustard and shepherd's purse, so it might be better to buy seeds.

The seed can be cleaned from the chaff and stalks. Much of this cleaning can be done by removing the seed from the stalks, then rubbing it between the hands and gently blowing off lighter chaff and lightweight small seed.

Seed should be kept in paper bags, carefully marked as to variety and date, and stored in a cool, dry place. Most seed can stand a few degrees of frost, provided it is dry, but will mold or spoil if it is damp.

Root crops should be stored in a cool (but above freezing), dark area with some humidity. The earth floor of a root cellar provides these conditions. If crops are stored in an insulated, built-in root storage in a house, a pan of water under the bench will provide the humidity. The onions, squash, marrows, and pumpkins will store much better in a dry place. They will do quite well in a warm, lighted place if no cold, dry area is available.

W. A.

HOW WE GREW BUCKWHEAT

My husband, like many men, always enjoys buying a new piece of machinery when he thinks he needs it. I teased him a lot when he and a neighbor bought a small combine a year ago last spring. "Dan is planting buckwheat so he can buy a combine," I told everyone. Actually, we discovered that there were some other good reasons for planting buckwheat besides offering an excuse to have a combine.

Our hive of bees had come through that winter, weak but alive. Hope of finally taking some honey from them for our own use was one reason we planted the buckwheat. Another was to add some home-grown grain to our winter food supply. Our third reason was that we had read that buckwheat is a good soil conditioner. Therefore, we planted our crop in the worst half acre of our field. What soil there was between the never-ending rocks looked like a good candidate for the dust bowl.

To prepare for sowing, we picked off the largest of the rocks and cultivated with the rotovator and tractor. Since buckwheat grows well on poor soil, we didn't use any fertilizer. Finally, we broadcast the seed at 20 pounds to the acre. Several days later, the plants began to sprout, quite sparsely. This rate of seeding was not enough. This year we are trying about 60 pounds to the acre. Incidentally, we were surprised to see the first plants—two little greenish-yellow leaves attached to a red stem. Buckwheat is not a grass but a broader-leafed plant related to rhubarb.

When the plants began to bloom, we watched our hive fill up with honey. The blossoms did not come all at once, but new ones were opening out continually. Most of the nectar flow, however, is early in the morning, before ten o'clock. Our bees were a little too lazy to take full advantage of it. Many mornings the fields were filled with bumblebees and only the occasional honeybee. In spite of this laziness, however, we would have harvested quite a few pounds of buckwheat honey had not some robber yellow jackets caught me and the bees off guard while Dan was out on a fire. This year we have bought a hive of Italian bees, which we hope will be more industrious and take full advantage of the early morning nectar flow.

Our buckwheat ripened as unevenly as it bloomed. Little brown teardrops weighted down the spindly stalks. When the fall rains came, we were still waiting for the last of the grain to form. And by the time September Indian summer came and we were able to harvest it, many of the seeds had dropped to the ground. The old combine made a great clanking and rattling as Dan on the tractor pulled it slowly through the field. Down went the buckwheat; wooden paddles guiding it up a wide conveyor belt into the great machine. Out and into a bin shot the buckwheat seed, mixed, to our dismay, with bits of straw and several times as much lamb's-quarter seed. Our combine obviously needed some repair. But in order to beat the weather, we continued in this manner. Soon the buckwheat was down and only stubble remained on the field and heaps of straw where the combine had dumped them in regular fashion. We should have plowed all this under that fall, but we postponed this task until the spring. When the harvest was over, we had about 300 pounds of buckwheat mixed with lamb's-quarter seeds.

We have one recommendation for harvesting: the grain should be harvested in time to be stooked and allowed to dry in the field. Our grain was not dry enough and did not grind well. This year we have planted our buckwheat early, around the first of May. In this way we hope to harvest when most, but not all, of the grain has formed in the dry August weather. Our plan now is to mow the field with the hay mower and stook it by hand. After drying the bundles in the field, we will feed the bundles into the combine by hand.

Because of our mistakes, preparing the buckwheat for eating was a bit tedious. After cleaning out the lamb's-quarter seeds as much as possible with a sieve, we set a pan of buckwheat on the warming shelf of the stove. In a few days it was dry enough to grind. Pancakes or waffles made with buckwheat flour and buttermilk were good. I made some all-buckwheat noodles, which were too crumbly. Noodles made of half buckwheat and half wheat would be worth a try. There were many batches of buckwheat bread. A few cups of buckwheat flour for four loaves of bread is plenty for flavor, and any more will make the bread too crumbly. We also had buckwheat pizza crust, and it was surprisingly good.

Here is a recipe worth trying:

Buckwheat Squash Cakes

 2 Tbsp. honey
 1 cup buckwheat flour
 2 cups cooked, mashed squash
 ¼ cup milk

Mix ingredients. Add more milk or flour to bring batter to the thickness of mashed potatoes. Drop spoonfuls of batter in a fry pan to make cakes 3½″ in diameter. Fry until well browned on both sides. Serve plain as a side dish or topped with applesauce for breakfast.

We had expected that our buckwheat would be good for eating and for bees, but its added value as a soil conditioner amazed us. When we plowed the same field this spring, the dusty soil looked black and lovely. We plan to use buckwheat again as a green manuring crop. I have planted it in a section of the garden, thinking it will not cause a weed problem the next year the way clover does. In our fields, we plan to harvest only half the buckwheat as a grain. The other half we will plow under as soon as most of it has bloomed. Then we will seed again and, we hope, grow some more blossoms for our bees, plowing under two green manuring crops in the same year. Buckwheat seems like something that will be useful to us in many ways in the years to come.

E. & D. B.

 MULCHING

Three years ago I put in five rows of raspberries and mulched them heavily with moldy hay.

Last year's crop was heavy, but this year the canes are seven feet tall and the crop is excellent. One thing I have found is that the mulch tends to make the suckers grow between the rows, and these have to be kept pruned down. On raising the hay, one finds oodles of worms on the surface of the soil converting the hay to humus.

I have a perforated pipe lying down the rows for irrigation, since I find that overhead sprinkling leaves a deposit on the berries and spoils their looks, though the flavor is very good.

For fertilizer I use a little blood meal and bonemeal early in the spring. Epsom salts are also good for raspberries.

I have two varieties: Himrod, which is a large, firm berry, good for freezing, with very bland flavor; and Cuthbert, an old standby, which is a good bearer with good tart flavor.

Reasons for Mulching: To conserve moisture, encourage microorganisms, feed worms, replace humus and trace elements, repel insects, control weeds by bringing roots to surface, create a breeding ground for wood bugs and beetles, keep ground cool. The timing of laying the mulch is important, for each plant has its own requirements for heat and moisture.

Materials: Hay, leaves, straw, manure, grass cuttings, ground refuse and compost, shavings and sawdust (must use nitrogen fertilizer underneath), bark, stones, flat rocks, gravel, boards, newspapers, black plastic.

Organic Fertilizers: Rock phosphate, blood and bonemeal, granite dust, greensand, kelp meal, fish meal, linseed meal, sludge, cottonseed meal.

Notes on Materials

Hay—lay on 6–10″ thick, old and moldy is best. If laid too thin, it will compact, allowing the moisture to escape and weeds to grow.

Leaves—should be mixed with other material, since they compact easily.

Manure—two inches smothers well. It enriches the soil and is excellent for worms.

Test soil for needed trace elements. Some manures, such as sheep, hen, and pig manure, may be too high in nitrogen for certain crops.

Grass Cuttings—compact quickly, hold moisture, are high in nitrogen, and are good for carrots against the fly.

F. G.

STARTING A BERRY PATCH

This is the time to start a berry patch or add to the old one. Raspberries, blackberries, strawberries, and currants all *prefer* an acid soil. Newly cleared bush land is acid, unless there is a large amount of calcium in the soil, in which case the soil is usually neutral, which is still OK for berries.

The best way to start a berry patch is to go to someone who has berry bushes, preferably of the kind and variety that you like. We got our raspberries from neighbors. We knew that one of the rows in their patch produced large, tasty, and easy-to-pick berries, and we decided to plant most of our raspberries of that particular variety. We also have a few bushes that produce fewer, harder-to-pick berries, but they are sweeter.

The way to get raspberry or blackberry starts is simple. Just dig up shoots that arise from lateral roots from the main plant. The easiest ones to get are those that grow between the rows, rather than those in the row. Don't transplant too early. (But wait until the plants have stopped growing. That way, the transplanting becomes less of a shock.)

I plant raspberries two to three feet apart in a row. I dig a hole about one foot deep and fill it with good topsoil. It is best not to put too many nutrients in the hole (like old manure or compost) because that would cause the plants to grow too rapidly the next spring and to produce a leafy, rank growth rather than a stocky, sturdy cane.

The first spring there will be a few flowers and a few berries. The second summer after planting the first real crop will be produced. From the third summer on, there will be lots of berries, providing you look after the bushes.

Since our raspberries are planted in rows, I have put a heavy fence post on each end of the row. About three feet above the ground, I have nailed a two-foot-long piece of 2×6. Two heavy parallel wires connect the two 2×6 pieces on the posts. After the leaves have dropped off, I cut the old canes at the base with pruning shears. The new canes are tied to the parallel wires and raffia, old "twisters," baler twine, or whatever may be available.

In the spring, after most of the snow has melted, I prune away the thinner canes, leaving three to five canes to each plant. At that time, I also prune off the top of each cane to induce branching.

After the snow has gone, I cover the ground between the plants with six inches of sawdust—preferably sawdust that decomposes readily, like white pine, birch, or cottonwood. Cedar sawdust is least desirable because it takes too long to rot. I put manure on top of the sawdust. The manure can be of any kind, fresh or rotten, depending on what is available. The nitrogen in the manure fertilizes the microorganisms that help break down the sawdust, thus allowing the nutrients in the sawdust to become available. The sawdust also eliminates weed problems, and the soil does not dry out easily with such a heavy mulch.

To start currants (red, white, and black) and gooseberries, look for old bushes that have been neglected. When this type of berry bush is not pruned properly, the larger, outside branches lower themselves to the ground. Whenever a branch is in contact with the ground for a couple of years, roots develop. It is simple to check all the lower branches on the perimeter of a currant or gooseberry bush and then to cut off and dig up any branch with roots. You can also layer off branches intentionally to touch the ground. The next step is to prepare a place for the bush the same way as for a raspberry or blackberry bush. I put ours at least five feet apart. They do not have to be planted in rows and will grow almost anywhere. They need light, water, and nutrients. Nutrients can be supplied the same way as for raspberries.

Pruning of currants and gooseberries consists mainly of replacing old wood and young thin canes that crowd the bush. Currants and gooseberries start to bear on two-year-old wood, but as the branches become older and more gnarled, they become less productive. I try to keep the bush open to allow light and air in. Without adequate light, the berries do not ripen well. Both heat from the sun and air circulation help dry the berries after a heavy dew or rain, preventing the development of fungi on both the leaves and the berries.

Strawberries are best started in the spring. It is a good practice, however, to start planning in the late summer. Strawberries produce runners on the end of which new plants

grow. As soon as the new plant looks like a plant, roots begin to enter the soil. When a basic root system was developed on the new plant, I cut the runner that connects this plant with the parent plant. This way the new plant does not depend on the parent plant any more but rapidly develops its own root system. All that needs to be done in the spring is to dig the plant up and transplant it into a bed of its own. We thin the plants in the spring so that they are 10–12″ apart in the bed. Since the older plants tend to be less productive after a few years, we thin out the older ones and try to keep the second-year plants. We pluck the blossoms off the first-year plants to give the plants a chance to develop. Some people just prefer to have alternate beds.

J. B.

TIPS FOR GROWING CORN

I poked early hybrid corn seed (unsoaked) about the end of May and transplanted the seedlings when they were about five inches tall, "puddling" each of them with a cup of fish emulsion fertilizer. The rest of the corn seed I planted directly into the garden—several rows, one week apart until the end of June. During this period it really rained, and later on we did far too much overhead sprinkling. The hotbed corn received just the minimum amount of water necessary during its sprouting stage and seemed to withstand the rain and sprinkling and thus was the *only* row this year to produce ears! The other rows were overrun with suckers and produced nothing. The hotbed corn was also the only row to receive a good mulch of hay and pulverized goat manure raked up from the goats' favorite trail. Next year I think I'll start all the corn in the hot bed—anything to foil the weather!

If you plant your corn in a rainy period, it might just be too much for the corn. You can protect the corn from the rain by making canopies with wire hoops and plastic.

M. C.

CREATING NO-DIG GARDEN SOIL

Another project with which I am involved is no-dig gardening. Initially the grass sod is well irrigated, then chicken manure or blood meal is applied lightly to provide nitrogen in order to rot the sod, and the whole is covered with a thick mulch of rotten straw or preferably rotten alfalfa hay (bales can be soaked six weeks before). The whole is then well irrigated to settle the mulch, and a light sprinkling of wood soot is spread on the surface to blacken it and thereby absorb more of the sun's heat rays and stimulate bacterial action as well as providing minerals, particularly potassium. Next spring, I will part the mulch to allow the soil to warm up, then dribble dark-colored compost in the rows before planting. The seaweed-soaked seeds are then planted in the compost strip to their proper depth. Mushrooms might grow well in the mulch also.

Yet another project involves the transplanting of kale, mangels, parsley, celery, and some herbs into holes where the sods are removed and the earth pounded out of the sods back into the holes. This procedure is done to retain the organic humus but not the raw organic matter (which will end up as compost) and also to retain the useful bacterialike nitrogen-fixers and mycorrhizal fungi that feed the plants. I use a little blood meal and bonemeal and seaweed in the holes (1:2:2 ratio) before planting and a foliar spray of seaweed on the leaves of the plants as they are transplanted. The whole is mulched, wood soot is applied, and watering is done not more than once a week, giving plants a good soaking each time. Cold frames will be placed over some of the plants later in the season. Manure tea will be prepared with herbs and used occasionally, as will additional seaweed sprays.

E. S.

REUSING KITCHEN WATER

In reply to your earlier question about what to do with kitchen waste water, a friend uses the following system with enormous success: Water flows into a dry well or sump that is designed to drain slowly. (Theirs is in sandy clay. In rocky or well-drained ground, you could line the sides of a dry well with unmortared brick, closely packed rock, or a cedar box of 2×6s with holes drilled in the sides.) An overflow pipe takes water from the dry well into the compost pit and keeps it well watered. The runoff from the compost seeps into my friend's cucumbers and raspberries, and you can imagine the results! These instructions presuppose that your house is located uphill from your garden.

Theoretically, you could water and fertil-

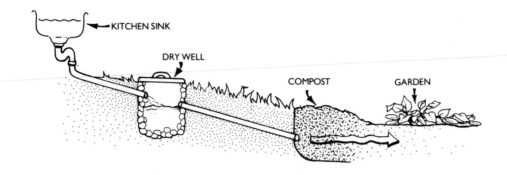

ize those plants that detest overhead sprinkling but need plenty of moisture by setting up a series of small ditches and dams and turning on the kitchen faucet.

M. C.

EASY SLUG CURE

To get rid of slugs in the garden, try putting a board down at night where they are likely to be, and in the morning they should be clinging to the board and can be removed. This past summer, we didn't have any bug problems in the garden. We mulched, used companion planting, and planted herbs around the garden. Maybe that will help too.

C. D.

COFFEE GROUND SLUG REPELLENT

If you're into coffee at all, I have found that a healthy mulch of used grounds keeps slugs

away entirely. The other thing I do is to leave a sampling of "weeds" because, after all, that's what they eat normally. Good luck.

J. D.

GARDEN PLANTING HINTS

When you are planting in rows in the vegetable garden, care should be taken to alternate the strong feeders—the cabbages, cauliflowers, cucumbers, celery, and spinach—with the plants that take little from the soil—the leguminous plants, carrots, beetroots, radishes, and onions. This is rather important, as the greedy feeders will gradually rob the soil of its nutrients if they are planted in the same position each year.

It is also advisable to plant the higher-growing peas and beans and so on around the lower-growing plants—say, several rows of beet together. This ensures protection against wind and frost, provides shade, and gives protection against drought. The *Helichrysum* plant has a great attraction for butterflies, and for those who wish to attract these insects to their gardens, a few plants of this half-hardy annual will be a magnet.

Sunflowers are heavy feeders and require a generous amount of compost. In return they provide a great deal of potash, but the stalks are rather hard to compost. A mulch of oak leaves round the plants is said to keep slugs away.

Nasturtiums have many uses in the kitchen garden. Planted near broccoli they will keep the plants free from aphids, and under apple trees they will repel the woolly aphid. They have even been tried among potatoes with beneficial effect. Plant leeks near carrots and the carrot fly should not strike so severely—if at all.

B. T.

PLANTING FOR THE BIRDS

As we have developed our one-acre organic garden over the past four years, we have discovered a great deal of pleasure not only in planning it from an overall aesthetic standpoint but also in planning it to provide a small haven for birds and other wildlife. If you are developing a new property, or even if you are renovating an established garden, you might enjoy the additional challenge of making it as attractive as possible from a bird's point of view!

In addition to being as vital a part of the beauty of our garden as the shrubbery and flowers, these small friends are constantly busy performing a most valuable insect-control service. Even the much-maligned starling is welcomed here, since we realized that during the nesting season it feeds almost exclusively on those pesky leatherjackets!

When we select a tree or shrub, we ask ourselves whether it provides one or more of the following: (a) food for the birds (we look for a variety to provide food during all seasons), (b) protective cover (from winter winds and predators), (c) nesting sites.

The accompanying chart will give you some idea of the plants that will provide these services, and most of the plants listed are very attractive to people as well as to birds. As a further guide, you can observe the native plants used by the birds in your area and try to incorporate some into your landscape plans.

It is as well not to be too tidy in your gardening. An absolutely immaculate garden is not the most attractive to a bird's eye. Let some of your flowers and vegetables go to seed. You will be amazed how these seeds disappear during the winter months. The marigolds that you use for companion planting in the vegetable garden produce quantities of seed enjoyed by the finches and juncos. And it is astonishing how many seeds one small radish can produce! Don't forget to plant giant sunflowers in a corner too—you can never plant enough of these.

If space allows, you might be interested in establishing a "thicket" area or woodland—a project we have embarked upon now that we have completed our basic landscaping of shrubbery borders, hedgerows, flower beds, vegetable garden, and so on. Our woodland will eventually be about 100 feet by 75 feet, but even if you have only a limited space, a densely planted corner along your fence line can be a welcome addition. At the rear (north) of our woodland we have planted a mixture of 20 native cedars and 20 alders, which should develop into a very dense area eventually. Five pin oaks will form the backbone of the rest of the area (spaced 25 to 30 feet apart), and between these we have an assortment of smaller trees, such as dogwood (which has to be the perfect tree!), birch, vine maple, wild cherry, and elderberry. Since underbrush is every bit as important to birds as are the larger trees, we are establishing ground covers of snowberry, honeysuckle, and mugho pine. As the shade becomes more dense, we plan to incorporate rhododendrons, lily of the valley shrub, ground dogwood, and ivy (all of which we are starting from cuttings). Along one side is an arborvitae hedge, and on the other side we plan to group several Scotch pines to serve as a windbreak and shelter. Along the border to the east in a sunny spot, we have planted about 60 feet of multiflora rose hedge (grown from seed and in less than two years already 5 feet high and 5 feet wide—an excellent source of food and protective cover; we might even manage to save some of the vitamin C–rich rose hips for ourselves). We estimate that in six to eight years our woodland will have become well established, and we look forward to strolls along our own tiny wooded pathways.

As well as planting for the birds, there are, of course, other ways of attracting them to your property. Providing water is very important. We have two shallow concrete baths that we made ourselves, one on a brick pedestal, and the other set into the ground— both in open lawn area. Fresh, clean water is as important as food, both in summer and in winter, so it is necessary to keep the baths well scrubbed and filled at all times. In the winter some ice chipping may be required, but some open water should be provided in the cold weather.

Feeding the birds can become a major project in itself and one that can provide a great deal of pleasure—especially through the bleak winter months. The point that can't be stressed enough, however, is that if you begin a feeding program during the winter, don't neglect it, even for a day. The birds do become dependent upon your feeder as a source of food, and in cold weather they may not be able to locate an alternative source of food quickly enough to survive. We use a mixture of equal parts of wild birdseed mix, chick scratch, yellow millet, and sunflower seeds. Pieces of suet hung in trees are very popular with downy woodpeckers, juncos, and chickadees. A special treat and a nutritious one for colder days is a "pudding" of melted suet, ground peanuts, and yellow millet. This can be packed into molds and when set turned out into feeding trays. A few raw peanut halves are a special treat for the chickadees, who can hardly wait to dash off with them the minute they are set out each morning.

An ideal spot for a feeder is on a 5-foot post in a location sheltered from the wind but at least 10 feet from any low shrubbery in which a lurking cat might hide. A grouping of evergreen trees not too far distant will provide a spot birds can fly to quickly for protective cover.

I have some precautions to suggest regarding feeding: (1) Go easy on bread (particularly white bread). It will tend to fill the birds but will not provide the nutrients they require. (2) Avoid the use of metal on your feeders. In freezing weather, there is the danger that their moist eyeballs may come into contact with the metal and adhere to it. (3) Avoid painting the inside of feeders (paint chips can be toxic). (4) Wash your feeders frequently. (5) Worried about cats and birds? Our cats wear ¾″ bells on their stretch collars, and this seems to provide quite good warning. In addition, we have booby-trapped a few spots where they tend to hide. Along our hedgerows we have strung a couple of rows of garden twine a few inches above the ground to serve as an inconspicuous trip-cord for pouncing cats. It throws off their aim rather nicely! We also have fenced off and made cat-proof a sanctuary at the end of our house, using six-foot grape stake fencing—a lovely private sitting area in the summer and an excellent spot for feeders in the winter. (6) One last precaution—but not the least. Please keep in mind that birds and pesticides are not compatible. It hardly seems fair to attract birds on the one hand and then endanger their lives with pesticides on the other.

As you can see, birds in your garden can become a very major pastime—and a most rewarding one as well.

S. D.

SOME TREES & SHRUBS ESPECIALLY ATTRACTIVE TO LOCAL BIRDS

Species	Food Source	Nesting	Cover
Trees			
Alder	Excellent	Some	Fair in mass plantings
Arborvitae	Good	Excellent	Excellent
Birch	Good	Good	Some
Cedars or junipers	Good	Good	Good
Wild cherries	Excellent	Some	Little
Cornelian cherry	Good	Good	Good
Flowering crab	Good	Good	Good
Dogwood	Excellent	Excellent	Excellent
Fir	Good	Good	Good
Hawthorn	Good	Good	Good
Hemlock	Good	Excellent	Good
Holly	Excellent	Excellent	Excellent
Mountain ash	Excellent	Fair	Fair
Norway spruce	Good	Good	Excellent
Oak	Excellent	Good	Fair
Pine	Excellent	Excellent	Excellent
Russian olive	Excellent	Good	Good in hedge form
Serviceberry	Good	Fair	Fair
Spruce	Good	Excellent	Excellent
Maples	Good	Good	Some

Species	Food Source	Nesting	Cover
Shrubs			
Arrowood	Good	Good	Good
Wild blackberry	Good	Good	Good
Black haw	Good	Good	Good
Highbush blueberry	Excellent	Some	Fair
Buckthorn	Good	Good	Good
Highbush cranberry	Good	Good	Good
Elderberry	Excellent	Some	Good in mass plantings
Japanese barberry	Good	Excellent	Excellent
Mapleleaf viburnum	Good	Good	Some
Multiflora rose	Good	Good	Excellent
Siebold viburnum	Good	Fair	Fair
Snowberry	Good	— —	Good in mass plantings
Tatarian honeysuckle	Excellent	Good	Good
Zabelli honeysuckle	Excellent	Good	Good
Vines			
Bittersweet	Good	— —	— —
Hall's honeysuckle	Good	Good	Good
Matrimony vine	Good	Good	Good
Virginia creeper	Excellent	Good	Good

B. T.

 MAPLE SUGAR IN B.C.

One day my friend Ralph was reading an old pioneer book when he came across a reference to Indians who traded maple sugar at a trading post in Kamloops, B.C. His curiosity aroused, he read on. The book explained that the Indians cut a *V* in the trunk of a maple tree on a sunny day, just after a cold spell. The sap that had been drawn up the tree by the sun on its bark would come back down through capillary action and gravitational force and would pour down the *V.* After collecting the sap in a container, the Indians would pour the sap into a hollow log. Then they placed red-hot stones from a nearby fire in the log until the water from the sap evaporated, leaving a thick syrup. The syrup was allowed to cool until it hardened into blocks. The resulting maple sugar had a flavoring of bark, twigs, dirt, ashes, and leaves—but it was apparently good enough for there to be a demand at the trading post.

Ralph had a good number of broad-leaved maple and vine maple on his property, but the book said the maples out West and particularly down near the coast were not suitable for sugaring. Undaunted, he thought he would give it a try. He found that under favorable conditions, he would get about a gallon of sap a day from a tree six inches in diameter, and further, that it took about 12 gallons of sap from a broad-leaved maple and 15 gallons of sap from a vine maple to make a pound of sugar. If he went out and tapped 100 trees in one day, by the time he'd tapped the hundredth tree, it was time to collect the sap from the first tree tapped.

For those interested, Ralph recommends that you first locate and identify your maple trees. The best producer appears to be the broad-leaved maple (also known as bigleaf maple, Oregon maple, or B.C. maple), *Acer macrophyllum*. Douglas maple (also known as dwarf or Rocky Mountain maple), *Acer glabrum* var. *douglasii*, also produces good maple sugar. So does the vine maple, *Acer circinatum*, though it is not quite as sweet. For reference, refer to *Trees, Shrubs and Flowers to Know in British Columbia* by C. P. Lyons (J. M. Dent and Sons, 1973), or *Native Trees of Canada* by R. C. Hosie (Fitzhenry and Whiteside Ltd., 1979).

Equipment
- taps: ½" copper water pipe, 8" long
- rubber hammer to bang in tap without clanging
- 2-gal. plastic bags to collect 1 gal. sap each
- wire or twisters to secure bag to tap
- ⅝" drill to drill initial hole 2½" deep
- evaporator: wood stove with large pot
- cotton cloth for straining: 3 thicknesses; can be pillow slips, sheets
- a container, 5-gal. or more, to collect the sap from the bags
- a pair of clippers to cut plugs for old holes
- candy thermometer from hardware store

Time of Year
According to Ralph, the sap in the trees starts to run in the Lower Mainland around the first sunny day in February or as the weather warms after a cold spell. If there's no sun by February 15, put your taps in and just watch until it starts to run. The light-colored syrup is the best. Early or late in the season the syrup is darker and apparently of lower quality. This syrup is used in chewing tobacco and not maple sugar.

Procedure
1. Drill a hole 2½" deep, near the bottom of the trunk and on the sunny side of the tree. The exact location depends on the bags you are using to collect the sap. You want the bag to rest on the ground when full so that it will not pull off the pipe.
2. Drive ½" copper water pipe halfway into the hole with the rubber hammer. Be sure to drive it in straight.
3. Attach your 2-gal. plastic bags to the pipe with wire. The sap should be able to run directly down the pipe and into the bag without exposure, thus avoiding fruit fly contamination in areas where temperatures aren't below freezing. That's why buckets can't be used in the Lower Mainland.
4. If you're tapping a tree with a 2' diameter, you can insert up to four taps, but make sure they are all in a row on the sunny side of the tree. Be cautious here; it is better not to overtap your tree.
5. If the trees stop running, leave them for a week. When the weather changes again, they will continue to run. If they don't run again by the end of the week, plug the hole up by cutting a small plug from a nearby

vine maple or other tree and tap it into the hole. Ralph uses a 2″ vine maple plug, which he says prevents the bugs from getting in and helps the tree to heal quickly; it is analogous to stopping the blood after cutting yourself with a razor.

6. Once a day, take your 5-gal. milk can or canner and go around collecting the sap. Take it to a location near your evaporator and strain it through three thicknesses of cotton. Do not use cheesecloth, because its holes are too large. Strain the sap into the container you intend to use in the evaporating process.

7. Bring the sap to a boil and skim off the foam, which contains the impurities. Continue boiling until the mixture thickens. (If you are doing this in the house, you'll find it smells the house up with sugar and coats your hair, etc.)

8. Strain the thick syrup again and then boil, using a candy thermometer. Boil until the temperature reaches hard boil, or 260°F. Be very careful to avoid boiling over and burning. Alternatively, drop syrup into cold water until it forms a hard ball.

9. Remove from the stove and whip with a wooden spoon as it is cooling until it sugars (looks like homemade fudge).

10. Let it set— in whatever shape or size of mold you wish, so long as it has been buttered to avoid sticking. Also score the sugar, for an hour later you'll need a hammer to break it. Ralph says it's advisable to make sugar from syrup because syrup molds if it is not canned. It's simple enough to get the sugar back to syrup by simply adding hot water in a ratio of about 2 cups of water to 1 cup of sugar. The sugar should be stored in a dry place. Finally, tap in a different area of the tree

from year to year, ensuring that you've plugged your old holes. The old hole will by this time be dead hardwood. Apparently, this process does not harm the tree, because the average tree produces approximately two tons of sap a season and your plug prevents insect damage and promotes early healing. If you are lucky, you'll run into two or three days of good weather and end up with a good supply of homegrown maple sugar.

F. F.

TAPPING AND MAKING BIRCH SYRUP

We thought you might be interested in our experiences with making birch syrup. We made it at the end of March, before the leaves came on the trees.

First, we found two good-sized trees (12–14″ in diameter) and drilled a ¾″ hole in them about 3' from the ground and 2" deep, on the sunny side of the tree. Then we cut a 6" piece of ¾" pipe and tapped it in with a hammer. We hung a five-quart bucket on the pipe, but it would be better if you used a larger size, because our buckets overflowed at night. We checked them morning and night, dumping the full buckets into a big enamel pot.

It is best if you boil the sap over a wood stove, because it takes about 7 hours and then you wouldn't use up all that electricity. Also, it would be good to do it outside, because the steam is sticky and there's lots of it. We stopped when it coated a spoon and was a deep amber color. Our syrup was fairly thin, but it went further. The proportion of sap to syrup was, for us, about 40 to 1. We used a bit over 20 gallons of sap to produce half a gallon of syrup.

If you are expecting the syrup to taste like maple syrup, you will probably be disappointed, because it has a very strong flavor all its own. For those of you who have tasted sorghum syrup, someone told us it had an undertaste very much like it. Be sure and plug up the hole when you remove the pipe to keep from harming the tree.

R. V., J. T., P. T., G. Q., J. Q.

ORGANIC SPRAY INSECTICIDE

20 cloves of garlic, peeled
1 onion, chopped
1 qt. water

Blend ingredients for one minute and strain through cheesecloth. Add 1 Tbsp. of non-detergent liquid soap and 4 Tbsp. of glycerine to 1 gal. of water. Mix together thor-

oughly. Useful for mosquitoes, bugs, flies, slugs, and worms.

B. T.

KICKING THE PESTICIDE HABIT

There is something basically wrong with our modern use of chemicals to kill weeds. Weeds are a symptom of a problem, not the problem itself. The real problem is in the quality of the soil. Soil that is compacted and has the topsoil removed, such as the soil at dam sites and clear-cut logging sites, is going to be more vulnerable to weeds. Weeds are the first step to bringing land back to a healthy state. Some of them add nitrogen to the soil. Some have long roots that bring nutrients from down deep up into the higher levels of soil. The roots break up the soil, aerate it, and improve its structure. Weed roots are attractive to earthworms and allow them to penetrate to lower depths in the soil. Weeds hold soil in place and protect the land from erosion.

Using chemicals destroys the microbial life in the soil. Microbes are important in the breaking down of the fiber in the soil; without them there is no humus formation and nothing to support plant life. When a chemical is applied to an area, the weeds go away; but when the chemical wears off, new weed seeds will take root in the poor soil, and chemical application is needed again, sterilizing the soil even further.

The long-range management of weeds is to improve the soil. This can be done by using cover crops or by directly adding organic matter. A stable community of suitable vegetation can be encouraged to keep out undesirable plants.

It is interesting to note the similarity between the word "humans" and the word "humus"; perhaps we are more connected to the quality of our soil than we realize.

How to Kick the Pesticide Habit in Your Garden

In the transition period from weaning your garden from insecticides, pest damage will become more noticeable until the natural balance is restored. If you are patient, natural controls will conquer the problem. Some things to do while you are waiting:

- Eliminate persistent pest-problem plants from your garden.
- Learn to recognize natural predators and encourage their presence.
- Learn organic control methods.

Some Easy Alternatives for Common Pests

Onion Maggots: They are most attracted to white onions. If you have a problem, try the more resistant yellow and red onions. Reduce damage by setting out transplants after mid-May. Add a little wood ash to the soil. Rotate onions yearly and keep the garden clean.

Earwigs: These are not generally a problem. They can chew holes in leaves of lettuce, beets, and carrots and live in the husks of corn, but usually they are beneficial in that they feed on decaying plant matter, insect larvae, aphids and slow-moving bugs. If they are a problem, they are easily caught inside shady shelters like rolled-up newspapers.

Cabbageworms: All are larval stages of moths and butterflies. A spray of soapy, garlicy water will bring them out of hiding so they can be handpicked. Rotenone and pyrethrum are effective against them, but the best of biological poisons is *Bacillus thuringiensis,* sprayed weekly. Companion planting, with rosemary, sage, thyme, and nasturtium, will help. Alternatives do exist, but funding has to be provided to develop them. All of us can encourage our government officials to support alternatives to pesticides.

Compost

We can go to any dump and see an abundance of organic matter that if separated from the glass and metal could be used to increase the humus in our soil and decrease the amount of money we have to spend on waste disposal. Japan has an incredible recycling system that we could learn from and expand on. We need help from government agencies to use this wasted resource.

Composting in Your Backyard

Save kitchen scraps, grass clippings, leaves, and weeds pulled from your garden. Put them into a 45-gallon drum painted black, add some soil (soil microorganisms are needed to start the composting process), add some water, and turn the drum every few days. In the heat of the summer, you will have rich compost for your garden in less than a month.

B. T.

ALL ABOUT NETTLES

While you are planning your garden so that you can eat fresh, organic natural foods, why not also think of the foods that God has naturally planted around us? Many plants are very useful, nutritious, and free for the gathering.

Stinging nettles are considered by many, including me, to be of the greatest value to

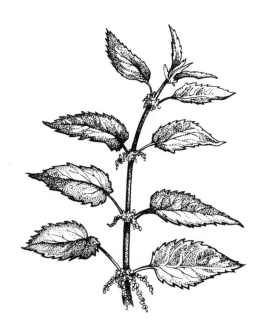

days. The mature stem of the branch can be broken and the juices rubbed on the itch. This mysteriously stops the irritation. If you are able to recognize dock, you can bruise the leaves of this plant and rub the juice into the nettle itch. The sheath on fiddleheads can also be used. These two plants are often found fairly close to nettles.

It is wise to wear gloves or use the thick leaves of mullein when gathering nettles. I was recently told that once the plant is up-rooted it no longer stings. I have not had a chance to find out whether this is true, but then it isn't necessary to kill the plant to gather the leaves.

In the spring the young shoots make a very good pot herb, but as summer comes, all but the young leaves get too tough to eat. There are some people who pinch the tops and eat them raw; supposedly they have little or no sting. The greens are normally steamed two or three minutes. Nettles are one of the tastiest wild greens and possibly the richest nutritionally.

Nettles are rich in protein. The greens contain large amounts of vitamin C. They are also a good source of vitamins A and D. Not many plants contain vitamin D. They also contain a lot of blood-enriching chlorophyll and minerals—phosphorus and iron in quite large quantities, with smaller amounts of so-dium, potassium, calcium, and silica.

The roots can be forced in the cellar through winter for continuous shoots. Extra greens can be canned or dried. Nettles can also be used for chicken and cattle feed. The seeds mixed in with the animal's fodder add shine to the animal's coat. When the whole plant is dried and ripened in the hay, it makes a valuable protein food for livestock, rivaling other meals. Ground leaves mixed in

humans, since they are found in many areas all over North America and Europe. Nettles are usually found on the edge of moist, shaded areas, as well as along roadsides and in waste areas. Their presence often signifies fertile soils.

Many people are familiar with the appear-ance of nettles because they have been stung by them and so look at them carefully to avoid them in the future. For those who are not familiar with the plant, here is a brief description: The plant ranges from one foot to four or five feet tall. It has an erect stalk with oval-oblong leaves in pairs opposite each other. The leaves are coarsely toothed and come to a point. Later in the season, flowers of light green appear, hanging in clusters from the axil of the opposite leaves. Fine hairs cover the leafstalks, stems, and undersides of leaves. These hairs exude the stinging formic acid.

If left alone, the sting will go away in an hour or so. If irritated, the sting may last for with chicken feed keep the birds healthy and free from disease.

Nettles are also extremely good to use as a mulch or fertilizer. When fully grown, they should be gathered, dried, and ground, then spread over the garden. If nettles are soaked in water for a week, the strained liquid can be used as an insect repellent, which is especially good for aphids in the cabbage and broccoli.

In Scotland, the nettle plant was once used just the same as flax was for linens. The fibers are very strong and can be twisted to make twine. Paper can also be made from the stock fibers. In Europe nettle beer is quite popular. An infusion of nettle leaves relieves not only the itch from the plant itself but also other itches and hives. A tea made from the leaves also has medicinal qualities. It is good for worms, diarrhea, dysentery, piles, inflammation of the kidneys, phlegm, fever, colds, and la grippe. The tea is also used as a hair tonic. Boiled leaves applied externally will stop hemorrhaging. A substitute for rennet can be made by boiling the leaves to make a very strong tea, which is then mixed with salt (two parts salt to three parts tea). A tea can also be made from the roots. A yellow dye can be made by boiling the roots.

Now that you know, can you turn away from the nettle the next time you see it?

G. B.

 ### IN PLACE OF POISONS 1

The gardener who does not wish to risk poisoning the birds he feeds in winter, or building up a dangerous dose of any of the cumulative poisons in his baby's body fat, has no need to gamble that the famous scientists who warn against chemicals are wrong and those who sell modern pesticides and belittle their dangers are right. He can change over to safer and often cheaper methods, which may be more trouble, just as shelling peas may be harder work than opening tins, but they stop pollution by pesticide at his garden gate.

Safe General Pesticides

Any good garden shop should sell derris and pyrethrum. There are many makes of both, and mixtures of the two are stronger than either separately, capable of killing caterpillars and a range of pests, including aphids of all types, listed on the tin or bottle. They are sometimes mixed with lindane and other organo-chlorine compounds, and these should be refused. Derris is available as a dust that is most effective against the flea beetle, which eats holes in the leaves of brassica plants and radishes. Since it began as a Malay fish poison, do not let it trickle into the goldfish pond. If you keep bees and have to spray anything on flowers, use pyrethrum in the evening and it will have killed your aphids and be harmless by the time your bees start work in the morning.

Quassia — The Safest Pesticide

Quassia has the advantages of cheapness, not killing ladybirds (ladybugs) that are eating your aphids, and sparing bees when sprayed against apple sawfly or raspberry beetle caterpillars at blossom time. Chips of the wood of *Picrasma quassioides* keep dry for years in a tin and can only be ordered through a good pharmacist, because it is still used by district nurses to kill nits in children's hair. Boil four ounces in a gallon of water for two hours, pour off the yellow liquid when cool, and dilute with five parts of water for an all-round garden spray for aphids and small caterpillars. A 1:3 mixture will kill gooseberry sawfly caterpillars that can strip the leaves from a bush in four days.

Homemade Pesticides — Nicotine

The cheapest powerful pesticide is nicotine, which is now difficult to buy, but it is easily made by boiling four ounces of non-filter-tip cigarettes (or a half pound of filter tips) in a gallon of water for half an hour. Strain the clear brown liquid through a nylon stocking, and it will keep several weeks in a stoppered bottle. Dilute with four parts of water to one of nicotine for an anticaterpillar spray or for anything hard to kill.

Water it along rows of young peas and beans when their leaves are eaten out of shape by the pea and bean weevil, a tiny, clay-colored beetle that hides under clods, so you rarely see it. Mix a quart of the solution with one ounce of soft soap or soap flakes and spray on spring cabbage plants, broccoli, and late Brussels sprouts in the autumn to kill mealy cabbage aphids, cabbage whitefly, and cabbage moth caterpillars before they burrow in the hearts. This strength kills celery and chrysanthemum leaf miners.

If you have a euonymus hedge, syringe it thoroughly with nicotine in November to kill the hibernating caterpillars of the small ermine moth that are the curse of these hedges, and the winter stage of the black fly on broad beans. These also winter on viburnums (all species), and if everyone sprayed these we might wipe out this pest. Squirt nicotine hard into the gnarled bark at the base of old rose bushes in November because it is here that greenfly hibernate.

Nonsmokers can obtain ashtray emptyings from cinemas and public houses, and the best way to keep free nicotine is as cigarette ends

in a tin. Do not spray it on anything you are going to eat within a fortnight, so the rain can wash it off, and label any that is already boiled "POISON." It breaks down quickly in the soil, unlike DDT and other organo-chlorine compounds, which are permanent pollutions, for "organo" does not mean "organic," like derris, but synthetic copies of molecules that natural agents like bacteria cannot take apart. Although nicotine costs nothing when made from boiled cigarette ends and is powerful, keep it for weevils, large caterpillars, and anything tough, wash your hands after using, and remember, it is a poison.

Homemade Pesticides for Aphids

For greenfly on roses use something weaker. Cut up three pounds of rhubarb leaves, boil for half an hour in three quarts of water, and strain. When cool, dissolve one ounce of soap flakes in a quart of water, mix the two, and use as a general spray for any aphid. It can also be made with three pounds of elder leaves; this mixture was used in the past as a spray for mildew on roses.

L. H.

IN PLACE OF POISONS 2

The Safe Fungicides

A great many plant "diseases" are not virus attacks but deficiency symptoms, and many organic gardeners who regard compost as a cure-all are merely gaining from giving their crops a better-balanced diet. Most gardens have only one bed sunny enough for outdoor tomatoes, and this bed gets wood ashes or sulfate of potash so often that the excess potassium locks up the magnesium, producing the familiar yellowing lower leaves in which the veins stay green. Organic gardeners who use only fish meal can have the same trouble, for too much phosphorus also puts magnesium out of the reach of roots. So does overliming, so this yellowing is common in chalky gardens.

To return leaves to normal, dissolve two ounces of Epsom salts (magnesium sulfate) in a two-gallon can and water on a square yard. Magnolias and other lime-hating shrubs can be "cured" of yellowing leaves by Epsom salt waterings, which locks up the lime they dislike. Before you dig up and burn any expensive shrub believing it has a virus, water with Epsom salts, for it may only be short of magnesium and good for many years yet.

Bordeaux Mixture

This is still the best and safest preventative for potato blight in potatoes and tomatoes, to be sprayed on every fortnight from mid-June till the end of September, especially in cool, wet summers. Most gardeners gamble on missing it, and there are resistant potato varieties, but no tomato other than the tiny "red currant" varieties is resistant. It can still be bought ready to mix and should be used according to the directions on the tin.

Burgundy Mixture

Always make this fresh by dissolving three ounces of copper sulfate in a gallon of water in a plastic bucket (copper sulfate reacts with zinc, so plastic is also best for Bordeaux Mixture—this is why syringes are brass) and leave overnight to cool and finish dissolving. Stir four ounces of washing soda into a gallon of cold water, mix the two, and spray, but never on anything with leaves. Protect near evergreens with polythene.

This is an excellent scab killer for apples and pears. Its great advantage over lime sulfur is that many varieties are "sulfur shy," and if you do not know what your trees are, you are safe with Burgundy Mixture. Spray it on gooseberries for mildew spores in January, on peaches for leaf curl and leaf blister in February or March just as the blossom buds begin to swell, and on roses for mildew spores in December and January. It has another great advantage over lime-sulfur in sparing *Anthocoris nemorum*, one of our best and most versatile pest eaters, so by giving up winter tar oil washes and using Burgundy Mixture instead, you are killing no friends.

Lime-Sulfur

This can be bought ready-made and used according to the directions on the tin, but read carefully to see that it has no expensive and deadly addition. Although it can be used against rose mildew at 1 part to 60, its most valuable use is sprayed on black currants at the rate of 1 pint to 2½ gallons when the first leaves are the size of shillings, to catch the big bud mite that is spreading then. Pick off and burn all big buds, which are quite distinctive, not only because the mites weaken the bush but also because they carry Reversion—a genuine virus.

Solutions for Specific Pests and Diseases

Only a few can be given, and many more will be found in our booklet *Pest Control without Poison*, but we are constantly searching for new ways round pest and disease problems, ideally those that do not even involve safe sprays, for all spraying is hard work, and even the safest can kill the predators that we are finding out how to help. Details with illustrations of these garden friends will be found in our booklet *Biological Pest Control Report No. 3*.

American Blight (Woolly Aphid)

Paint the patches with a mixture of two parts

paraffin to one of creosote, or with the petrol and oil mixture sold for two-stroke engines.

Ants

Mix equal parts icing sugar and powdered borax very thoroughly and sprinkle where the ants are. If this is in the open, sprinkle on a piece of slate and prop another piece over it to keep the rain off. This nonpoisonous method is very effective indoors and is also excellent against cockroaches. Excess boron is toxic in the soil, but millions of antfuls of boron well scattered do no harm.

Apple Aphids (or Black Aphids)

Summer-prune apples and pears by removing a quarter of the length of the leading shoots in July, and the side shoots after the second leaf, not counting the little ones around the base, and prune as normal in winter. This slows down the growth by reducing leaf area and leaves no soft shoot tips for the aphids to attack. There is no need to summer-prune every year, but summer-pruning and stuffing the tips in the dustbin or burning them gets rid of even the worst attack.

Black Spot on Roses

Spray with Burgundy Mixture in November, gather up and burn fallen leaves, and spray again in February. A mulch of peat, Pompost (composted cider waste) or lawn mowings in April will prevent the rain from splashing the old spores onto new leaves.

Cabbage Caterpillars

Use nicotine up to a month before eating the cabbage, but after that use derris, or stir four ounces of common salt into a two-gallon can of water and apply with the hose. Squirt the nicotine well under the leaves, especially for cabbage aphids.

Cabbage Root Fly

Cut six-inch squares of tarred roofing felt and punch or snip holes in their middles. Push the root of your plant through the hole before planting so that the "collar" sits on the surface. It is also possible to make a slit in from one side so that the felt can be fitted on after planting. The stem grows and fits the center hole tightly, and the fly cannot lay its eggs through the felt. This trick also beats the cutworms or surface caterpillars that eat through the stems, for they will not cross the tarred surface.

Carrot Fly

The traditional remedy is planting onion sets between the carrot rows because the flies hunt by scent. Sawdust or sand soaked in paraffin between the rows also keeps up the scent barrage. Masking the carrot scent only works at a distance—the flies that hatch in your garden use their eyes. Dig over the bed that was attacked, shallowly, two or three times in winter to give the robins and other birds a chance to snap up the tiny chrysalids.

Clubroot

There are many remedies, and none are completely effective. The clubroot fungus dislikes lime, and if you apply a dressing of three pounds a square yard in spring, then plant nothing of the cabbage tribe till the following spring, a small attack will often clear. A promising method still under investigation is to sow summer spinach in March or April and dig it in when it has bolted before planting the cabbage crop. This could lead to a cure.

Currant Aphid

This aphid crinkles the leaves awkwardly, so it is hard to reach by spraying. It migrates to nettles in summer and returns to winter on the black currants, ready to attack again in spring. Spray with nicotine in February or March before the bushes are in leaf to kill it sleeping.

Gooseberry Mildew

Spray with three ounces of washing soda and

one ounce of soap flakes in a gallon of hot water that has been allowed to cool before use. Burgundy Mixture in winter completes the cure, with safety for unknown varieties that may be sulfur-shy.

Mildew on Roses

Add one dessert spoon full of carbolic acid (which can still be bought at a good pharmacist's) to a gallon of cold water and stir in two ounces of soap flakes. A weaker mixture is to dissolve two ounces of the carbolic soap used for dogs in a gallon of water and let it cool before spraying. Burgundy Mixture in winter is the best remedy.

Millipedes and Wireworms

Trap these by bending perforated zinc round a broom handle and sewing the edges and the bottom together with wire to make a cylinder, or by punching the sides and bottom of a tall can full of holes. Fill either trap with potato or carrot peelings and bury upright in the border with a wire handle sticking out. Lift by this handle about once a week and dump the contents in strong nicotine or throw in the run to give the chickens a treat. This was the standard garden remedy 60 years ago, but you need enough traps to make an impression on the pests.

Moles

Removing moles from a garden is a problem best solved with a moped motor-mower with a two-stroke engine. Connect a hose to the exhaust pipe and lead it down a main runway, which can be found by digging through a large hill, ideally where the mole appears to have burrowed into your garden. Start the engine and run it slowly so that it goes pop-pop-pop and does not purr or drone, which is known as four-stroking. This produces most carbon monoxide gas and, if the two-stroke has petrol lubrication, adds a lasting smell of burnt oil, which will prevent the moles from using the burrows for hunting again. The carbon monoxide will kill any caught underground. Those who like moles will do this job in the dusk so they have a chance to break ground under cover of darkness and escape. A scrap radiator hose from a garage should first be fitted to the exhaust pipe as an adapter, because modern plastic hoses melt fast as they get hot.

L. H.

IN PLACE OF POISONS 3

Blackfly on Broad Beans

Sow your beans in November, and when the first blackfly appears on the tips, remove the top eight inches of stem. Blackfly can only start on soft new growth, and if you remove enough there will be only tough bark left. Failure with this old trick comes from leaving the stems too long.

Onion Fly

Stop growing onions from seed and grow them from sets, which dodge the fly completely. This is our perfect organic remedy.

Potato Blight

Plant a second crop early that will keep, so it will have grown most before the attack, like Duke of York. Grow a blight-resistant variety like Maris Page, Maris Peer, Pentland Dell, Pentland Beauty, or Ulster Ranger. These are worth searching catalogues to find, for they are not stocked by chain stores and garden centers.

Raspberry Beetle

Responsible for grubs in the fruit. Spray with derris 10 days after the first flowers open and again 10 days later. For blackberries and loganberries, spray 15 days after flowering and again 15 days later. This will kill bees, so beekeepers who will have most bees on the blossom should use quassia. The beetle pupates in the ground between the rows, so digging between them at October pruning time and again in winter gives the birds a chance to eat the chrysalids.

Scab

Although Burgundy Mixture is a good anti-scab spray, some 80 percent of the spores overwinter on dead leaves. Sweep up your dead leaves in the orchard and stack them for leaf mold—they decay quite safely with a year in the stack. If you have a large lawn and little time, let them lie till there are plenty and run a rotary mower, like a Hayter, over them. This will break them into fragments that the worms can take under easily, building up the humus under your lawn as well as feeding your spores to the worms. Even with ornamental trees and no scab to worry about, this saves wheeling leaves and helps the lawn.

Slugs

The best slug trap is a soup plate, dog drinking trough, or anything china, wide and shallow, sunk level with the ground, and filled with a mixture of equal parts of beer and water sweetened with a dessert spoon full of Barbados sugar to the pint. The trap can be cleared of dead slugs with one quick swish of a broom and refilled from a can of the mixture. One trap makes little impression—you need a dozen. Your local bar will provide a bucketful of beer from the contents of the drip tray for nothing, and this is quite good enough for slugs. The object of the beer instead of the milk often recommended is to stop cats from drinking it, and though hedgehogs may take it, modern beer diluted to half

strength is not enough to intoxicate them. The sugar makes the traps collect codling, tortrix, and yellow underwing moths, which are responsible for the cutworm or surface caterpillars. The dead slugs are not poisonous to birds or anything else that may eat them.

Wood lice

Wood lice in the open are little trouble, but they can be a problem in the greenhouse. Buy a bottle of cloudy ammonia, turn off the lights, and sprinkle it quickly on the floor—when the house is cleared of plants. This will gas the wood lice and a whole number of pests, as well as killing at least the surface growth of the weeds. Come out quickly; it is a powerful smell, but it soon clears off. It is the cheapest and least poisonous greenhouse fumigant.

Worms in Lawns

Chlordane worm killer (banned in some areas) kills worms, but it goes on giving a less than killing dose to worms that crawl in it for the next 15 years. When birds eat these worms, the chlordane accumulates in their bodies and concentrates in the fat of their eggs, which become infertile. Chlordane also penetrates the skin, so there is a risk for children playing on the lawn. Amateur gardeners have been made seriously ill by playing bowls on chlordane-treated greens and licking their fingers as they handled their "woods." This may be a tiny risk, but why take it? Why not let your worms alone? They are among the gardener's best friends.

If you must kill the friendly earthworm, at least kill it so that you do the least harm to wildlife and leave no poison in the soil for the next gardener in your house if you move while the chlordane is still in the soil. Dissolve one ounce of potassium permanganate in a gallon of water and water over a square yard of turf. The worms will come up quickly and can be swept up and dumped in the dustbin. This, like most of the remedies described here, is a great deal cheaper than the permanent poisons they replace.

Birds and Greenfly

The ideal way of getting rid of greenfly on roses is to thrust long bamboo canes slantways into the bed and hang fat from the tips to dangle about a foot above the bushes. While the birds are waiting for pecking and clinging room, they will clear the hibernating greenfly from the gnarled black bark round the bases of the roses. December and January are the best months for this treatment.

Ladybirds and Hoverflies

Using nicotine, either bought or made as directed earlier, spares ladybirds and their larvae, which are both aphid eaters, and hoverfly larvae, which are even more effective. Hoverflies (there are 270 species, 30 of which are aphid eaters) usually look like slim wasps, and when you see them poised in front of flowers on wings moving with invisible speed, they are hunting for aphid colonies to lay their eggs among. There are two generations a year, each averaging 140 eggs a female, and every larva eats about 600 aphids before it becomes adult.

The adults feed on pollen and nectar, not aphids, and because they have only short tongues like all flies, not long ones like bees or butterflies, they can only feed (as distinct from searching) from flowers with an easy way in. The two leading hoverfly attracters seem to be buckwheat and convolvulus tricolor. Sow a row of buckwheat in April three inches between the large seeds (they keep three years) next to your broad beans, or anywhere in the vegetable garden. The white flowers are good bee fodder, last well in water, and keep flowering till October. The convolvulus grows six inches high. It is an annual without the lasting white roots of its wicked uncle bindweed, and its deep blue saucer flowers with white and yellow centers are hoverflies' delight. Sow in April in half-inch-deep furrows six inches apart and thin to six-inch spacing. The thinnings will transplant. The best variety is the dark blue Royal Ensign. If you want to watch your hoverflies feeding, a sunny morning between 8:30 and 9:30 is best.

L. H.

This 3-part article comes from England. The booklets mentioned are published by the Henry Doubleday Research Association, 20 Convent Lane, Bocking, Braintree, Essex, England.

 SPRINKLING FOR FROST PROTECTION

To L. P. re sprinkling plants with water for frost protection: Yes, it does work very well. The more water you apply, the more protection the ice will give. We had nature do the job for us just last week when it rained very heavily in the evening. The next morning our truck windshield was white with frost and the temperature read a cool 27°F. This would definitely have been a killing frost, but not one of our plants was in the least bit damaged. Our plants include white shasta daisies, a clump of columbines still in bloom, as well as peas, broccoli, etc. In a research report available from Beaverlodge on the Experimental Farm, Mile 1019 Alaska Highway, it says under "Frost Protection with Sprinkler Irrigation":

- "0.047" water per hour protected to 26.3°F.
- "0.085" per hour protected to 22.3°F.
- "0.110" per hour and higher protected to 19.0°F.

S. W.

NEWSPAPER MULCH

A number of years ago when a correspondent of *Organic Farming & Gardening* raised this question, I called one of the senior staff chemists of International Pulp and Paper at Gatineau, Quebec, and asked him about the danger of poisoning the soil with newspaper mulch. He replied that the chemicals used would be harmless to both the vegetation and to the animal organisms in garden soil. On his advice, I used newspapers extensively as a mulch, and this year I have put down a couple of hundred pounds of the stuff. It has helped and is helping the cultivation of the garden and, I am sure, the quality of the produce.

I use newspapers between the rows of vegetables, where they keep the soil damp and weed-free and encourage the propagation of earthworms and countless other small organisms that contribute to the health of the soil. Newspapers, folded or spread out, fit neatly between rows of vegetables, at whatever distance apart you choose to plant them. Earthworms consume them, printer's ink and all (printer's ink is mostly carbon black, the essence of all organics), and you will find the

worms lying between separate sheets of paper after they find out how good it is. Underneath the papers you will also find the light, well-chewed soil that the worms have passed through their digestive systems, and this can be swept up for rich potting soil. As a bonus, if you want worms for fish bait, just go to the garden and roll back a few sheets of newsprint and you'll pick all you need right off the top of the soil.

Putting the newspapers and similar paper products on your garden is the ultimate in recycling, giving good forest products back to the earth that produced them.

N. S.

PLANTING ASPARAGUS

Once established, a well-planted bed of asparagus will yield tender, succulent stalks for at least 20 years. Having experienced planting of two such beds, and reading extensively on the subject, I hope this article may be of interest to some readers of *The Smallholder*. First, do not make the mistake (as I did) of planting the original bed right in the location my husband had chosen for putting a cement slab. Having to uproot and relocate meant a loss of another couple of years before harvesting could begin! Second, I learned it was a serious error to plant five rows, each three feet apart. Just try crawling about on hands and knees trying to weed among a growth of tender young shoots without breaking at least some of them off. Third, the original bed became infested with the weed horsetail. Underground roots from nearby growth of this pesky thing soon became almost impossible to cope with, as the roots intertwined with those of the asparagus.

Preparation of the ground for an asparagus bed should begin at least several months before the actual planting, as it is of the utmost importance that any weeds such as those described above be eradicated first. Then two long, deep trenches should be dug—two feet deep is about right. Fill with manure and rich soil up to about six or eight inches from the top. Let this mixture settle for some weeks—more can be added if the fill seems to be sinking too far down.

Where to obtain the necessary roots for planting can pose a problem; to just dig any old roots from around orchards is really not satisfactory, and it is usually difficult to find a nursery that handles roots for planting. Sometimes they are available for a short period in the spring; if they are imported, they will appear as a bundle of pretty dried-out "fingers" of rhubarb roots. They should be at least two years old.

If you succeed in finding the roots, put a few shovelfuls of sandy soil on top of the material in the trench and place each "crown" on top, making certain the "fingers" are well spread out in every direction. Press the roots down and put a few inches of soil on top, not filling the trench by any means. As the roots take hold and begin to send up shoots, the trench can be gradually filled in so that by the end of the growing season the top of it is flush with the ground level. Plants should be 18″ apart.

With any luck, the plants will send up shoots and then put out a crown of fernlike tops. This top growth will die down when frosty weather comes along. The following spring should see lots of shoots appearing; but don't touch! Let them grow and make

good-sized crowns first; then the following spring you can steal a few for a short period only (never cut past mid-June). As with rhubarb, if you pull all the stalks all summer, the plant will die.

Another way of starting an asparagus patch is to begin with seeds, which are readily available at any nursery or seed supplier. This is a rather long process, although in many ways it is well worth the time and effort. Asparagus plants are both male and female; all plants will bloom, with an insignificant little yellow flower (which, incidentally, bees love), but only the female plants produce red berries. Ideally, all female plants should be discarded, if one wishes to have the best bed. The male plants put out much thicker stalks than the females, which send up numerous thin shoots; further, the berries from the female plants infest the bed, and the result is undesirable seedlings coming up everywhere. I made extensive inquiries about the possibility of purchasing only male roots, but without success. Most nursery operators stated that they were totally unable to distinguish the male from female roots; one well-qualified man said he could only guess right at times, in that the male roots were inclined to have a few large "eyes," whereas the female roots had lots of smaller "eyes." When I dug up the seedlings for putting into the permanent bed, I was only able to guess correctly in about 75 percent of cases. Hence, I retained the bed of seedlings, and as the permanent plants began to produce berries, I upheaved them and replaced them with what I hoped were male plants.

As a long-range gardening project, the planting of an asparagus bed can be most interesting. Also, this vegetable is particularly bug-free, the asparagus beetle being one enemy, but fairly easily controlled. An annual top-dressing of well-rotted manure during fall or winter is about all that is required in the way of fertilizer. Since asparagus grows natively near the seaside, it appreciates an occasional dressing of salt.

J. W.

 GARDENING IN A COLD CLIMATE

Although friends tell me of gardens in the Yukon, I can't believe it. Conditions can't be much worse than here. With work and ingenuity, my garden gets better each year. Planting is the first week of June. Frost can occur anytime, even in July or early August. So be prepared; learn about mulching; start plants indoors; build cold frames, hot beds, a greenhouse. They don't have to be fancy. I built a cold frame of 2 × 4s scraps, odds of plywood, black plastic, an old window, leather for hinges, and carpet scraps tacked around the edges for sealing. Learn about all the new short-season plants. Beans that mature in 50 days; broad beans in 65 days (Bread Windsor Long Pod from Stokes); carrots in 56 days (Klondike Nantes from Stokes); cauliflower in 48 days (Stokes Early Abundance); corn in 53 days (Stokes Polar Vee); if you don't get frost, hybrid squash maturing in 47 days for zucchini and 50 for baby crooknecks, Stokes Alaska tomato maturing in 55 days. Take shortcuts. If you cannot grow your own bedding plants, buy them. The time you save will be worth it. Be willing to improvise. Keep an eye on the weather. A maximum/minimum thermometer may be a help,

though I don't have one. Keep notes on weather and crops. If it looks like frost, don't take a chance; run out and cover your tender plants. It'll become a fever—beating the weather, growing enough food for your family in three months. It's a challenge some of us can't let alone. Remember, despite the short season, the days are long. Even here it is light by 4:00 A.M. and not dark until 11:00 P.M. (in May).

Other hints: white fences around gardens reflect heat and light into the garden. Shrubs or berry bushes planted around the garden protect it from cold winds and frost.

L. P.

 WINTER VEGETABLES

Last winter we harvested kale and Jerusalem artichokes all winter, plus we left carrots and parsnips in the ground. Fresh salad all winter!

We covered the root crops with several inches of mulch, so when the ground was frozen, I could just pull up the mulch and the ground was left soft enough to pull the vegies up without breaking. Other winters have kept in salsify, broccoli, and Swiss chard.

C.

 RHUBARB TEA FOR MAGGOTS

A lot of people in our area have had root maggots in the garden. Some people use diazinon, which is supposed to be the safest chemical, and it does work. We didn't have them very badly and decided to experiment with rhubarb leaf tea. I put about six leaves in a gallon of simmering water, and when it was cool I poured a cup on the roots on everything that might be affected. One row of broccoli was keeling over and the roots were riddled. The next day when I looked, only one plant was dead and the rest were looking better. When I looked at the roots, they were crawling with red ants, which are the root maggot predators! So now I don't know if the tea worked or if it just weakened the maggots enough that the ants could move in and finish them off or if the ants came by coincidentally and the tea had nothing to do with it. Anyway, as a preventive measure, it seems to have worked; nothing else in the garden got infested. The broccoli recovered completely.

C.

REMEDIES FOR GARDEN PESTS

I've been meaning to write for some time now, but most other seasons just leave me with too many things to do, so letters fall by the wayside.

Having trouble with tent caterpillars? Here's a method for getting rid of the critters: let them hatch. Don't burn or cut down trees. The caterpillars will go out to feed. In daylight, midday, go out and rub the web trail they leave on branches. You don't need to rub it all off, but make a break in their trail about two feet long at least. They won't be able to find their way back to the nest (it helps to destroy it as well). When they're

young, they will die, as they can't stand the cold. This method is much safer than burning.

Looking for a cheap way to fence in your garden from marauding deer and the like? Put up fishnet. Search around the harbors where fishing people hang out. You'll likely be able to pick some up free. It usually lasts a couple of years. We string it between six-foot poles. Works like a charm. Haven't had any raccoons into the corn either (except for the time someone left the gate open one night).

R. D.

ESTABLISHING COMFREY

You had an article on comfrey. The most important year is the first one. Keep it well weeded and mulched. After that it acts as if it is a weed! This spring I dug up some old comfrey to transplant. I cut the long roots into two-inch lengths and planted these root cuttings two inches deep, parallel to the top of the ground. I had a real good stand of new comfrey plants, although the older plants produced top growth a lot sooner than the transplants. Rabbits and geese love it. Bye for now.

R. D.

SUCCESS WITH LAVENDER

This is in reply to some of the matters raised previously. I too have found lavender very hard to start but have finally gotten a couple of plants. For a couple of years I have been starting some of the more difficult plants by germinating the seeds before planting. I cut a little square of cloth for each type of seed, mark the name on the cloth with crayon (since it doesn't dissolve in water), and fold each kind of seed in its own particular cloth. All the little packets are laid in a shallow pan, covered with sponges, and left damp in a warm part of the house—behind the stove or up high. I wet them with warm water every day that I remember, but the sponges keep the packets damp when I forget or when a hotter fire tries to dry them out faster than I expect. As the seeds germinate, they can be planted with the aid of tweezers. If they are let go too long, the root grows into the cloth and will be damaged when you remove the seed.

I got some rosemary this way and have had good results with slow-germinating parsley. But the process yielded only one lavender that survived. So this year I cut the ends off some tin cans and embedded them in the garden, pressed the seeds into the top of the soil, and left them, figuring they would know better than I when conditions were right. There are now two tiny lavender plants, despite the cold, wet weather. I plan to keep all three plants indoors over the winter so as not to take chances, although I understand they are perennials.

J. M.

kinds, in our compost heaps. We use the stuff first for bedding and to sop up the mud around the barn. Then we stack the mix in the compost heaps and empty our pee buckets into it. The urine furnishes nitrogen to balance the almost pure carbon in the sawdust, and it rots pretty well. While it is in the compost heap, you can add lime, ashes, etc., to manipulate the pH. We have found the result quite helpful in lightening our heavy clay soil.

J. M.

FEATHER FERTILIZER

This year we discovered a gold mine in organic fertilizer with an extremely high nitrogen content. (Rodale says 15.3 percent nitrogen.) It's poultry feather. In our area we located a good source by looking in the yellow pages for a wholesale poultry supplier. The farmer was delighted to have us clean out her feather shed. It's important to keep the feathers dry till they are dug in, since they break down easily when wet. An easy way to incorporate them into the soil is to dig one-foot trenches, spread the feathers, then cover with the broken topsoil.

S. T.

VERSATILE SAWDUST

About using sawdust: We have been using sawdust and planer shavings, cedar or other

GARDEN PEST CONTROLS

Root Maggots

Buy a sack of builder's lime at the local builders' supply. It is hot lime, used in making cement. For every gallon of water, use about a cup of hot lime or a little less. Place the lime in a large container and pour the water over. Stir and let set 24 hours. Pour off clear water and in the *afternoon* pour about a half cup of water at the base of each infected plant. Actual measurement is not necessary—I use somewhere between half a cup and a cup. Just pour at the base of each plant, since the water does seem to irritate earthworms. If any worms shoot to the surface, I usually pick them up and dip them in clean water, then place them in another part of garden, and they are okay. One application is usually enough.

Cabbageworms

The best method for me is to plant under nylon screens. We have *hundreds* of cabbageworms in this area. A friend of mine says to take rye flour, place it in a coarse woven burlap sack, and early in the morning walk along the rows giving the sack a little shake above each plant. This is supposed to be good even for heavy infestations, so I'll try it next year.

Apple borers

Anyone with good ideas? I have been using soft soap smeared on the limbs. I have heard of using coal tar, molasses, whitewash, etc. Do they work? Four little apple trees surrounded by bush loaded with borers is a real worry.

W. C.

EGGSHELL MEAL

Here's a tip I'd like to pass along: instead of using bonemeal in our little garden, I use ground-up eggshells. I wash and dry the shells and, about once a month, grind them in my blender, then store. I use them the same as bone meal.

E. K.

DUELLING SQUASHES

May we suggest that yellow crookneck squash is more prolific than zucchini ever dreamed of being?

J. & A. K.

GROWING GRAIN IN A GARDEN PLOT

I would like to share my enthusiasm about growing grain on a garden plot. We just harvested 125 pounds of rye from about 1775 square feet of a rather weedy patch, which is the equivalent of about 55 bushels per acre. We now know that one can grow a year's supply of grain in a garden.

Last September, I tilled a patch that had had sunflowers and fava beans and lots of weeds in it and sowed it to winter rye. It soon showed as fresh green grass and was right out and up when the snow was gone in spring. I had meant to till it under then, but when coming back from tree planting all in a flurry to get the garden going, I decided to let it go and see what it would do for grain.

By the time I had planted the rest of the garden and begun to weed, the rye was six feet high and heading. In particular, I was struck by the fact that while I was hoeing and pulling weeds from in between corn, the rye was shading its ground with a six- to seven-foot stand and handicapped the weeds quite a lot. They were there, and I pulled a fair bit of stinkweed, but I did no other weeding. When it came to cutting the rye with a sickle, the weeds came a bit into the lower half of the bundles but did not otherwise interfere. I made the bundles about six inches in diameter where they were tied. After a while, I first tightened them with an old leather belt, which saved the skin on my fingers. No, I have not yet learned the art of using the straw of the grain. Then the bundles were leaned against each other in a shock, using a tripod of slim poles, which we usually use for drying hay, in the center.

Since the weather was so dry and hot, the bundles were ready to thresh within a few days. A friend who had done wheat that way before helped with the flailing, which was done by hitting the bundles against the floorboards in the house and also beating them with an old German carpet beater of woven willow. That work was light and gentle, and no hard pounding flail was needed since the grain was so dry. We had cleared one corner of the room and made "thresh-holds" on the two open sides, using boards and benches about 18″ high. (We had discovered the origin of the word "threshold" before, when we were beating out wheat in a small cabin and some of the kernels kept going out the open door—until we put a big board there. The amount of grain being harvested did not allow for waste on open ground or under the hoofs of horses running in a circle!) One wants the doors and windows open because of the dust.

The main facts to remember, for me anyway, are: fall-sown grain has such an early start in spring that weeds cannot grow with it and so there is less work than with other crops; and fall-sown grain matures so early in summer that the weather is likely to be good and dry and there is little trouble with harvest and threshing, which is otherwise a problem here, where fall-harvested grain is often damp and sprouts in the bins. (When the grain is dried again and then ground into flour before it gets bad, the result is malted grain and naturally sweet bread—part of the European secret of good-tasting bread, particularly in the northern parts, where weather is often damp.)

There was some lodging, or laying down in storms and heavy rains, of the standing rye. At first it would stand up again, but after a while the whole center of the batch was almost flat and I did not count on much grain harvest. But, as it turned out, that was no hindrance to either the harvest or the ripening of the grain. I would still like to find a variety of wheat and rye with a short stalk.

There was also some ergot in the rye. That is an easily discernible, glueish, almost grotesque-looking outgrowth on kernels. Ergot is poisonous, causing St. Vitus's dance, a nerve disease, and is better not eaten. I sort the few much bigger, easily found kernels out when I pour the grain on a big cookie sheet (with rim) to toast it. I have lately been eating toasted ground grain quite a bit. Mixed with some ground sunflower or sesame seeds, or a little oil, it really tastes very good. At first, it is very dry in the mouth, but as the saliva begins to penetrate, it gains sweetness, and I chew it well. I believe I get a lot of goodies from grain eaten that way. There is no cooking, my digestive system is not diluted with water, and I obviously can work on such a diet. After a couple of hours I feel thirsty all right, but then it is hot these days too.

Since we are at it (again: food) I may as well tell you about my fudge: finely grated red beets and ground sunflower seeds. Or added to this, some ground home-grown sweet corn. Try it, if you can stand it in your mouth.

We also grow sweet corn in quantities to dry on the cob. On fall and winter evenings we rub the kernels off the cob and grind it when needed. That is also so good and sweet that I grind it with some sunflower seeds and eat it raw—without oil. Again, you have to get used to the dryness in your mouth. I pour a little in the grinder (a cup or three) and then have my meal.

R. E.

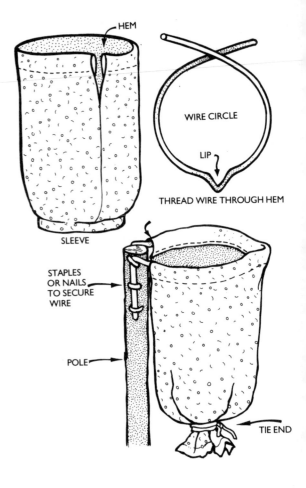

 HANDY FRUIT PICKER

If you can't reach the fruit at the top of your fruit trees, try a picker made from a coat hanger, a piece of old shirtsleeve and a long pole. Bend the coat hanger into a round that will take your largest fruit easily. It should have a small beak or lip at one end and two loose ends at the other. Loosen about three inches of the underarm seam of a foot-long section of sleeve and sew a hem on it to thread onto the coat hanger. Open the ends of the wire and bit of open seam matching. Now bend straight ends to about a 45° angle and attach these ends to the end of a long pole with horseshoe staples, bent nails, or what have you. Close the bottom of the sleeve with string or tight elastic. When picking, drop

fruit into larger circle, then slide stem into narrowed section and pull. The bag can catch about six apples.

I. M.

 POTATO STORAGE

Some friends of ours kept potatoes in their root cellar in excellent condition until mid-May by putting them in wooden boxes and covering them with several inches of moss. It kept them from drying and shriveling, and it was dark enough that they didn't sprout.

M. S.

COMPLETE GUIDE TO GARLIC

During the past years, our friend Oswald has displayed his garlic and other vegetables at the fall fair and has taken several first prizes home. He is now 72 years old. It is August, and all his garlic is dried and ready for use. He sells it from his backyard. Here's how he grows it:

First of all you should have good, loose soil with good organic fertilizer. I use seaweed from Okanagan Lake and alfalfa hay—but it must be well rotted before it is good in the ground, and then you keep your garden well wetted or it will take the moisture away from the vegetables.

You should hand-water, not use a sprinkler. Vegetables that bloom and onions and garlic should not be sprinkled. The sprinkling kills a lot of the blooms. The water should get to the bottom of the roots; just give them a good watering every three or four days.

You plant your garlic in the fall, two inches deep; if you plant too close to the surface, the roots will push the clove right out of the ground. So stay with the two inches, then the roots go down about four inches. Then you cover it with leaves just in case you get a wet fall. In the spring you take the leaves or whatever other mulch you are using off the garlic and water it good even if the ground seems cold.

When you see the seed on the Canadian fall garlic, pinch it off; otherwise it will weaken the bulb. You can let the seed grow strong and later plant it. It will get good and strong too. But I prefer just to use the cloves, and I plant them approximately eight inches each way, leaving enough space to get through with a cultivator. When your two bottom leaves are grown, then your garlic is about ready to be taken out, even if it looks green. Don't let it get too ripe, because then the earth will eat away the outer skin and remove the protection of the plant and pretty soon the cloves will split open. Take a garden hose and wash the dirt off, then put them to dry in the shade. You cannot dry them like onions. When the tops and roots are dry, cut them off, store the garlic in a drafty place, and they are ready for the market. Never dry them on a cement floor or hang them on a cement wall.

Oswald says not to be discouraged if the first crop doesn't turn out with big bulbs. The crop will improve as the soil improves.

R. R.

STARTING TOMATOES IN TINS

I seeded my tomato plants in empty tin cans. At planting time, cut the bottoms of the cans with a can opener, and by pushing the cut bottoms up, the whole plant slides out of the can with no damage to the roots. Saves the plants a couple of weeks recuperating from root damage. Make sure the soil is quite moist to keep it from crumbling. Also, when you are late with thinning, use a pair of old scissors and cut the seedlings at ground level, rather than pulling plants out and damaging their neighbors' roots.

R. R.

STAKING SMALL TREES

In districts where the wind is fairly continuous from one direction, the usual method of tying the trunk to a vertical stake driven in close to the roots can be improved upon. Unless the stake is exceptionally massive, it tends to be pulled over the tree if placed vertically. If, however, it is driven at an angle, facing the prevailing wind, very strong support is provided.

Additional advantages are that termites are not attracted to the base of the trunk, and there is less likelihood of damage to the roots. Also, there will be more space between the trunk and the stake for weeding.

B. T.

HAIR SCARES OFF DEER

In an arboretum in the state of New York, scientists have been testing the value of human hair as a deer repellent. Evidently, deer don't like to come near human hair—in fact, they would not come closer than a yard from the balls of hair that the scientists had hung on the branches of about a thousand shrubs and young trees at the arboretum.

This seems to be an idea well worth testing in our own gardens and orchards. Why not

put up hairballs at one-yard intervals around the garden fence and watch what happens? Then send in your observations to *The Smallholder.* Some of your gardeners may already know of this folk method; if so, please let the rest of us know if and how well it works.

The hairballs in the New York experiment were fist-sized and wrapped in nylon netting. (If you don't cut your hair, you can get some from your local barber instead.) Chances are, though, that unwashed hair will work best, as the scientists speculate that the repellent may come from the sebaceous gland at the base of the hair follicle.

S. T.

FRESH HERBS YEAR ROUND

Herbs taste really different when freshly picked, and growing your own on a windowsill isn't that hard. In winter, though, herbs need at least three hours of direct sunlight (more in summer), but you can also use balanced fluorescent tubes intended for growing plants. Although this sounds expensive, buying herbs at the store is even costlier.

Good herbs to grow indoors are rosemary, sage, basil, and bay. Although rosemary will die back in the garden during winter, indoors it will be green the whole year round. Rosemary needs soil that is constantly moist when growing in a living space (as compared with a humid greenhouse, where it grows well even if the soil dries out between waterings). The soil should be loose and rich.

Only some species of sage will do well indoors. Two of the best are *Salvia coccinea,* and *Salvia rutlans* (sometimes called *elegans*). The same soil as for rosemary works well for sage, but sage requires even more sunlight, if possible.

Basil plants tend to sprawl and get leggy, but *Ocimum minimum* is a small basil and good for potting. It needs the same care as rosemary and grows well indoors.

Sweet bay is wonderful when fresh and can grow up to six feet tall. It's actually a small evergreen and very beautiful. It will grow in the same soil as the others, but between waterings the soil should dry out more.

These herbs are sensitive to temperature. They are temperate-climate plants and prefer a cooler space than most other houseplants. They do well near a window for this reason too, but make sure that their leaves do not touch the glass, freezing the tips, in winter.

An ideal spot is a sunny window above a sink where moisture is always available. If this is not possible, they'll need lots of misting, especially in the dry months.

S. T.

WATERING TEST

A very old test of water needs for the garden from an old farmers' bulletin, from 1902:

> The amount of moisture in the soil may be determined with sufficient accuracy for the needs of the plant by examining a sample taken a few inches from the surface of the ground. If it clings together when molded in a ball and shows the print of the fingers, there is moisture enough present. If the earth falls apart when the hand is

opened, irrigation is needed. As stated above, this point is passed some days before the plant shows indications of suffering.

B. T.

COMPANIONS FOR CABBAGES

We've printed information before on companion planting. It seems, though, to judge from our experience here, that a reminder sometimes may be helpful. Here's a list for those of you whose cabbage family plants are attracting white butterflies and other destructive insects. Mint (peppermint, spearmint, and pennyroyal) is a companion to cabbage and tomatoes; nasturtiums are companions to the cabbage family, cucumbers, and tomatoes; sage is a companion to cabbage and carrots.

B.

TRANSPLANTING WILD TREES

The March issue of *Rural Delivery* includes a few hints on transplanting trees from the wild for windbreaks, hedgerows, decoration, or whatever. The first thing to consider is root pruning:

> In root pruning, a tree is selected in the wild (no bigger than 10' in height) and one merely cuts down with a sharp shovel, all around the trunk (say a foot to 18 inches

from a 1-inch diameter stem). No attempt is made at this time to lift the tree or to remove any soil from the site. Simply the roots are severed, which forces those that remain intact to sprout a massive fibrous system close to the trunk. Tag the tree, and return the following year for a specimen that will be better prepared for the stress of moving.

Another recommendation is to prune the top of most deciduous trees to balance root loss (a third to a half of the original woody growth may be removed) at the time of transplanting. For birch, the author suggests that "the number of branches may be reduced by cutting closely to the trunk, leaving a well-balanced head, equal on all sides. This is really the only way a birch may be pruned without in some way compromising the grace of its natural appearance." Spruce is particularly affected by competition from grass or other vegetation in the new site, and cedar requires plenty of water. "Very often good results may be obtained by leaving a hose trickling into the planting hole for several days."

B. T.

CLOCHE GARDENING

I have been wanting to write to you about our experiences with cloche gardening. We live at 3200′ elevation, and frost in July has been a common experience for us. Rather than limiting our garden to frost-hardy vegetables, we have devised a system that allows us to raise even the most sensitive plants with some

peace of mind and to extend our season considerably.

Our garden consists of raised beds, each 4′ wide and 20′ long. For each bed we have built two cloche frameworks, each 10′ long. These are made very much like a sawhorse, only of 1″x material and without bracing, since they don't need the strength. They are very light and easy for one person to move around. Over each bed we place two cloche frames, end to end, so that the whole length of the bed is covered. A length of clear plastic (6 mil for durability) 20′ wide is wide enough to cover the frames with enough length at the bottom to be secured with rocks. The sides are easily rolled up and secured with a rock on the top of the frame when you need to work in the bed or let the rain in.

The advantages we have found in cloche gardening are: (a) You can extend your gardening season considerably, planting early and harvesting late, without fear of damage to frost-sensitive crops. (b) It conserves moisture, which you would normally lose to evaporation, and provides a nice humid atmosphere for your plants. (c) It magnifies and conserves heat. Even on a cool, cloudy day, the temperature inside the cloche will be pleasantly warm. (d) It keeps out an overabundance of rain. This spring, which was a very wet one, our garden flourished while many others were drowning in the torrents of rain that lasted for half of May and all of June.

On a hot day, it is necessary to open the cloches fully or partially for ventilation, as the temperature inside can soar very quickly under a hot sun. I have also seen cloches made by using ¾″ black plastic pipe cut in pieces long enough to make an arch over the garden bed, spaced at four- or five-foot intervals. These are secured at either side by driving a slender stake into the ground and fitting the ends of the pipe onto the stakes. The plastic is then draped over this framework.

For individual plants that are not under a cloche framework, we cut the bottoms out of gallon juice or wine bottles with a bottle cutter (clear glass is best) and set these over the plants. The lids can be removed for ventilation, and the whole bottle must be removed on a hot day. This method is good only while the plants are quite small.

On another topic, we use a black plastic pipe cloche frame over our sleeping bed during mosquito season. We nail a slender stake on either side of the bed where we want a piece of pipe and fit the ends of the pipe over the stakes. This is a convenient framework over which to drape mosquito netting. If you use ¾″ or narrower pipe, the netting can be held in place on the pipe with clothes pegs.

B. C.

BASEMENT WINDOW GREENHOUSE

We use our basement window as a greenhouse. The walls are stone with insulation on the outside. The east, north, and west sides are underground, and the south side is a 24′ × 5′ double-glazed window set at 70° to get all the heat we can in midwinter. There is a 30″ stone wall under the window, which is also below the ground.

The greenhouse is most effective energy-wise. I would fully recommend building below ground in this climate, but do not put earth upon the roof; it is a poor insulator

and, being very heavy, causes much expense in ceiling construction. The benefit of being below ground is from the warmth stored in the earth. Ambient temperature here is 44°F. in winter at a depth of 8′.

Now, about the greenhouse: plants do very well in the window, and it is possible to have tomatoes and other vegetables year round. We do find, however, that by mid-November and until mid-February everything stands still, owing to short days and low light intensity. So plan to have most things mature by mid-November, and don't plant seeds until mid-February unless you have artificial lighting to compensate. Very little extra heat is needed in this structure, but shutters are needed below 0° F.

P. & J. P.

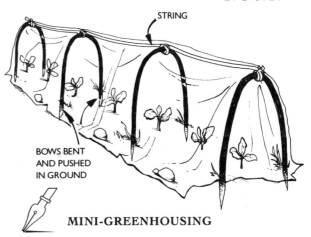

MINI-GREENHOUSING

In the garden we often make mini-greenhouses over raised beds or rows, using clear plastic. For supports we use cedar bows sharpened at both ends and smoothed up slightly with a hatchet. We run a string between the bows to prevent them from drooping. These cedar bows are reusable for several years.

We have found that mulching does not

work well here because of the slugs; however, we do cover the beds and rows in the winter to prevent leaching of nutrients by heavy rain. In the past we have used black plastic for the covering. This year we are trying something new. We got a lot of used tin roofing, more than we needed for immediate roof repair, so we are using it in the garden. Each row is cleaned up of old crops and weeds, then heavily dressed with compost. Then we cover the row with a sheet of roofing, which is held in place with cedar bows. In this way, the growing area is protected, but you can still walk between rows without worrying about damaging the plastic. In the spring it will be easy to uncover the rows one at a time as needed. So far the only problem has been with the wind, which tries to lift the sheets and throw them around. They must be securely held down. Another idea, which we haven't tried, is to use old carpets in the same way.

S. & F. M.

SLUG AND DEER DETERRENTS

Dry and crush eggshells fine and put them where slugs are bothering plants. The shells stick fast to them and the slugs soon die, since they cannot go anywhere with the shells sticking to them. Also, use sand in the garden rows to keep slugs away.

To repel deer from fruit trees, mix goat manure with water. Dip a broom into the liquid and spray onto the trees. (Other manures will probably do as well.) It has to be done again after a rain.

J. & H. G.

STORING ZUCCHINI OVER WINTER

We had an abundant crop of zucchini this year. Toward the end of the season, we left many on the vine. Of course they got quite large, but they also developed a tougher skin, which is slightly yellow in places. We keep them like any squash in a dry and cool (but not too cool) place, carefully separated by newspapers so they don't touch. It is mid-January now, and we still have three fine firm zucchinis left. It is definitely more than a "summer" squash.

S. & F. M.

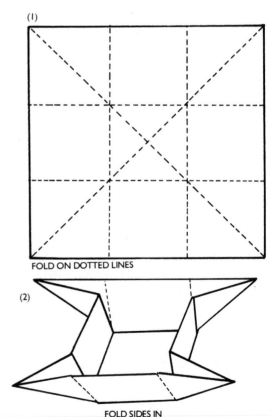

(1)

FOLD ON DOTTED LINES

(2)

FOLD SIDES IN

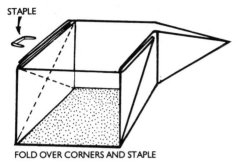

STAPLE

FOLD OVER CORNERS AND STAPLE

STARTER BOXES FOR SEEDLINGS

S. A. gave us the model of his homemade starter box. He takes three sheets of newspaper, cuts them into 6" × 6" pieces, and staples them together (see figures above). He plants his seeds in these boxes, then transplants them into the ground without removing the box. Because the roots are not disturbed, he believes that they transplant very well.

B. T.

THE REMARKABLE STINGING NETTLE

Hardly any other plant has such beneficial properties as the stinging nettle for humans, animals, plants, and even the soil. It should have truly an honored place in the garden. But it also grows wild along sunny creek banks, on wasteland, on the margin of cultivated land, and often around garbage dumps.

Being a perennial, it can be propagated by root cuttings. It is best to transplant the root after cutting off most of the top in late summer.

Use for Humans

The young plants, which are rich in vitamin C, chlorophyll, and minerals (iron), can be cooked as a delicious spinach. Its blood-cleaning properties make it an excellent spring cure.

Tea, made of fresh or dried leaves, helps against rheumatism and hemorrhoids and is a diuretic.

Juice of the fresh leaves, if diluted 1:4 with water, cleans the respiratory system, works against catarrh, and helps for kidney and bladder ailments. Undiluted, it stops gum bleeding (use as a mouthwash) and nose bleeding (use a cotton dipped into the juice).

Finally, a decoction of the root rubbed onto the head is said to prevent hair loss.

Use for Animals

Rheumatism in dogs may be cured with a lotion of stinging nettles, cabbage, and celandine (let the leaves macerate in rainwater for two days). If young chicks are fed with leaves, the "inner fire" of the stinging nettle can serve as a substitute for any missing brood warmth. In addition to chicken starter, we fed our chicks chopped nettle and dandelion leaves, mixed with homemade cottage cheese, and they did very well.

Some people advise feeding pregnant animals a few weeks before they give birth with stinging nettle hay as a simple measure to ensure vigor and health of the livestock.

Added to the winter fodder of dairy cows, it promotes the production of milk with a higher butterfat content.

It should also be mentioned that the stinging nettle is the host of many caterpillars, like the ones of the common tortoiseshell and the peacock butterfly. I read a beautiful observation that the plain, insignificant flowers of the stinging nettle seem to manifest their potential for color in the splendor of these butterflies!

Use for Plants

Stinging nettle is a very important companion plant for numerous herbs since it increases the content of the aromatic oils (especially of peppermint, sage, marjoram, valerian, etc.). It also aids the family of the nightshades (like tomatoes and peppers) as well as mustard and coriander (increasing the seed yield by 30 percent).

There are various methods of using stinging nettle as a manure tea or pest repellent. Four and a half pounds of fresh leaves and stems (gathered before the plant has gone into seed) are put in 2½ gal. of water for 24 hours. The juice is to be sprayed against any kind of larvae or caterpillar. The treatment should be repeated twice within a few hours.

If the liquid is left for some weeks, until the leaves are decomposed and have a strong smell, it has a potent effect on growth. Plants that have suffered from attacks by aphids can be helped by spraying a dilution (1:10) on the soil in the early morning and watering well a few hours later. Repeat twice within a short period of time. The fact that the sap begins to flow again more vigorously will cause the aphids and often also fungal attacks to disappear.

More diluted (1 cup to 2½ gal. of water), the manure tea can be used to water toma-toes, cucumbers, spinach, cabbage, etc., as a general tonic and to support strong leaf growth and the formation of chlorophyll. There should never be more than three successive applications, however, or the quality of the produce might suffer.

Effect on Soil

R. Steiner likens the part the stinging nettle plays within the soil organism to that of the heart within the human organism. Being closely connected with the iron process (the same as it is manifested in the human bloodstream), the nettle helps to bring about the right balance of nutrients in the soil.

It also organizes and harmonizes soil life and influences the formation of fertile soil. Growing on wastelands and garbage dumps, it fulfills the task of turning raw organic matter into humus.

Compost made completely of stinging nettle gives you one of the finest soils, suitable for the most delicate crops.

Stinging nettle is also one of the bio-dynamic preparations. If you bury faded plants for one year in the soil and then add stinging nettle to the compost in very small quantities, the manure will become inwardly sensitive and "will not suffer any undue composition to take place nor any improper loss of nitrogen."

The effect of stinging nettle on the activity of earthworms, which are so important for the creation of fertile soil, should be mentioned here too. Research has shown that earthworms are very attracted by stinging nettle. Test fields treated with manure tea or compost made of stinging nettle showed a much higher population of earthworms compared with other fields. This effect could be measured even when the above-mentioned preparation was put into a little glass tube in the soil, which might suggest a strong radiation of the nettle.

Concluding, I'd like to say that I didn't gather this information only to show the beneficial properties of a single plant but also to point out that in agriculture, we don't work so much with substances or matter, but rather with *forces*. And in my opinion, it is the task of a sound agriculture to become aware of these forces—how they permeate all life, from the soil to plants and animals to human beings—to take care of them, and to work with them.

M. W.

HEAD START FOR GARDENS

To give potatoes a head start, about mid-March or early April put small seed potatoes in a clear plastic bag. Add a tablespoon of water and tie the bag. Hang it in a window or lay it on a windowsill in the sun. Turn occasionally. Small tight leaves and sturdy roots will form. When the ground is warm enough, untangle and plant whole. If a little cool, cut the bottoms from plastic jugs and place over the spot. A depression can be left to hold the jug, banking it up well. Leave lid off.

These jugs are also fine to protect tomato and other plants. When the weather is warm, you can thread a wire through the jug handles and hang them away for next year.

Save wood ashes and keep them dry for fertilizer. They contain potash, which is necessary for growth. It's essential for the ripening process, so about mid-July add a generous dusting around the tomato bushes.

Paste tomatoes are easy to grow. Since they are drier than normal t[...] lovely for salads. They are a[...] making sauce or thickening[...]

If you are making tomat[...] ter, etc., use your biggest roaster in [...] oven—the larger surface of pulp to cook down means that there will be less scorching and it will be easier to stir; thus, there will be no need to stand over it.

Winter Welch onions are so useful. They are a perennial; they don't form a bulb but produce seeds after several years to replenish the patch. Always leave some plants to grow big. They will be ready earlier if you pull some leaves from the outer edges of the plant. Leave the middle to seed. A few feet of row will produce all the green onions needed for a family.

Lettuce seed planted in August and cared for will usually winter over and begin bearing early in spring. We put hoops over in the fall and then clear plastic over that in early spring for a heat-tunnel effect. Our hoops are off a horse-drawn hayrake. Heavy wire could be used (about 3' long). Bend to push into the ground. An old garden hose, cut in about 1½' lengths and put onto the wire, will protect clear plastic put over a row of seedlings. Bury plastic in the ground on each side and leave each end closed till too warm; then open.

Pole beans can be planted two weeks earlier under plastic, and other seeds will benefit. Rhubarb and asparagus come fast. We usually use plastic on both and on onions in late April.

A generous sprinkling of road salt will kill weeds and improve asparagus and raspberry plantings. It keeps weeds down and improves soil.

The CBC gardener recommends crumpled-up newsprint as a fertilizing agent. In addition, it holds water when put in the bottom of the trench below planted seeds. Even the ink is organic — not colored stuff, though.

Make use of sawdust and leaves for mulching your raspberries. In a few years' time, it will become soil and more will be needed. Blueberries do well with heavy mulch. Potatoes thrive in leaves, but only if they are chopped up; leaves lie too flat otherwise and stay cold.

M. L.

 SCABLESS SPUDS AND TRANSPLANTING LEAFY VEGETABLES

When I still lived in England, I used to garden in an allotment garden along with many other city dwellers who shared a garden space, each working on his or her own small plot. I learned much from the other gardeners, most of whom were elderly people. These two tips I pass on to you as ones that really do work:

1. To keep your potatoes from having scab, plant them in between layers of fresh green grass. Just pull off a handful to put in the hole before you put in the potato, then put another handful on top and finish filling the hole with earth.
2. Cutting leaves down to half-size before transplanting leafy vegetables lessens the area for evaporation of water and gives the plant a better start with less shock.

S. W.

 GREEN MANURES

Green manures increase the total organic matter in the soil through their use of solar energy to convert inorganic materials into complex organic structures. When green manures are turned under, they decompose and foster the bacteria that are essential to a healthy soil. Fertile soil has organic materials in all stages of decomposition, ranging from recognizable chunks of plants to compost to humus. Green manures replenish the top of this sequence.

Green manures help keep weeds under control. Weeds specialize in rapidly covering bare soil. Green manures have a wonderfully calming effect on weeds by out-competing them for light. Buckwheat is probably the best green manure for weed suppression, although the grains such as oats and rye are quite effective if seeded thickly. Clover is the weakest in its early growth, although once it is well established, it competes with weeds effectively.

Legumes accomplish all of the above and have another special quality for increasing soil fertility. Living on the roots of the legume in little nodules are certain strains of soil bacteria that help feed the plant the nitrogen compounds vital to its life. Here our soils are typically quite poor in nitrogen, the element that promotes dark green, vigorous leafy growth. Air has plenty of nitrogen, but it is in a form that plants cannot use. The bacteria that live in symbiosis with legumes can convert the nitrogen in the air into compounds that enable the bacteria to grow and reproduce. As they die, they decompose and are assimilated by the plant. Thus, legumes can often thrive in nitrogen-poor soil. When a legume green manure is turned under, nitrogen from the air has been added to the soil for the next crop.

I use mainly fall rye, oats, red clover, and buckwheat for my green manures. Each has its particular strengths and uses. Oats are extremely cheap (I use chicken-feed oats), grow well on fairly poor soil, and thrive in cold, wet weather. I use them in both fall and spring. When the peas are done (say mid-August or so, depending on how early I plant them), I take them to the compost heap, rake oats generously into the soil, and water well. I sprinkle them until they're up and let them grow until late fall, when I dig them in. They will not live through the winter—an advantage for beds that will be planted in early spring.

I use oats in the spring in beds that had crops, such as Chinese cabbage, too late into the fall for getting any other green manure established. The secret to spring oats is to get them into the beds as soon as the soil can be worked—here, usually early April. I've planted them when there was still a little corn snow on the soil, and they've done very well. Spring frosts don't seem to affect oats at all. By early June the oats will have made good growth and will be ready to turn under.

Fall rye is planted from late summer through midfall, lives through the winter, and starts growing vigorously as soon as the snow melts. Its emerald green blades are especially welcome in early April when so little else is going on in the garden. My experience has been that rye does not get well established if it's planted too late. I prefer not to plant any later than early October. Corn and potatoes are excellent crops to follow with fall rye. When the potato patch is finished, I dig the potatoes, compost the stalks, lightly rake over the bed, and rake in fall rye seed. This works well if you rotate corn and potatoes, since they are both planted late enough (mid- to late May) that the rye will have made good growth. I like to dig it in when it's about a foot tall (taller is okay, as long as it's still green and succulent). I cut it with a sickle a few days before turning it under to make the spading a bit easier (if it's too long, you have to tuck it under). It needs to be upside down if you want to plant the bed immediately. Don't worry about the odd bit of greenery sticking out here and there or the roots sticking out all over—everything just settles down and disappears. I often plant on the same day I turn under the green manure, contrary to some books I've read. The only problem is that raking and incorporating compost have to be done with some care in order not to turn up great gobs of rye.

Buckwheat's strengths are its ability to smother weeds and its extremely quick growth. It is frost-sensitive, so it has to be used in the summer and early fall on the odd bit of empty ground you might have. I often use it after I have used up a compost pile to grab some of the nutrients leached into the earth underneath the pile. Friends of mine here who use buckwheat say it seems to have a special ability to bind sandy soil into some kind of structure. It doesn't do as well on poor soil as oats or rye. It matures quickly, has lovely little flowers much favored by bees, and if you don't want to dig it in, can be easily pulled out and added to the compost heap. Because of its quick maturity, it would be easy to grow your own seed.

The clovers need to get planted fairly early in the season (say by mid-August or so) to get well established and live through the winter. Clover seed seems expensive compared with the other green manures, but it is actually cheap when you consider how thinly it can be sown. Each clover plant is much bigger than a rye stalk, for example. Clover starts more slowly than the other green manures and does not compete well with really vigorous weeds. It will survive under fairly low light situations, and I have been planting red clover in the corn patch around late June. By then I have gotten the weeds under control, the corn is well on its way, and the clover gets established under the corn. When the corn is all picked, I cut the stalks off at the roots, rather than pulling them up and disturbing the clover, and add them to the compost. By this system I think corn might actually be a soil improver. This same system can be used with annual flowers such as petunias. Because clovers are slow early growers, they should be left in as late in the spring as possible.

Green manures do have some drawbacks and problems. Sometimes it is hard to get early spring oats established because flocks of birds discover the seed and eat all of it. Getting it in really early and well covered with earth helps, but occasionally I have had to cover it with tarps until it has rooted.

Rye is often eaten by deer in the spring because it's the greenest thing around (this just slows it down a bit). If you let your green manure get too big, go to seed, get too coarse and stemmy, you can have problems dealing with it. Start small until you are sure it's worth the trouble for you. You might have trouble getting over the notion that a garden consists of a few healthy plants and lots of endlessly cultivated bare soil, and that soil isn't ready for planting if you've just turned under a bunch of plants and their roots are sticking out all over. For potatoes and corn, this isn't much of a problem, since their seed is big and vigorous. For small seeds, you just have to rake each furrow open with some care.

For me, the benefits of green manuring far outweigh the drawbacks. I have coarse, sandy soil that loses nutrients quickly and badly needs the binding action of the green manures. I don't have a pickup, don't particularly like to buy and haul animal manures, and believe they should go back to where they came from in the first place, if possible. I dream of a truly self-sufficient garden, whose fertility is maintained or even improved with little or no subsidies from the outside. But finally, on an emotional level, turning under a lush green manure crop just feels right, like making some kind of sacrifice to the gods of the soil.

T. Z.

HARVESTING KELP

With my last year's supply of kelp rapidly diminishing, I find myself looking forward to making a trip to the coast to replenish my stock.

Late May is the time my friends and I usually gather kelp. We choose this time because the new kelp leaves are at their prime—they are a good size but not too weather-battered yet. It's necessary to choose a time when there will be a fairly low tide, preferably in the early morning. The amount of the harvest varies according to how low the tides are.

We usually plan on staying for a few days

in our makeshift camp on one of the Gulf Islands. It is best to choose a site where the water traffic is minimal, or else your kelp may be somewhat polluted. A site with a rocky point is good, since the kelp beds lie beyond these. The weather needs to be sunny. This is the hardest part in choosing a time to harvest—co-ordinating low tides and sunny days.

It takes us about half a day to assemble the drying racks out of wood we find on the shore. We make our racks by jamming poles into rock crevices and keeping them in place with rocks if necessary. The two poles should be about six feet or more apart. The poles stick out of the crevices on an angle so that they are about five or six feet off the ground at their farthest end. By placing cedar strips across these two poles, we form a rack. Cedar strips are made by splitting long pieces off cedar driftwood logs. If it is a windy day, these strips may need to be tied down.

To gather the kelp, we go out at low tide in an 18' canoe. We've tried a 12' canoe, and it wasn't successful because the waves bounced it around too much. Any sturdy boat should do. We head out to an exposed kelp bed. One person anchors herself to a kelp plant, while the other lovingly cuts the stem just below the bulb and hauls it into the meticulously clean canoe. Sometimes you can watch whales play while you work!

Upon returning to the shore, carefully put the kelp in sacks to avoid contact with the sand. We've found that plastic net onion sacks suit us best to haul the kelp from the boat to the racks. If there is no low morning tide, it is possible to gather kelp at a low tide later in the day or evening and store it in the sacks in the water until the next day, when it can be dried. The sacks should be securely tied below the low tide mark.

Carry the sacks to the racks and set them on clean rocks nearby. Pull the kelp out one bulb at a time. Holding the bulb, tear off the leaves and drape them over the cedar racks. Avoid letting the leaves touch each other, because they will stick together and dry more slowly if they touch. A breezy day makes this almost impossible, however. If the days are hot and sunny, your kelp should dry in about two days. The kelp has to be taken off the rack and rolled in tarps at night so that the damp sea breeze doesn't wet it.

After drying on the racks for a couple of days, the kelp is then laid out on black plastic (or tarps) stretched out on the rocks. This gets it crunchy dry. After a day of this (or until crispy), it is put in a barrel and beaten with a mallet (or it can be crunched on the plastic with your hands). This last step in the drying can be put off for a few days (or longer) if the weather changes. We've had to do the final drying at home in the yard.

Kelp stores best if kept in sealed plastic buckets.

Once your kelp harvest is in, it's time to enjoy! I use kelp every day in cooking and baking. When recipes call for salt, I just throw in a pinch of kelp. We always keep a jar of it on the table to sprinkle on our food.

Besides the good taste kelp adds to your food, it is a very good food for you, filled with vitamins and minerals. Many healing properties have been attributed to kelp, including treatment of arthritis, rheumatic fever, heart pains, and high blood pressure. So, happy kelping!

E.

COLD FRAME CELERY

This past winter I discovered an excellent way to keep fresh celery—in the cold frame. In past years I've tried storing whole celery plants in the root cellar or an earth pit. With those methods, I found half the stalks rotted by Christmas. In the cold frame, however, the celery plants remained healthy and crisp until March. They would have continued longer, but I'd eaten all the stalks by then!

I dug up the plants from the garden in October, before a heavy frost. It's a good idea to dig deeply so that the roots come out unharmed in a large clump of soil. Then a wheelbarrow ride brought them to the cold frame. My cold frame is dug into the earth at a slight slope. This way the plants are closer to ground temperature, and the window glass faces the low sun. I dug the celery plants into the sandy soil that lines the cold frame. A little water finished the job.

I watched with trepidation as the coldest nights plastered frozen celery leaves to the glass. Some winter evenings I lifted the window and cut frosty, crystalline stalks for a soup pot. But for some reason I never bothered to cover the cold frame with any extra insulation. No matter. The plants lived on. By late January, new little leaf growth was sprouting from the celery stumps whose stalks were all harvested. By March, all the plants were showing bushy new stalks.

Now it's time to think about making room in the cold frame for new spring crops, primarily tomatoes. When the tomato plants are ready for the cold frame, the celery plants can move back to the garden. There—if all goes well—I can look forward to a harvest of celery seed.

Maybe this has been the mildest winter in recent memory. But if a little care and watchfulness are exercised, I think celery will demonstrate its frost-hardy succulence most winters in the cold frame. Near-freezing temperatures and plentiful moisture are ideal for wintering celery. What better way to perk up that cabbage and carrot salad, those sprouts, that regular spaghetti or stir-fry? Next year I'll try to keep a few more celery plants in the cold frame to last until it's time for fresh bok choy, the prolific "summer celery."

N.

ADVICE ABOUT FRUIT TREES

I'd like to share with you some information on fruit trees that Tony Netting, of Owl Meadow Nursery, gave us. When we described the soil conditions of where we wish to plant our trees as sandy glacial till, Tony responded:

Take heart. Your pristine glacial till is probably on its way to becoming that "deep, rich, and well-drained loam" beloved of orchardists and gardeners. Just a couple of million years! If you're not in a mood to wait, you have to concentrate the available humus under your fruit trees. *Humus,* not compost, not manure. The trees want to sip nourishment slowly over many months, season after season.

I have come to believe that the best start is to fill a large hole with rotted wood, or half-rotted, or even chunks of green wood, especially fast-rotting wood like aspen or birch. Fill in with duff from the forest floor, sod, rotted hay—any rough organic material. Save your topsoil (if any) for the area right around the roots. Well-rotted compost, peat moss, dead leaves could be added here. Also a few handfuls of bonemeal and ground limestone. What you're after is to endow the tree with a fund of *gradually decomposing* organic material.

After planting, you *must* eliminate the grass from a 5' (better, 10') square area— use rabbits (with wire around the tree), chickens, geese, bark, chips, black plastic, cardboard, sheet metal, tweezers, anything!

After the first season, you can judge how much additional nitrogen the tree will require by how much it has grown. The shorter and spindlier the shoots, the more nitrogen you should add. In November— just before the snow comes—or in March—just before it goes—spread manure, compost, urea (homemade or bought) in a doughnut around the tree.

That's the basic recipe: a humus bank under the tree, an absence of grass around the tree, and some annual feeding of nitrogen to maintain optimum growth. You can fine-tune with foliar spray of soluble fish every 10 days from the time the leaves come out till July, added seaweed extract for trace nutrients, phosphate rock spread every few years, wood ashes (for potassium) especially at petal fall, ground limestone or dolomite also every few years; watch for symptoms of boron deficiency and use foliar spray if indicated, but probably none of these supplements is crucial, like vitamin pills on top of a good diet.

Tony gave us further suggestions on how to deal with suckers on rootstock: "True rootstock suckers should be removed as soon as you see them. If numerous, they suggest something wrong with the trunk of the tree—winter or mouse damage, canker— which prevents sap from moving up."

We asked whether or not we could grow our own rootstock by trying to root the pruned suckers in water.

He thought they were unlikely to root in water but suggested growing our own rootstock, using seeds from any local apples. Such seeds would produce standard-sized trees rather than dwarf varieties. Standard-sized trees, he said, would be better suited to our marginal fruit-tree-growing location anyway.

The concept of planting trees in a humus bank is very appealing to those of us who have little spare compost at the best of times. Rotted wood we have lots of. So Tony's advice opens up whole new possibilities at a grass roots level. We send our thanks.

S. & Y.

HEALTHY LEEKS

Leeks are biennials, so even though bulbs are usable in the first year, the plants do not mature and bear seed until the second growing season.

Plant your leeks along an outside edge of the garden where they may be left undisturbed. If your asparagus bed has extra room, it's a good place for the leeks. Planted between rows of asparagus, the leeks' oniony aspect may help deter asparagus beetles.

Before a hard frost, bank the leeks halfway up with rich, sandy soil. Then cover the tops with a heavy mulch of chopped leaves or other materials—this way, they can be lifted as you need them (using a garden fork so that you get the whole plant).

Be sure to leave a few of the best and strongest for your seed-bearing crop. Let them grow undisturbed through the second growing season and collect the seeds when they mature.

B. T.

BEER BAR FOR SLUGS

Earlier a reader gave us several ideas on how to keep slugs and snails out of your gardens. Later another reader wrote that she had tried these methods with the result that the slugs "just charged right through." We came across this description of an old, successful method.

You will need only a bottle of beer, a soup bowl, and a trowel. Scoop a depression in the soil, place the bowl in it with the rim close to ground level, and pour in the beer. During the night, mollusks will be drawn to the volatizing alcohol and grain factors in the beer. Coming from as far away as some yards downwind, they imbibe, get drunk, and drown. The allure of the beer, unless cut short by rain, will continue through several nights, after which the gardener is in for a dismal cleanup job. The best way is to dig out a shovelful of dirt beside the bowl, tip the contents into the hole, and cover with dirt.

Boozing them to death is an effective control (you may need to set several bowls in several locations) and fairly narrowly aimed at slugs and snails. True, there are a few

harmless or valuable forms of insect and other anthropod life that may come and drown, together with the mollusks, but birds and animals won't be harmed by the brew even if they lap up the entire contents of the bowl.

B. T.

ALUM SLUG CURE

I was sorting some old papers and found the following slug cure: ¼ lb. powdered alum mixed in 1 pint water. Put in a watering can with a fine-holed sprinkler and sprinkle around plants. Or sprinkle the straight dry powder around the plants. The water goes down the slugs' holes, though, and gets the eggs and the young.

I don't know how this works or the effect of having alum on your garden soil. I use a yeasty soft dough or diatomaceous earth. The slugs are attracted to the dough by the yeasty smell and get stuck. Diatomaceous earth kills them by cutting their skins and breathing pores.

W. C.

TOMATO TRENCHING

In *Earth Garden* we found some useful gardening information:

Tomato trenching means laying plants in the ground lengthways when transplanting, so that root growth takes place over the full length instead of just from the bottom.

Readers might be interested to know that a succession of new plants can be taken from any healthy tomato plant to save buying seeds or plants or growing a new one.

Simply choose a few of the laterals that you normally pinch out and allow them to grow to about one foot in length. Break off at the base and plant in the trench manner. Keep moist for a few days, and the roots will grow quickly—you have a new tomato plant!

Allow about two or three inches of soil and mound up soil to support the above-ground part of the plant.

B. T.

CITRUS DOESN'T APPEAL TO MAGGOTS

We wish to submit our experiences in trying to control cabbage root maggots. About two years ago, we read in *Organic Gardening* that any citrus peel would deter cabbage root maggots from attacking our brassicas.

We experimented with this, since we eat a tremendous amount of grapefruit, oranges, etc.; also, we love cabbage. We put the peels on top of our wood stove to dry out. We then put the dried peels in our blender to grind them up but have found out that this is not necessary if you chop them into half-inch pieces. We put the peels around the plants on the surface or dug in a few inches. It works!

We would warn you that the earthworms do not like the peels—so you have to take

your choice. (Nematodes don't like them either.) We would like to suggest that a good source of citrus fruit would be a Meyer lemon grown inside the house or greenhouse. It does tolerate mild temperatures and is decorative and pleasing. The peel is thin, so it would take quite a few.

Or another solution: in northern Europe we have seen "orangeries" devoted to citrus plants in the late 1800's. Part of my early years, I lived in an orange grove. We even had a dog that loved to eat oranges, with no ill effects.

B. & M. F.

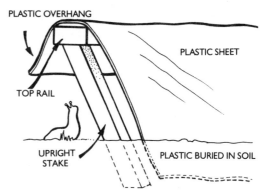

SLUG FENCE

A friend of mine has had some success with a slug fence. Last year, after one year, he seemed to feel it was worthwhile, since he'd often find slugs trying to crawl up the outside of it but none on its inside surface.

Build a low, light-rail fence, about 10–12" high, around the periphery of the area you wish to protect. Over this framework, place plastic sheeting so that one edge is buried in the earth, just inside the upright stakes, and the other edge is hanging down (weighted, possibly, or just stable because it goes around corners). The hanging edge must be out far enough from the other part of the plastic that a slug's body cannot bridge the gap.

My friend says that if the fence is built on an angle, the plastic edge hangs well away from the fence and the slugs can't negotiate that turn. If the fence is upright, the flap will touch in some places along its length. He swears he's seen slugs crawling away with disgusted looks on their faces. I can't vouch for that.

This may not be 100 percent slug-proof the first year, of course: if eggs have been laid inside the garden, they'll hatch. Be sure that the outside of the fence is clear of any brush and weeds the slugs could climb.

My friend also found that his snake population increased with a high slug population. So it might be worthwhile to ensure good living conditions (including conditions for overwintering) for garden snakes. (They didn't keep up to a slug explosion, however.)

S. W.

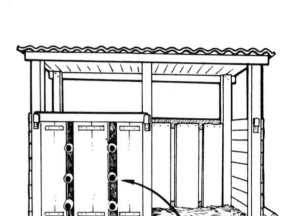

½" DRILL BIT

HOLES ABOUT 3" APART

1¼" TUBING

PIPE PLACEMENT IN COMPOST BIN

AIR TUBES FOR COMPOSTING

A small booklet, *Compost with Ease*, provides details for construction and use of an improved composting system. Written by Russell Wold, the booklet outlines an idea so simple that the response is, "Now why didn't I think of that?"

The key to Wold's system is the use of perforated polyethylene tubes, which provide a continuous air supply to the composting mass in lieu of turning the compost or punching holes. The tubes eliminate the chore of hand turning and also keep the material from losing heat — an improvement that reduces the physical effort and the time required to complete the composting process. The author says that he has found this method the least odor-producing one he has ever used.

The tubes are laid horizontally in the material at vertical intervals of about a foot, with slots made in the sides of the bin so that as the mass heats and settles, the tubes sink with it.

The air tubes are cut from a 100' coil of black 1¼" polyethylene water pipe, with pieces cut 5' long for a total of 20 pipes—enough for two bins with 10 tubes each. The resulting five pairs per bin, if spaced evenly throughout, can ensure adequate air for a good composting operation.

After finding that larger holes cool the mass too much and that smaller ones tend to clog, the author settled on a half-inch drill bit to make the air holes, spaced at six-inch intervals along the pipe. The drill goes through and out the other side to make holes along the bottom as well. Then, he turns the pipe and makes another row of holes in the same way, at 90° to the first holes and centered in between them at three inches.

The pipe pieces should be long enough for the ends to protrude outside each side of the bin to prevent plugging and to allow free access for air. Wold sets the horizontal pairing of the tubes so that the air does not have to travel more than a foot to supply any part of the bin.

B. T.

TREE DOCTORING

Two years ago our favorite apple tree, a dwarf tree bearing an unknown variety of big red apples, suffered severe damage. In a nighttime raid, a bear stepped up into the tree to reach the higher fruit and split the crotch nearly to the ground.

We cut an old inner tube into a long narrow spiraling strip. First we tied a short length of the rubber strip around the split trunk, pulling it as tight as possible, just to hold the trunk while we painted pruning paint over the wound. When the paint was dry, the long piece of rubber was wound around and around the trunk and tied so that the split was held under tension.

Now, two years later, the tree is still producing good apples, and the split seems to be healed, with new growth visible in the scar.

I'm reporting this very simple remedy to you just because it seems to have been effective and because it almost didn't happen. When we first saw the damage, it was so bad that we were sure nothing would save that tree.

B.

GROWING TOMATOES

I have had good results with a wire-enclosed mound of finished/new compost mixture, including grass clippings, etc. I put the plants *outside* the mound, on their sides, in compost. Then I water the *compost* occasionally and thoroughly. This year I also used liquid manure and have leggy plants without much fruit; other years I've used a little liquid seaweed, and I've had enormous plants with perfect fruit (Moneymaker, a coastal, medium-sized tomato, mostly) and lots of it, with no cracking or other problems, and great massive roots when I pulled the plants at season's end.

They didn't get wet/dry cycles, so I guess the compost held the moisture well. I had lots of ripened fruit and great quantities to pick green and have lasting till Christmas.

My circles were about 2½' diameter with four plants around—I'm sure size could vary with available space and wire. I believe this would greatly reduce splitting even in cherry tomatoes. It would work well also for other heavy-feeding, thirsty plants, like cucumbers.

S. W.

 CLOVER AND RYE FOR GREEN MANURE

I have had some additional thoughts on small-scale green-manuring that I would like to pass on. Clover and other legumes are the most valuable of the green manures, thanks to their nitrogen-fixing properties. Unfortunately, they are also the most difficult to include in a garden plan without removing some of the garden from production.

Clover needs to be planted by early September, at the very latest, and mid-August preferably, if it is to live through winter. Most of its growth is in May and June of the following summer. Since the garden is in full growth in August, I've been experimenting with planting red clover in with already-growing crops. Best results have come with broccoli and onions. Both of these crops let in enough light and air for the clover to thrive. I plant the clover in early to mid-August, after the food crops are growing well and weeds are under control.

I've tried planting clover in corn with mixed results. The problem seems to be some sort of fungus that rots the clover. There is not enough air circulation and light for the clover once the corn is tall. It takes several weeks for this fungus to show up, so I'm going to try again this year by planting the clover as *late* as possible—around the third week of August. Then, as soon as the corn is finished, I'll cut it down and hope that the September sun will establish the clover for winter.

I've also been using green manures in annual flower beds with success. Mainly, I've put in fall rye after the petunias are finished—about mid-September here.

In summary, my green-manuring program looks like this:

1. I plant fall rye in any ground where crops are finished from mid-September to mid-October. Typical crops to follow with rye are potatoes, squash, tomatoes, and celery.

2. Peas are a special case. Contrary to general advice, I've grown them in the same place for years. Since I plant them very early, there's not much sense in planting rye, which makes most of its growth in spring. So I plant feed oats or wheat as soon as the peas are done, around mid-August. Oats are cheap and make surprisingly good growth by winter. They don't overwinter, which is fine for a spot where early crops such as peas go in.

3. Any crops that will let clover grow well with them are planted in red clover about mid-August. Broccoli and onions are especially good crops for this. Corn may work—see above.

4. In very early spring, I plant oats in any leftover ground that has nothing on it and that won't get planted until late May to early June.

By following this program, most of the garden is growing something all the time. What little is not gets green-manured by rotating crops.

T. Z.

GERMINATION TEST

On a completely unrelated matter, I'd like to pass on something that has worked well for me. I often make germination tests on old seeds to see if they are still in good shape. I take a small piece of newspaper and fold it to about a three-inch square. I put the paper in a saucer, open up one fold, and sandwich in about 10 or so seeds. Then I put another saucer on top and flood the paper and seeds with tepid water. After a day or so, I drain the water. The upper saucer keeps the paper from drying out. The seeds can be easily inspected, and any number of varieties can be tested by stacking many saucers and newspaper squares. Water can be added later if necessary.

T. Z.

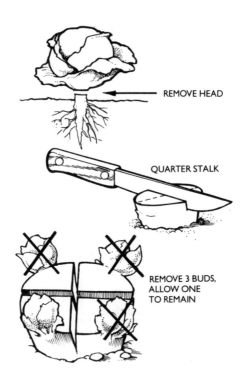

REMOVE HEAD

QUARTER STALK

REMOVE 3 BUDS, ALLOW ONE TO REMAIN

SOYBEAN DEER FENCE

On the radio I heard that planting soybeans around your garden will prevent the deer from eating the vegies.

B.

TWO CROPS FROM ONE CABBAGE PLANT

Here's a good trick for getting two crops off the same plant. Unfortunately, it only works for cabbages and some types of head lettuce, but it's a neat trick nevertheless.

When your cabbage has reached harvest size and well before the first frost, carefully cut the head off the taproot, leaving as much as you can above ground (two or three inches at least). Carefully trim this stock of any weak lower leaves and make sure the top of it is flat and clean. Then take your knife and score to make four quarters (cut a cross in the top of the stock). Cut down about a half inch but no more.

Soon a tiny cabbage head will form on the edge of the stock in each quarter. Select the healthiest "bud" and pinch off the other three "buds." This way, all the nutrients will flow to the one head, and it should get quite large before the frost finally gets it. These second-growth heads are often harder and denser than the first growth, and sometimes sweeter. If they don't get very large, you can always cook them like Brussels sprouts.

We've had a few reach two pounds. Neat, eh?

Remember to keep pinching off the smaller buds as the second growth progresses.

B. & G. W.

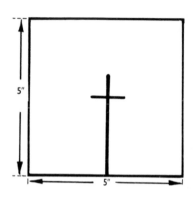

ROOT MAGGOT GUARD

I don't know if others suffer from root maggots, but if anyone is interested, here are the results of years of research. Nothing suggested in any book works (noxious chemicals, of course, excluded). We have had to find our own solutions.

To protect carrots completely, drape the row with old chiffon curtains, fastening down the edges. This is not handsome; you had better put it in a back corner. However,

it is very effective, and the carrots don't seem to mind at all. This will work equally well to protect radishes, turnips, and Chinese cabbage from their scourge, the cabbage root maggot.

However, for the bigger plants—cauliflower, broccoli and cabbage—we use plan 2. Cut plastic bags, such as a garbage bag, into 5″ × 5″ squares and then make a cut to the center, as shown in the figure.

The little flaps will help the square fit tightly against the stem. When you put your transplants out, put on their guard right away. Wrap it around the stem like a shawl, overlapping the edges so that you are left with three corners, and press those three corners down into the earth to anchor the guard. The guard should be tight around the stem. The plant will have no trouble expanding as it grows, but you don't want to leave a gap for the female fly to lay her eggs in. Put this guard on right, and you won't have to do any more for the rest of the plant's life.

"Perseverance Furthers."

B. B.

COPPER WIRE AND TOMATOES

An unusual experience in tomato growing is reported by F. Brimble of Geelong in Australia in *Earth Garden*, May/July, 1984.

He writes that when seedlings have a stem thickness of a lead pencil, he inserts a three-inch-long piece of fine copper wire right through the stem at a point just above the soil level. He says that one strand from seven-strand grounding wire is ideal.

The wire should be pulled through so there is an equal length on each side. About 8 days after the wire is inserted, the plants take on a greener, healthier look. They also grow more vigorously and withstand the attack of all tomato pests and diseases. The copper wire also has the tendency to enlarge the fruit. I have lost only about 5 plants to wilt over 37 years of growing tomatoes in Victoria.

He said he learned this from his father, who heard it from a Chinese market gardener 50 years before telling his son.

B. T.

HEAD START WITH LIGHT

Although I have for years had a small fluorescent light setup in my basement and have also presprouted many seeds, such as corn, peas, and beans, just this year I have put the two together for starting heat-loving plants.

Our earth-floored basement stays about 50–60°F winter and summer—too cold for melons, lima beans, etc., but the light setup consists of two 4' units on shelves, one above the other, so that the lower one supplies bottom heat to the upper shelf. By enclosing the shelves with insulating materials (pieces from an old fiber-filled jacket and a scrap piece of Styrofoam), I can maintain about 80°F when both lights are on and 70°F at night with only the bottom one on. This is ideal for melons, eggplants, cucumbers, peppers, etc.

On May 11 I soaked cucumber seeds. On May 12 I put them in wet paper in a plastic bag, put them on the top shelf, and went away for four days. (The top light is on a timer.) When I came home, there were little cucumber plants with roots 1½" long, ready to be potted up, and 10 days later they were outside in raised beds under old storm windows—with two pairs of true leaves.

Just once have I grown successful limas, by presprouting and then planting them under plastic; but *this* way I can keep them in recycled Styrofoam cups under lights until the ground outside has warmed enough to be hospitable to them.

When going away for four days, I was afraid that all my plants would die of thirst, so I tore up a piece of old flannelette sheet into one-inch strips, wet them, and squeezed them out, then buried one end in each pot and put the other end in a large pot of water. The plants took up water through the wicks as they needed it, with the result that all were sturdier than if they had depended on *my* estimate of their needs.

I tried something else for the first time this spring. In grafting pears and apples, I have for several years dipped the scions in melted wax to prevent them from drying out, and I have always used raffia and wax on the union. Being in a hurry this year, I dipped them as usual but then simply took a rubber band, cut it to form a strip about five inches long, and wrapped the union tightly, tucking in the free end. Never have I had such a high rate of success—almost 100 percent, if you discount the scion I put on upside down.

Growing things is like magic, except that I am not the sorcerer, only the sorcerer's willing apprentice.

H. B.

ENABLING TIPS FOR DISABLED GARDENERS

For gardeners who still want to continue to tend their gardens even though they have physical handicaps, the Garden 1985 issue of *Farmstead* has a wealth of ideas.

Thelma Honey, author of the *Farmstead* article, says she has redesigned her garden to provide closely spaced supports, convenient handholds, and resting spots, and she has reduced her garden space by 50 percent through the use of intensive gardening in raised beds.

Her method of planting peas shows how she meets the challenge of limited physical ability. For making holes, she uses a spading fork with a line painted across the tines. "Each time the fork is pushed into the soil to the red line, four holes are made for peas." She carries seeds and other supplies in a cut-off gallon plastic bottle strapped around her waist through the handle. The peas are dropped one at a time in a 2½' long 1" PVC pipe, then the holes are filled and tamped as she walks along. Peas are planted along a fence. Other vegetables are planted with more ease in raised beds, where little weeding and mulching are needed because the plants are set closely together.

A small gardening cart is one of her enabling tools—18" × 30" to fit her space and her strength. She can load fertilizer or peat moss into the cart by dropping the front to the ground, then tipping the cart upright again—the same method works for raking leaves and debris into her cart.

A hoe replaces a cane in the garden and is used with the thumbs up, as one would hold a broom, in order to reduce the need for bending and thus straining the back.

The *Farmstead* article lists some other enablers and their suppliers. One such enabler is the kneeler stool, or Easy Kneeler. It can serve as a kneeler or, turned upside down, as a stool, with a foam pad for use either way. It has high handles to help you get up and down. Another is a tool that is like two small shovel heads that work with a scissors-like action to pick up piles of leaves, grass clippings, etc.

Some companies also sell tools made of a superlight aluminum alloy, as well as tools designed as back savers, with the bend in the handle rather than in your back. The bend delivers pressure directly to the tool head to do the work.

We send our thanks to *Farmstead* and ask our readers to give us your ideas and experiences with other enabling tools you've found to meet the challenges that come when you find you're less flexible than you used to be.

B. T.

IDEA FROM A BLIND GARDENER

The article on tools for less flexible gardeners made me want to share this with your readers.

I have a blind friend who wants to spend some time usefully in the garden. He has raised beds in a wooden framework. That way he knows clearly where each bed is and will not damage the plants by accidentally stepping on them. He can mow the grass between the beds, work the soil by hand, and weed when the vegetable plants are large enough to be identifiable (they are planted in single rows to enable this). This is a city friend without much spare time; doubtless, there are many other techniques someone with more gardening time would find.

S. W.

MULCH SLUGS AWAY

From *The Ruth Stout No-Work Garden Book* by Ruth Stout and Richard Clemence (Rodale Press, Inc., 1974) comes this question and answer on a perennial problem to *The Smallholder*'s readers, if we judge from the number of times it's mentioned in your letters:

Doesn't mulch attract slugs, since the earth under it is always moist? I never thought so (I have no slugs), but I didn't know how to answer this question until I read what the *Encyclopedia of Organic Gardening* has to say about it: that a well-mulched garden, after there is plenty of humus in the soil, attracts earthworms and that tends to make the soil alkaline which slugs don't like. Isn't that a break? If slugs are really a problem, try the beer treatment.

B. T.

ROCK DUST FOR
REMINERALIZING SOIL

The results of using rock dust (any good mix) for remineralization have been spectacular. I used a small amount last spring from a local

rock crusher with excellent results. Trees set grew better than last year; two cuttings of lilac and honeysuckle that had just sat with nil growth for two years despite manure really started to grow. And possibly more significant, I sprinkled only a small amount around a few five- to six-foot pines, badly infected with mistletoe and pine beetle, thinking they were a lost cause anyway. This fall, there was no deterioration; they look better than in the spring. I think it is quite possible the beetles would simply "bug off" if caught early enough and remineralized.

B. T.

PLASTIC BOTTLE
WITH CUT-OUT

MOTH TRAP FOR FRUIT TREES

Here is an idea we would like to share with other readers. In the spring we hang containers with a mix of sweetening and water (¼ cup sweetening—molasses, honey, or sugar—to 3 cups water) in our fruit trees to catch certain types of moths. To prevent rain from diluting the mix, we use plastic bleach, vinegar, or juice jugs in which an opening is cut on the side, and a length of wire or twine is put through the handle to hang the jug on a tree limb. When the season is over, we clean out the jugs and put them away until next year. We clean out handfuls of moths each year.

H. & J. G.

SWING SET GREENHOUSE

In *Organic Gardening* for October 1987, there's an imaginative idea for using the swing set your children have grown too old to use. Move the frame to a place near your garden and set it up with the long side facing south. Drive four steel fence posts into the ground along each side; fasten a 2 × 2 perpendicular to the top of each set of posts. Attach a few more 2 × 2s between the ridgepole (frame of the swing) and the posts. Cover the whole structure with 4-mil plastic; edges can be fastened together with duct tape. For an entrance, leave one corner free. If your new greenhouse is in reach of electricity, you can use a heat lamp in it on cold nights to extend its season.

B. T.

HARVESTING SEAWEED

Here is some information on using seaweed in the garden. Seaweed is a very practical

fertilizer on the coast but one that needs more research.

Like all living organisms, seaweeds go through a life cycle. This cycle follows our seasons from spring, summer, autumn, and on into winter. Our water temperatures vary from 45°F in the chill of winter to as much as 55°F in the warm summer, promoting incredible growth in a very short time.

Our use of these seaweeds is also cyclical. It begins in early March, as the herring come to spawn. Their eggs are so thickly layered on rocks, seaweed, everything, that it resembles a heavy frost on the shoreline. At low tide we gather as much of this herring roe on seaweed as possible. The best is that laid on the huge kelplike fronds called laminaria. This is the West Coast relative of the Japanese kombu. These are washed carefully, then dried around our wood stove. Each frond gets up to three feet long and eight inches wide. We break the dried fronds into finger-size pieces for munching, like potato chips. This has been a native delicacy on the coast for centuries.

We not only eat this seaweed/roe as a treat but also collect any seaweed that might have roe on it. This seaweed is then bagged and carried along a ¾-mile cedar boardwalk path to our gardens, where it is buried in the garden. A trench is dug two feet deep and one foot wide. One foot of seaweed is then put into it. Next to it another two-foot trench is dug, and the dirt from the second trench is placed onto the first. This process is continued until the entire garden has been fertilized. As the seaweed rots, it warms the soil, speeding up the growth process. Also, since our water supply is directly dependent on rain, this added moisture allows us to water much less in the heat of summer, once the young roots reach the layer of seaweed.

Come late June, our seedlings are up and in the garden. Moisture on the surface of the soil is quickly used up if a mulch is not applied. Off we go to a bay just down from our garden area. Here huge bull kelp grow up to a foot a day. In the sun their round-ball heads are bobbing on the surface, with their beautiful amber streamers trailing behind. These heads are cut and the streamers hauled into the boat. They make an excellent ground mulch to keep the roots cool, and should it rain, this kelp then rehydrates to hold that moisture as well.

By early September, the bull kelp fronds have melted into the soil. It is time then to harvest and mulch with seaweed once again. This time bladderwrack is used *(Fucus gardneri)*. It grows very high on rocky beaches and, in the autumn, washes onto shores, where we gather it and lay it thickly over all the gardens. Because of its tough, leathery nature, this seaweed will take the entire winter to break down. It fertilizes slowly, as well as stopping weed growth. It's a great home for worms too. Come springtime, it is dug into the trenches with the herring roe/seaweed.

And so the cycle continues, Nature granting us as much fertility as we have the energy to gather and harvest. Each year is a bit different, bringing its own surprises as we continue to live and learn by watching the world around us. My husband and I have lived on light stations together for eleven years. During this time we have gardened extensively, as well as harvesting local food sources.

J. S.

PROTECT FRUIT TREES IN WINTER

This tip comes from the Cooperative Extension Service of the U.S. Department of Agriculture in Montana:

In this region, alternate freezing and thawing damage fruit trees during winter. A suggestion is to paint the trunk of the tree with white latex exterior paint (not lead-based paint). A sunny winter day can raise under-bark temperatures above thawing only to fall to the prevailing night temperature. The painted trees tend not to thaw, reducing damage.

B. T.

GROWING TOMATOES IN A COLD CLIMATE

We've been noticing our neighbors' ways of producing ripe tomatoes outdoors, since most of us get ripe ones only in the greenhouse. One neighbor painted a sheet of plywood black to absorb the sun's warmth and planted her tomatoes against it in rich soil, tying the plants to cords running up the plywood. The ripe tomatoes against the green plants and black background add an unusually attractive touch to her garden. Another has a rock wall at the base of her house's south-facing side. She lines her tomatoes up close to this wall, and they always ripen well. Someone else grows Sweet 100s in pots on a sunny balcony, gets lots of ripe tomatoes all late summer, then brings the pots indoors to finish ripening the remaining ones in a bright window. The most promising method is that of another neighbor, who grows each plant inside an old rubber tire. He adds a second tire as the tomatoes grow higher, so staking is unnecessary. The black rubber holds the sun's heat so well that these tomatoes ripen earlier than our greenhouse ones.

B. T.

GOOD YIELD OF RIPE TOMATOES

My father, a Latvian tomato gardener, maintains that the only way to get a good yield of ripe tomatoes is to pinch side shoots from the main stem once a week. It works for me!

A. K.

PLANT AIR PURIFIERS

Most of us have heard that spider plants purify the air in our homes. Now a two-year project by NASA (National Aeronautics and Space Administration) researchers confirms this. The spider plant *(Chlorophytum elatum)* removed 96 percent of the carbon monoxide and 86 percent of the formaldehyde from a sealed test chamber in a 24-hour period. English ivy *(Hedera helix)* removed 90 percent of the benzene in the same circumstances. Other plants with a similar pollutant-removing record are golden pothos *(Epipremnum aureum)*, peace lily *(Spathiphyllum "Mauna*

Loa")*, Chrysanthemum morifolium,* and several species of *Dracaena.*

B. T.

RUE KEEPS CATS OUT OF PLANTS

A reader's tip in *Organic Gardening,* January 1990, suggests crushed rue leaves to keep cats at a distance from your house plants. Rue leaves are, she says, "very repulsive to cats."

B. T.

VEGETABLES ON THE WINDOWSILL

For several years I have had success with planting lettuce seeds in early fall in containers sitting on an indoor window sill. In this way my family can enjoy fresh lettuce salads long into the winter. Looseleaf and buttercrunch and bibb are the kinds I've had best luck with; the outer leaves can be picked regularly on these varieties. We've also been able to add Tiny Tim tomatoes to our salads since I learned that I can do the same thing by digging a tomato plant just before frost hits and bringing it indoors, potting it. A neighbor grows eggplants indoors and gets good eggplants, small but tasty.

J. W.

Index